Praise for *RESULTS Coaching Next Steps*

"*RESULTS Coaching Next Steps* invites leaders to function as coaches and clearly teaches them how to coach. It is truly transformational for those unfamiliar with coach leadership and for veteran coaches alike. This book transformed me as a school principal and continues to serve as a fundamental resource in training school leaders. It is without a doubt my top recommendation to anyone who asks how to learn coach-leader skills."

—Dr. Hank Staggs, ACC, Director
Governors Academy for School Leadership, Tennessee

"*RESULTS Coaching Next Steps: Leading for Growth and Change* clearly sets the path for transformational leadership that creates a culture of trust and communication in which the effectiveness of the organization flourishes when freedom to explore and collaborate are not just promoted but valued. The authors artfully articulate and demonstrate the leadership coaching behaviors and skills that help leaders shift organizational mindsets from negatives to positives and behaviors from isolation to collaboration resulting in new and innovative thinking and learning. The UAM School of Education faculty and staff have become fearless visionaries who work as a team to make yesterday's challenges today's successes."

—Dr. Peggy Doss, Dean
School of Education, UAM

"Finally! Another must-have for my professional library! *RESULTS Coaching Next Steps* speaks to education leaders who continue to focus on being a coach leader, no matter what their title or position. The book drives novice and experienced coaches to reconnect to the essentials and renews your commitment to never interact the same way again."

—Kim Richardson, ACC, Teacher Development Coordinator
Hampton City Schools

"Education is about change and growth in people. Results Coaching Global's first book *RESULTS Coaching: The New Essential for School Leaders* completely reframed educational leadership landscape. Now RESULTS Coaching Next Steps: Leading for Growth and Change brings out the details in the picture of leading learning systems. This book provides specific examples related to the mindset of the Coach Leader and thoroughly examines supervision versus coaching. Everything you need to create a culture of coaching in your district is laid out beautifully. As a superintendent, I've seen firsthand the impact this work has had on principals, midlevel administrators, and cabinet-level leadership. The bottom line—the significant changes we are looking for come from changing educators from within. It is a journey and *RESULTS Coaching Next Steps: Leading for Growth and Change* is the guidebook."

—David Curry, Superintendent
Union Hill School District, California

"*RESULTS Coaching Next Steps: Leading for Growth and Change* equips the 21st century leader to move past old paradigms of supervision and into the realm of influence. Next Steps continues the journey of transformation and challenges administrators to become coach leaders. The need for a coaching culture to support leaders makes this book a valued resource. To truly impact school environments, *RESULTS Coaching Next Steps: Leading for Growth and Change* is the first place to start!"

—Lezley Lewis, Executive Director of Teacher Learning
Ft. Worth ISD, TX

"*RESULTS Coaching: The New Essential for School Leaders* has served as the launchpad for authentic communication and academic success in our school district. The authors have developed an educator-friendly book that offers a practical approach, coupled with a dose of theory, to provide a solid balance for the ever-busy school teacher and leader. *RESULTS Coaching Next Steps* offers a communication framework, a review of essential communication skills, and an especially helpful section for school leaders and supervisors. *RESULTS Coaching Next Steps* builds upon its predecessor, and continues to support and guide for real change and results. For all of us who know that academic success is dependent on building relationships and communicating effectively, this book is a must-read!"

—Carl Dethloff, PhD
Superintendent, San Angelo ISD

RESULTS Coaching Next Steps

RESULTS Coaching Next Steps

Leading for Growth and Change

Kathryn Kee
Karen Anderson
Vicky Dearing
Frances Shuster

CORWIN
A SAGE Publishing Company

FOR INFORMATION:

Corwin

A SAGE Company

2455 Teller Road

Thousand Oaks, California 91320

(800) 233-9936

www.corwin.com

SAGE Publications Ltd.

1 Oliver's Yard

55 City Road

London, EC1Y 1SP

United Kingdom

SAGE Publications India Pvt. Ltd.

B 1/I 1 Mohan Cooperative Industrial Area

Mathura Road, New Delhi 110 044

India

SAGE Publications Asia-Pacific Pte. Ltd.

3 Church Street

#10-04 Samsung Hub

Singapore 049483

Executive Editor: Arnis Burvikovs

Senior Associate Editor: Desirée A. Bartlett

Senior Editorial Assistant: Andrew Olson

Production Editor: Laura Barrett

Copy Editor: Deanna Noga

Typesetter: C&M Digitals (P) Ltd.

Proofreader: Christine Dahlin

Indexer: Sheila Bodell

Cover Designer: Michael Dubowe

Marketing Manager: Anna Mesick

Printed in the United States of America

ISBN 978-1-5063-2875-1

This book is printed on acid-free paper.

SFI Certified Sourcing
www.sfiprogram.org
SFI-00453

16 17 18 19 20 10 9 8 7 6 5 4 3 2 1

Contents

Come—Let's go to a place of extraordinary results.
A place where every person feels a
deep sense of purpose and moral responsibility
to engage, invest, and achieve at high levels,
individually and as teams.

Come—Let's go to where trust triumphs over distrust.
Where vulnerability, honesty, loyalty, respect, joy, and
a sense of humor radiate.
Where people feel safe and willing to open up and engage
in thoughtful and honest conversations.
Where current realities are identified and examined.
Where successes, both large and small, are recognized,
valued, and celebrated.

Here, people listen first and talk later.
They seek to understand what is said, felt, and desired by others.
And when they talk, they talk with others,
rather than at or over others.
Here, people speak using intentional language that aligns with
current research findings from neuroleadership and
cognitive behaviors.

Here, thinking abounds and relationships flourish!
People value time for reflections.
They are willing to identify areas in need of
adjustments, improvements, revisions,
even eliminations,
as solutions are determined, goals set, and actions planned.

This journey is not necessarily an easy one to take.
There will be obstacles along the way.
Naysayers and outdated hardwiring to name a few,
tugging at us, trying to lure us back
to old habits and status quo.

It will take strong determination and
deep resolve to last this journey.
This is why we carry our TARP and our SCARF with us,
remembering that change takes
Time, Attention, Repetition, and Positive Feedback.
Recognizing that we all want to feel a sense of
Status, Certainty, Autonomy, Relatedness, and Fairness
as we travel together.

Come—Let's keep focused on where we are headed.
After all, we are well on our way.
And when we arrive,
we will know for sure
that this has been a journey well worth taking.

By Vicky Dearing, PCC
Results Coaching Global

Preface

You have picked up this book, *Results Coaching Next Steps: Leading for Growth and Change*, for a reason specific to you: Perhaps the title intrigued you and you wanted to know more, or maybe it spoke directly to your passion and personal desire to impact results where you lead and live. And possibly you are already familiar with our first book, *Results Coaching: The New Essential for School Leaders*, and were eager to find out what is next. Whatever the reason that brought you here, we are glad you did!

This book is the result of listening to the voices of leaders, like you, who continued to ask for more specifics and practical approaches on how to lead and coach others in ways that elevate results and strengthen relationships. While standing on its own merits, it best serves as a close companion to follow our first book, *Results Coaching: The New Essential for School Leaders*, and promises to provide multiple learning opportunities for you, whether new to the role of leader or well-seasoned. It is written to read on your own or with a group of dedicated colleagues.

On our behalf, the writing of this book has been like releasing a long and satisfying breath. It is full of new learnings and experiences with coaching after multiple years of inhaling research and practical examples from working with leaders from across the country. It is considered our gift to those who want more—are hungry for more—on best approaches, on practical ways to lead and coach for growth and deep change—for reaching meaningful results.

- Results that are inclusive of elevated thinking for everyone associated with the school.
- Results that represent advanced learning and behaviors for students, teachers, support staff, parents, and leaders.
- Results that reflect a culture of collaboration, respect, and personal regard for all.
- Results that last.

We wrote *Results Coaching Next Steps* because there is more to know, there is more to say, and oh, so much more to do to achieve the type of leadership environments that will produce results for students in schools as well as the teachers chosen to make it happen. We believe that leaders who have the skills and tools to coach thinking have the skills and tools to have powerful conversations that impact thoughtful reflection, self-monitoring, and self-assessment. Why did we write this book? We have so far to go. Thousands of leaders retire annually and younger less skilled hopefuls step into their shoes every year. The kids have changed, the teachers have changed, and the communities often have changed, and what is needed is the leader for all seasons: the coach leader.

This book is for all educators, leaders, teachers, or anyone who wants to make a difference: a difference in the results for kids and a difference in the environments and relationships found in most schools. This book is for anyone who engages in conversations desiring to influence the most positive outcome for any relationship.

In *Results Coaching: The New Essential for School Leaders*, we offered the focus on the leader's mindset, the power of Intention, the concept of "coach leader," and the language skills needed to influence and inspire REAL change. In the past 6 years, our work in schools and districts all over the country continues to return to the same issues and boomerang behaviors. This book shares the impact of what happens when leaders become a "coach leader" and walk in the mindset, intention, and language that changes results and people in ways that last—change that will impact student and adult learning and growth across the country. After all, isn't this what we all want?

Our purpose is to draw upon the coach leader mindset, skills, and tools of the first book and drill down for pure gold: the impact, the difference, the collaborative cultures that can be created. In this book, we drill deeper into the research as to why the coach leader mindset can produce such results—the science that offers compelling information to change. While we all know smoking kills, some people still choose to smoke; while we might pull out a typewriter if we had to, almost no one will today. Why? Because there is a better way! That's what we want to offer: work, life, relationships, collaborations; all can be improved with the mindset and skills of the coach leader. Four big reasons to buy and read this book:

1. We tackle the role of supervision and answer the question that coaching is the broader supervising option. We provide a model and language and tools to support every supervisor and the varying conversations demanded of the role and situation.

2. We present a deep review and expansion of the most essential communication skills expected of any leader and specifically how to use these skills more eloquently and purposefully.

3. We offer a conversation framework that will provide confidence and courage in holding thoughtful conversations, including those thought to be tough and difficult conversations.

4. We provide evidence of how individuals have created a culture of coaching by working on themselves first to make adaptive changes in their lives and thereby impacting and influencing the overall culture of their organization.

We hope you will experience for yourself how the information contained in this book holds the possibility to not only change but also to transform lives and leadership, including your own.

Acknowledgments

As in our first book, *Results Coaching: The New Essential for School Leaders*, our passion and desire to be the best students of coaching began with the life-changing work and teachings of Art Costa and Bob Garmston, to whom we will forever be indebted for "a way of being" that changed our careers and lives forever.

To Dennis Sparks, Stephanie Hirsh, and Dave Ellis for providing our rich exposure to the larger world of professional coaching.

To Francine Campone, MCC, who continues to be our mentor, teacher, and coach for more than a decade and who challenges us to be the best at our craft and pushes for ultimate possibilities in our mindset for coaching.

To John Crain, lifelong colleague, collaborator, and friend of Kathy and who shares the joy of our work and continual exploration of supervision and its power to transform with the "coach" mindset.

To David Rock, author of *Quiet Leadership*, who continues to inspire us to align our deep beliefs and core values to the life-changing NeuroLeadership research and its impact.

To our highly skilled instructors whose commitment to this work supports its life, energy, and dynamic impact: Reba Schumacher, Pam Smith, Dr. Lloyd Sain, and David Curry.

To all the people—authors and researchers—whose work motivates and energizes our work:

- Carl Glickman, our Supervision guru
- Susan Scott, *Fierce Leadership* and *Fierce Conversations*
- Daniel Pink, *Drive: The Surprising Truth About What Motivates Us*
- Daniel Goleman: *Emotional Intelligence*
- Robert Kegan and Lisa Lahey: *How the Way We Talk Can Change the Way We Work* and *Immunity to Change*
- Martin Seligman: Positive Psychology
- Barbara Fredrickson: Positive Psychology

To our students and fellow educators who love what we have learned and shared in our seminars and have been transformed in their leadership approach to impact real change and results in schools.

To the hundreds of leaders we coach each day, month, and year, whose courage to make a difference and impact the results of schools is ever present.

To our families who stand by our side and cheer on our passion and our joyful work as "coach leaders."

Thank you each and every one!

PUBLISHER'S ACKNOWLEDGMENTS

Corwin gratefully acknowledges the contributions of the following reviewers:

David G. Daniels
Principal
Susquehanna Valley Senior High School
Conklin, NY

Kathy Rhodes
Principal
Hinton Elementary
Hinton, IA

About the Authors

Accredited Coach Training Program
International Coach Federation

Each of the authors has a strong commitment and a personal passion for championing the power of coaching within education and business. They understand the difference that coaching makes in organizations and individual lives, and they have dedicated their time, energy, and efforts to moving the dream forward that coaching is the go-to way to lead and thrive in organizations. They are partners of Results Coaching Global, a company dedicated to supporting school leaders in achieving extraordinary results professionally and personally, as they become more confident, competent, and courageous leaders.

Each partner has received her Professional Certified Coach Credential through the International Coach Federation, and together they have created a school for leaders who wish to become credentialed coaches through the International Coach Federation. The school is recognized as an International Coach Federation Approved Coach Training Program, and their first book, *Results Coaching: The New Essential for School Leaders,* serves as the textbook for the school. The authors offer this next book as a dedicated example of their desire to continually support leadership development and growth within organizations and for individuals.

KATHRYN (HARWELL) KEE is a committed and passionate champion for the power of COACHING and what the impact, the mindset, and the skills of coaching offer to educational organizations, in particular, and to all places of work, in general. Having served in all levels of education since 1970, Kathy's 47 years have confirmed her strongly held belief system of how critically important leadership is. She believes a leader must be committed to the research and knowledge we have today in order to influence, motivate, inspire, and grow people to use their best thinking to produce their best work. Our schools seem so hardwired to traditional processes and behaviors that to realize real lasting change will require the patience of Gandhi, the determination of Martin Luther King Jr., and an army of committed coach leaders who want a different future and clear results for all children.

Kathy's credentials range from teacher to assistant superintendent in districts from Louisiana, Missouri, and Oklahoma, and, since 1978, in Texas. She also served as adjunct mentor for University of North Texas for new administrators coaching their new career beginnings. Kathy's experiences with leadership grew from being a student leader in student council and government and from teacher leadership to administrative leadership in gifted education, parent education, remedial reading, and campus and district leadership positions. A pattern a look back reveals is the power and magic of a leader's belief in one's potential and possibility. These *Results Coaching* books voice her purpose and passion and the legacy of leadership she desires to leave.

Kathy is a founding partner of Results Coaching Global (RCG); serves as a seminar instructor, mentor, and coach; and directs the Accredited Coach Training Program. She has authored numerous articles and was the lead author of *Results Coaching: The New Essential for School Leaders.* Other experiences and honors include past president and founder of the Texas Learning Forward; past president of Learning Forward; and recipient of Learning Forward's Lifetime Achievement Award.

KAREN ANDERSON believes coaching is her most significant work as an educator. She is passionate about working with leaders who are open to advancing their performance to a higher level. Leaders who "work on their work" in ways that challenge the norm, create a space for possibility, and include commitment to action motivate and inspire her as a coach.

Her dream is for every educator to have a coach *and* for every educator to "be" a coach leader. She wants her grandchildren to have a leader who looks for the best in all, values individual differences, and holds the highest standards and expectations for achieving one's potential. She believes coaching has the power to transform the place we call school.

Karen has been a public school educator for over 45 years. In addition to coaching, her expertise has been facilitating groups focused on working collaboratively to discover solutions and improve processes and delivery systems. She is a national trainer and has served as an adjunct faculty member at Texas A & M University-Commerce. From 1996 to 2004, she served as the Executive Director of the Texas Staff Development Council and was recognized as the recipient of their Lifetime Achievement Award.

As a founding partner of Results Coaching Global (RCG), Karen serves as a seminar instructor, mentor, and coach. She has authored numerous articles including "Coaching for High Performance" and "Leadership Coaching for Principals." As one of the coauthors of *Results Coaching: The New Essential for School Leaders*, she was recognized as the recipient of Learning Forward's Lifetime Achievement Award.

VICKY DEARING has been involved with coaching for over 20 years. She believes that coaching has been one of the most important and influential components of her professional career and personal life, and she wants to support others in experiencing the power of coaching. Vicky's expertise and experiences include 30 years of work within public education, serving as an elementary teacher; a central office administrator leading and supporting Gifted programs, Title I programs, and at-risk programs; and as a principal who received state and national recognition for leading a school to recognized and exemplary results. After retiring from public education, Vicky spent over 8 years working in the business and higher education sector, traveling across the United States on behalf of supporting education initiatives and leadership development before joining her partners in the Results Coaching initiative. Her leadership roles in the business field include consultant, director, vice president, and senior vice president.

Vicky understands the demands and the rewards of leadership, regardless of the level or the title, and the possibilities for reaching increased results and personal satisfaction when people work within respected and trusting environments, toward a shared purpose and vision, with clearly identified and articulated expectations, standards, and goals and have honest and open conversations, using intentional communication skills designed to increase clarity, expand thinking, and motivate people to move toward positive change. In addition to serving as a business partner and lead faculty instructor with the Results Coaching Global Coaching School, Vicky coaches school leaders, business leaders, and pastors from across the nation. She believes in the importance of ongoing development and the intentional practice of her own coaching skills and considers herself to be a life-long student of coaching.

FRANCES SHUSTER was an early adopter of the professional coaching model and is part of the first wave of students and active members of the International Coach Federation (ICF), the global leader in professional coaching. She has served in various roles and capacities in support of and contribution to professional coaching, both as a volunteer and as a leader, faculty instructor, mentor, coach, and partner in Results Coaching Global. Frances has also been active in the University of Texas at Dallas coach training program since 2008, serving as an instructor, supervising mentor, and assessor. She continues to be in conversation with the movers and shakers of the global coaching community, who are working toward maintaining the integrity and vitality of professional coaching now and into the future.

Frances is surrounded by a family of educators in the generations before and following her. Her public school career included teaching in elementary schools, coordinating and supervising gifted and talented and reading programs, and directing professional development and learning. She served in high-needs schools throughout the country as a literacy consultant, teaching literacy strategies, and observing and coaching teachers.

As a curious observer of human nature, Frances notices the patterns of behavior regularly associated in coaching interactions. The person who is being coached is frequently transformed in her beliefs, mindset, and actions because of the trust and belief of her coach. Just as often, the coach is transformed in her mindset and actions because of the trust and vulnerability that grows in the coaching relationship. Her life purpose, "to seek and share love, peace, wisdom and joy," is actualized in her work as a teacher and coach and in her circle of Very Important Family and Friends (VIFF).

Introduction

Results Coaching Global was created to support and serve educators in finding and living their best lives professionally and personally. As friends and colleagues, each having more than 40 years of experience in the education and leadership arenas and having experienced the power of coaching, have been on an unwavering mission to carry the message forward that coaching is a necessary factor required to transform schools and entire school districts. Coaching has the power to ignite, grow, and sustain thinking, motivation, and determination for action to achieve the extraordinary results desired and expected today.

We believe it is important for people and organizations to dream big. Our dream is for coaching to become the go-to way for adults and students to think, talk, create, act, and be within schools across our country and the world. We also believe that we have been positioned to be messengers about the importance of coaching and a conduit for teaching the "how to" for the dream to become a reality. Now thanks to our association with the International Coach Federation and professional coaching, and as we continue to work closely with school leaders from across the nation, we are ready to offer the next big message on Results Coaching, this time with elevated attention placed on leading and growing for change.

We propose that people, who are intentionally focused on leading and growing, are leaders with a deep commitment to be their best, lead their best, learn their best, and discover their best. We understand that school leaders have a magnitude of demands and expectations placed on them by well-meaning government officials, politically motivated groups, caring parents, and dedicated school systems. How could we possibly expect any one leader to walk unaccompanied into the reality of the work of today's schools? To lead and grow today, it is a moral imperative to support leaders with a coaching mindset and culture. We believe that every leader will want to know and use the skills and tools of coaching, to have a coach, and to be a coach to those serving the same mission. Now *that* is a bodacious dream and mission!

Education is a very different field today than it was in the past. Yes, people continue to enter the field of education because they love kids and they want to have a positive impact on them, just like most did in the past. However, today it is no longer a place for only some kids. It is a place for every child who enters the school doors, regardless of their race, or whether they are English speakers or not, irrespective of their economic status, religious beliefs, previous school experiences, special learning needs, or family backgrounds. And today it's not a place for teachers to come, unless they are all in and committed to high levels of learning for every student. Today, it is the teacher's responsibility to make sure that each and every student masters the multitude of curriculum learning objectives identified for each grade level. And it is the responsibility of leaders to support teachers in reaching these lofty results. To get to this place in our society, where all students learn and meet their potential and have equal opportunities for a productive and satisfying future, there have been many changes and demands of significant magnitude. Is it any wonder that schools are places of high stress? And when high stress and low trust are combined, the journey needed to accomplish such a daunting task seems almost impossible to make. And yet educators keep moving forward.

As we go to work with school leaders (from superintendents to teachers) across this country who are completely dedicated to meeting the high demands facing them today, our hearts go out to them because we feel the heaviness of the responsibility and the unwavering commitment to accomplish the task by holding on to their number one responsibility: teaching children, preparing children, celebrating with the children as they move through their years in school and toward their future. Today's school leaders inspire us and motivate us to support them on this journey through our work in coaching.

One of the first messages we deliver to school leaders is about what coaching actually is and is not. This message comes as a result of what we have learned over the last 13 years. It was about that time that school systems across this nation turned to coaching as the next best answer for helping achieve the daunting tasks of reaching and teaching every child. However, in many cases, there was no clear understanding of what coaches actually do and how they behave in support of teaching and learning. With good intentions, many coaches talked to, and not with, teachers about the work. Many coaches had as their main strategy to advise, tell, and direct. That doesn't work as one might think.

Then, in 2007, a message began to grow in size and volume. It had to do with leaders being mindful of the impact their behaviors and words had on the thinking and productivity of those they lead. People from across the world began to sit up and take notice of ways to lead and coach with the brain in mind. One of the early pioneers in this new leadership focus, backed by data and research, was and continues to be Dr. David Rock, founder of the NeuroLeadership Institute, author, and professional coach to business leaders across the world. Dr. Rock dedicates his time and effort to combining research findings about the brain and leadership in such a way that it becomes practical and usable, regardless of the business or organization.

Dr. Rock stresses the importance of leaders moving away from the management era to the coach leadership era of today and emphasizes that to increase performance it's the responsibility of the leader to increase thinking and to become the Chief Thinking Officer (CTO) of their business or organization.

Through the use of the iceberg metaphor, first offered by cognitive behavior therapy and other behavioral sciences (Rock, 2006), Rock reminds leaders that "performance at anything is driven by our sets of behaviors, our habits" which are "driven by our feelings, which in turn are driven by our thoughts." In other words, if leaders want high levels of performance, they can no longer deal only with surface-level actions and behaviors. They must dive deep and ask the same of others to better understand the thinking and feelings of every member of the organization. Thus, as Rock says, "if you want to improve performance, the most effective way to do this is to start at the bottom—to improve thinking." Hallelujah! Clarity at last about the importance of everyone thinking metacognitively and with others about the effectiveness and impact for results of their work, and about being aware how feelings impact thinking!

Rock was not alone in influencing our work as coaches. At about the same time, the world of positive psychology was also gaining momentum and seemed to walk hand-in-hand with neuroleadership and emotional intelligence. Many of the influencers associated with these three theories and others dedicated to improving leadership awareness and development are cited in this book. For their work and dedication we are forever thankful.

With growing evidence about the importance of elevating thinking of all to accomplish the daunting tasks of today, and because we also have scientific evidence that emotions impact thinking, leaders are called to lead with the brain in mind. They understand that each person they lead performs at higher levels when fear is reduced and motivation is increased.

When individuals and entire teams are given the opportunity to think and make personal connections independently and collaboratively, both energy and the desire necessary to move toward action are increased. It is almost impossible to accomplish bold goals without combining emotional drive with clarity of thoughts.

Today's successful leaders use intentional behaviors and processes to grow and improve people's thinking. They take on coach-like behaviors to influence and motivate themselves and others to reach for and achieve high levels of performance and results. Leaders of today are becoming coach leaders. Coach leaders demonstrate a commitment to listen fully to others and to use intentional communication skills to help others organize and simplify thinking. Coach leaders create space for thinking and provide language to support it. They ask powerful questions and create safe and supportive environments.

Thanks to the work of the NeuroLeadership Institute, we now have a simplified and concrete way to understand the key dynamics at play as people decide the degree to which they want to engage with individuals or teams, and it all has to do with whether or not they feel safe and emotionally rewarded for their work. David Rock's SCARF Model is opening the door to more intentional interactions.

The SCARF Model is a powerful tool for organization leaders, professionals, facilitators, trainers, coaches, consultants, teachers, social workers, and any "change agent" desiring to influence others. The additional payoff is "helping understanding and improving the quality of everyday interactions with colleagues, friends or family" (Rock & Cox, 2012, p. 1). We offer more detail about the SCARF Model in Chapter 2 of this book. Needless to say, it has strongly impacted the way we think about and deliver our seminars and coaching.

In 2012, David Goldsmith wrote, "I doubt you'll find many supervisors or HR managers who will articulate their decision-making thoughts in those words (how you think), but that's what is really going on in their minds. They consider whether a prospective leader or manager has the thinking skills to create new opportunities, solve challenges, and redirect the energies of others in order to achieve success. Looking at yourself from this perspective, you can see that your thinking skills set you and your organization apart from the crowd when you want to get ahead, and they keep you in your leadership position. As Warren Buffett has said, companies 'occasionally . . . excel because of luck. But usually they excel because of brains.' The rewards you've earned and those you have yet to seek—a new job, a better quality of life, higher income, or more respect—come down to your thinking skills. In other words, you are paid to think" (p. 1).

In the following chapters, exciting advancements are shared and built on as we deepen our goal of a new leadership model as coach leaders. This mindset and the rich skills that are aligned with it hold the power to transform leadership in our schools and therefore the educators and students within. It takes courage to be a coach leader, and the *results* and relationships will be the rewards.

CHAPTER 1: In Chapter 1, we explore the importance of the coach leader being a leader of self first, to provide the basis for leading others in an atmosphere of trust as a coach leader. We introduce the complexities involved in leading today and the necessity of developing the knowledge and skills to continue to broaden and build our personal capacity as leaders to move into increasingly complex interactions and situations. Leaders who have developed beyond the levels of the socialized mind and the self-authoring mind have access to those mindsets as well as the more complex self-transforming mind. The self-transforming mind allows the leader to take varying perspectives into account and respond accordingly in any given situation. Positive psychology and neuroscience underpin the importance of leading in an information-rich, diverse society.

CHAPTER 2: In Chapter 2, we consider some of the current research findings related to leading with the brain in mind. As leaders dedicated to motivating and inspiring others to produce at high levels and enjoy the experience, it's imperative that we think about the impact we have on others. We call on the work of Jill Bolte Taylor, who learned from her work as a neuroanatomist and from personal experiences about how the brain works and adapts. Bolte Taylor reminds us of the complexity of our brains and the impact our emotions have on our own thinking and responses, as well as on those with whom we lead and interact. We include information on how emotional intelligence, or lack thereof, impacts leaders. And we offer research findings on ways people respond in social encounters and include ways to reduce response regrets, something we all desire. You will read about the way Dr. David Rock has incorporated key research findings about leading with the brain in mind and created his SCARF Model, which is explained in detail. You will also find actual examples of ways to reduce stress and increase motivation woven throughout the chapter. And, if you read carefully, you may find stories about you or someone you work with who has solidly moved into the role of a coach leader.

CHAPTER 3: In this chapter, you will find the lessons learned with regard to the essential skills of coaching taught in our first book. While not intended to replace this foundational learning, our purpose is to expand and recognize the clarity that has emerged from our work with you as we have practiced committed listening, discovered the power of paraphrasing for ourselves, and witnessed the shift that is possible when asking questions that presume positive intent. With those skills integrated into our mindset and behaviors as coach leaders, we have honed the art of reflective feedback that delivers the message and keeps others engaged as we continue to grow and improve. You have taught us so much, and this chapter is a celebration of that deeper learning and understanding!

CHAPTER 4: This chapter offers an insightful look at the role of supervisor and the research promoting a new type of leader and supervisor. We offer an examination of our dependency on performance appraisals and positional power hoping for change that rarely happens. With Carl Glickman's permission and approval, we review his model of supervision as a powerful standard barrier for the role of coaching in supervision and walk through the model with examples and outcomes. This chapter was in collaboration with colleague Dr. John Crain and the use of his book, widely used by supervisors throughout the country, *The Documentation Handbook: Appraisal, Nonrenewal and Termination* (Crain & Kemerer, 1998).

CHAPTER 5: This chapter explores the power of conversations and especially difficult conversations. People fear and avoid conversations because they are anxious about how people will respond—and it's usually not well. Supported with language skills and a frame for powerful, succinct, and engineered conversations, even the most difficult can have positive results and produce real change in people and for the students they teach.

CHAPTER 6: This chapter answers three questions. *Why* is a coaching culture of critical importance in this century? *What* exactly is a coaching culture? And *how* does one make it a reality? We believe coaching is the leverage for transformation of the culture of a school or district, and we hold significant evidence of the "power of one" as the impetus for beginning that change.

Once again our goal is an essential 21st century leadership guide. Dennis Sparks's words from *RESULTS Coaching: The New Essential for School Leaders* described it best.

> When educators speak with clarity, possibility, and accountability and when they interact with others in respectful and mutually satisfying ways, they empower themselves and their organizations to produce extraordinary results.
>
> Such interactions add purpose, joy and energy to our lives and the lives of those with whom we relate and increase the organization's capacity to engage in demanding, complex tasks AND to sustain that effort over time. (Kee, Anderson, Dearing, Harris, & Shuster, 2010, p. 7)

REFERENCES

Crain, J. A., & Kemerer, F. (1998). *The documentation handbook: Appraisal, nonrenewal and termination*. Austin: Texas School Administrators' Legal Digest.

Goldsmith, D. (2012). *Paid to think: A leader's toolkit for redefining your future*. Dallas, TX: BenBella Books.

Kee, K. M., Anderson, K. A., Dearing, V. S., Harris, E., & Shuster, F. A. (2010). *Results coaching: The new essential for school leaders*. Thousand Oaks, CA: Corwin Press.

Rock, D. (2006). *Quiet leadership*. New York, NY: HarperCollins.

Rock, D., & Cox, C. (2012). SCARF in 2012: Updating the social neuroscience of collaborating with others. *Neuroleadership Journal, 4*, 1–14. Retrieved from www.davidrock.net

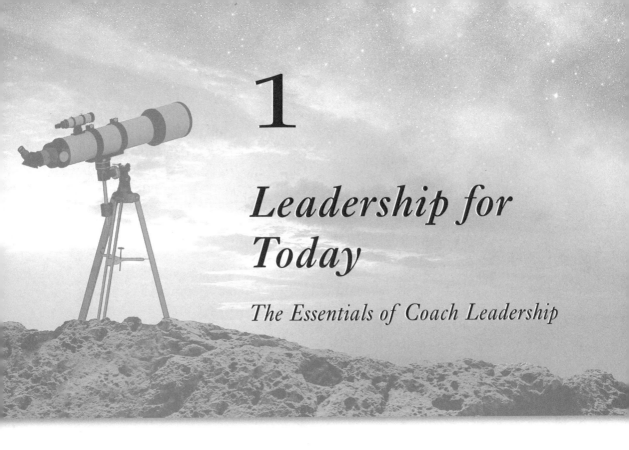

1

Leadership for Today

The Essentials of Coach Leadership

Yesterday I was clever and wanted to save the world. Today I am
wise and I am changing myself.

Rumi

The demands of leadership are great. In today's complex society, the
demands can at times be overwhelming. There is so much to know!
And so much that is not yet known. Leaders must be able to operate at
high levels of complexity, while broadening and building their own personal resilience and nimbleness. Great leaders lead themselves first, while
intentionally building relationships that focus and build on strengths of
others. School cultures built on trust, transparency, and belief in the
strengths and abilities of all—students, staff, parents, community—are the
ones that will not only survive, but will flourish.

WHAT GOT US HERE WON'T GET US THERE!

In the ever-changing modern world, it is increasingly common to read
about leaders today who cite listening as a major leadership practice that
springboards them to impactful leading. It is not enough to have a broad or
deep background of experience. The complexities of today's world cannot

be navigated with outdated or limited strategies or tactics. Even approaches that were highly successful in the past may provide insufficient fixes for the ever spiraling and complex new developments leaders must deal with on a daily basis. So they listen, listen, listen. They ask questions and listen to ideas that are compatible with their beliefs and to ideas that may not jibe with their current thinking. They listen with openness. While holding their own agenda and ideas, they make room for alternative pathways by really hearing thoughts of others.

In a webinar with David Rock, it was reinforced that as we enter a professional role and begin our job responsibilities there is a distinct set of skills related to the position that are essential, the basic skills for the position. In education it would be the essentials of being a teacher. In 2016, these skills would include the pedagogy of teaching and learning; effective teaching practices for meeting the needs of a diverse group of students; how to set up and manage a classroom; how to plan for instruction; how to use data; and how to design, create, and interpret assessments.

As one moves from teacher into a leadership role—to department or team head, or to instructional specialist or coach; perhaps on to assistant principal then principal and even to director to assistant superintendent, and finally to superintendent—the demand for a new set of skills emerges. This set of skills must now include those needed to lead others, and this takes people skills. It will now require emotional intelligence to achieve high levels of success as a leader who is there to inspire and influence and grow talent in others. Daniel Goleman (Harvard Business Review [HBR] & Goleman, 2015) suggests that as a person moves up the ladder in an organization into leadership, up to 90% of their success will be dependent on their emotional intelligence. It's not that IQ and technical skills are irrelevant—they do matter, but mainly as "threshold capabilities" or entry-level requirements. According to Goleman, "Without emotional intelligence, a person can have the best training in the world, an incisive, analytical mind, and an endless supply of smart ideas, but he still won't make a great leader" (HBR & Goleman, 2015, p. 1).

These five skills enable the best leaders to maximize their own and their followers' performance:

- Self-awareness—knowing one's strengths, weaknesses, drives, values, and impact on others
- Self-regulation—controlling or redirecting disruptive impulses and moods
- Motivation—relishing achievement for its own sake
- Empathy—understanding other people's emotional makeup
- Social skill—building rapport with others to move them in desired directions. (HBR & Goleman, 2015, p. 3)

Susan Scott offers in *Fierce Leadership* (2009), "As a leader moves up in an organization up to 90 percent of their success lies in emotional intelligence. In other words, nine out of ten executives who derail do so because they lack emotional competencies! The three primary derailers are difficulty handling change, not being able to work well in a team, and poor interpersonal relationships. *Yep, that would pretty much do it*" (p. 77, emphasis in original).

We are all born with certain levels of emotional intelligence, and we can strengthen these abilities with attention, intention, persistence, practice, and feedback from colleagues or coaches (HBR & Goleman, 2015).

In *What Got You Here Won't Get You There* (Goldsmith & Reiter, 2007), we are reminded that the higher you go, the more your problems are behavioral. "At the higher levels or organizational life, all the leading players are technically skilled. They're all smart. They're all up to date on the technical aspects of their job. You don't get to be chief financial officer without knowing how to count, how to read a balance sheet, and how to handle money prudently. . . . All other things being equal, your people skills (or lack of them) become more pronounced the higher up you go. In fact, even when all other things are not equal, your people skills often make the difference in how high you go" (pp. 42–43).

The latest research in neuroscience continues to be encouraging. More and more studies point to the neuroplasticity of the brain. Neuroplasticity is your brain's ability to reorganize pathways, create new connections, and, in some cases, even create new neurons throughout your entire lifetime. This means we have more control over our body, mind, and brain than previously thought. Your DNA changes continuously based on your experiences, emotions, thinking, and environment. This knowledge offers promise that we humans can create new and more effective ways of thinking and, therefore, leading.

WHY CHANGE IS SO HARD

While there is promise that change is possible, there is no doubt that change is *hard*—for us all. One critically important reason is that what knowledge and skill brings us into the job will not keep us in the job. The more one advances into leadership roles, it is less about what you know and more about how do you know people and can influence people. Emotional Intelligence in leadership is required for real deep change, mindset change.

Kegan and Lahey (2009) write of our natural immunity to change: our web of self-protection that often keeps us from achieving the very thing we say we want. From study and discussion of their incredible work, several concepts offer the potential for deeper understanding of why change is so hard. First, they teach us about three plateaus in adult mental complexity.

The plateaus are the socialized mind, the self-authoring mind, and the self-transforming mind. Each are defined as the following:

- **Socialized mind**: This plateau carries the attributes of being a team player, a faithful follower who is aligning, reliant, and seeks direction. At this level of mental complexity, one's goal is to fit in and be included. I may be strongly influenced by what I believe others want to hear. Additionally, the information I receive and attend to may be more about the implicit rather than the explicit message.
- **Self-authoring mind:** The attributes of this plateau include agenda driver; independent, problem solver; and self-taught leader who is aware of his or her own compass or frame of reference. Rather than sending messages I believe others want to hear, my messages are more about what I deem others need to hear to best support the agenda or my outcomes. Consciously or unconsciously, I have a direction, a strategy, and a point of view that may be in the right direction or misguided. When the self-authoring mind receives information, a filter is created that discerns what it will let through or not. While this level of mental complexity may be admired for the ability to keep and maintain focus, it can spell danger if the direction or the filter is off base.
- **Self-transforming mind:** When one gets to this plateau, we see the meta-leader who leads to learn, who is open to other points of view, who seeks solutions, and who is interdependent. Interestingly, this plateau also has a filter, yet the person is not fused to it. Kegan and Lahey (2009) say, "The self-transforming mind can stand back from its own filter and look at it, not just through it" (p. 19). As a result, the self-transforming mind resists one stance, welcomes collaboration, and seeks information that will advance the thinking and accelerate the work.

Further, Kegan and Lahey teach us that each plateau is higher than the preceding one because it can perform the mental functions of the previous level as well as the attributes of the current level. Regarding performance, a higher level outperforms a lower level. The startling results from numerous studies report that the percentage of people beyond the self-authoring plateau is very small.

A second powerful concept that illustrates why change is so difficult emerges from the work of Ronald Heifetz as reported by Kegan and Lahey (2009, p. 29). Heifetz distinguishes between two kinds of change challenges: technical and adaptive.

A *technical change* is defined as a well-known skill set necessary to perform complicated behaviors. It is not necessarily easy, nor are the results unimportant or insignificant. By considering the work of a highly skilled surgeon or an airplane pilot, we get the critical importance of the routines and processes to which they must adhere. We expect a high standard with regard to the technical aspects of their work when we are in the operating room or when we are flying from one destination to another.

The second change challenge is called an *adaptive change challenge*. These challenges can only be met by transforming one's mindset, which means advancing to a higher stage of mental development. Most of the change challenges we meet fit into this category, *and* the biggest error we as leaders make is applying technical solutions to solve adaptive challenges. No wonder change is so hard!

Third, we refer to the brain research from David Rock and others who have helped us understand that change requires TARP—time, attention, repetition, and positive feedback. Shifting from the notion of changing hard wiring to creating new wiring makes sense in terms of why it's hard work. We have practiced things a certain way for a long time. In fact, some of us have a "Grand Canyon" with regard to the patterns of language we have practiced for a lifetime.

What we know for sure is that scores of you are creating new wiring as you bring intention to new habits of mind with regard to your mindset and your language. Change is hard, and you are up for the challenge!

COACH LEADERS FIRST LEAD THEMSELVES

In our work with coach leaders across the nation, we are finding graphic examples of individual transformation that impact whole systems. The leaders we highlight here were excellent and well-respected leaders even before they transformed themselves into coach leaders. In the words of David Rock (2006), "If you want to improve performance, the most effective way to do this is . . . to improve thinking" (p. xxiii). These coach leaders lead by improving the thinking of others through listening, understanding, inquiring, and offering feedback for growth.

Dr. Lloyd Sain, director of leadership and teacher development in the school district in Little Rock, Arkansas, researched coaching models prior to bringing Results Coaching into the Little Rock School District (LRSD). His vision to train external executive coaches to coach school principals began with a broad gathering of respected leaders. Dr. Sain knew that the leaders who could only tell others how to lead and direct the activities of others through directive control were of a bygone era. Dr. Sain's vision to bring external executive coaches to LRSD grew to principals wanting to be more coach-like in their leadership by emulating the communication and coaching modeled by their executive coaches. As more and more leaders experienced the coach leader behaviors of their supervisors, more learning of the attitudes and skills of coach leaders was requested.

Results Coaching Global's partnership with LRSD began in 2009 and continues. The stories of personal and professional transformation abound. We enjoy the laughter and stories of Dr. Sain—before and after the influence of Results Coaching on his own leadership and personal style! Lloyd confesses that his former unproductive listening style was judgment and/or criticism. His personal transformation leaves that behind, and he is now the unofficial chief listening officer of LRSD. He is intentional about being fully present as a listener and asks the same of others. He has made a clear transition into the coach leader identity. Dr. Sain is now credentialed as a professional certified coach, and his work influences school leaders within LRSD as well as other school venues, both public and private.

David Curry, superintendent of Union Hill School District in Grass Valley, California, husband and father of three sons, and friend to multitudes, will tell you that he knows firsthand the power, importance, and transformational value of coaching and of being a coach leader. When Dave was executive director of educational services in the Tahoe Truckee Unified School District, a district where he spent more than 29 years of his career, he had a deep desire to see the district elevate the level of honest and open collaboration necessary to strengthen relationships and accomplish increased results for all students. Just as Dr. Sain did, Dave researched best approaches to consider for his district. Results Coaching Global was one of those approaches. As Dave tells the story, he happened into a Gift of Coaching Session held at a Learning Forward Conference in Washington, DC, and saw what was happening in a brief conversation between a coach and another person. He wanted that for his district. Thus began an 8-year partnership with the Tahoe Truckee Unified School District and Results Coaching. The amazing thing about this story, which could actually be a book in itself, was that Dave slowly and carefully began to take his dream from a place in his head and heart to a reality within the district.

While the journey was never without bumps and a few potholes in the road, Dave kept focused on the dream and the vision to transform the district into a coaching culture. And in the midst of the district transformation, Dave changed. By working with his coach, he moved the concepts from the pages of the materials he was studying and what he was hearing and experiencing in our coaching training to his own actual practice. He became willing to listen more and talk less. He invited thoughtful conversations with others, and he intentionally created space and established agreements for holding team conversations, including clarity on topics to be discussed and agreements on conversation processes to be used for listening, speaking, and making decisions. He sought and received his own credentials as a coach through the International Coach Federation. He became a coach leader. In the fall of 2015, Dave responded to a new dream growing from within himself to hold the highest position within a district and to do so as a coach leader. Dave is in the process of living this dream now, and we fully expect it is going to be a dream that unfolds into a reality that impacts all those fortunate enough to work and connect with Dave.

POSITIVITY BROADENS THINKING

Dr. Sain and Dave Curry are living examples of what Barbara Fredrickson (2009) in her book, *Positivity*, describes as experiencing firsthand the benefits of using positivity as an intentional way of changing how your mind works through broadening and building thinking. Heartfelt positivity has the power to contribute to moving one to higher levels of mental complexity—the self-transforming mind—which is open, flexible, and curious.

Individuals accomplish this transformation through developing their own self-knowledge and resilience: therefore stepping up to the next level of existence by broadening their mind and building their best future (Fredrickson, 2009, pp. 9–13).

According to Fredrickson (2009), "Whereas the narrowed mindset sparked by negative emotions were valuable in instances that threatened our ancestors' survival in some way, the broadened mindsets sparked by positive emotions were valuable to our ancestors in different ways and over longer time scales. Broadened mindsets mattered because—over time—such expansive awareness served to build our human ancestors' resources, spurring on their development of assets, abilities, and useful traits. These new resources functioned as reserves, better equipping our ancestors to handle later threats to survival, which of course were inevitable" (p. 22).

Fredrickson offers an example of how the *interest* from a positivity mindset broadens and builds our resources. With interest, your mindset is open and curious, drawing us out to explore. Because open mindsets produce exploration and experiential learning, they also produce more accurate mental maps of the world (Fredrickson, 2009, p. 23). We have known for a long time that we learn more when we feel upbeat and interested and act on that pull of curiosity. Fredrickson states that negativity and neutrality hold us back, constraining our knowledge and therefore our experience of the world. When a school leader encounters behaviors that may appear to be resistant or even sabotaging, because of her positivity belief, she is able to see possibility for growth rather than need for punitive action.

Fredrickson (2009) introduces us to 10 positive emotions that are the focus of a growing amount of scientific attention, and her recent research and the research of others has seen these 10 forms of positivity present in people's day-to-day lives most frequently and clearly (pp. 39–48). Fredrickson describes the 10 forms of positivity as:

1. **Joy:** Circumstances that spark joy are being in surroundings that are safe and familiar. Things are going your way or going even better than expected. The situation requires little effort on your part.

2. **Gratitude:** Gratitude comes when we appreciate something that has come our way as a gift to be treasured. It opens your heart and carries the urge to give back.

3. **Serenity:** Like joy, serenity enters when your surroundings are safe and familiar and require little effort on your part, but it is much more low-key than joy. It is a mindful state, and she calls it the *afterglow emotion*.

4. **Interest:** Something new or different draws your attention, filling you with a sense of possibility and increased attention on your part. You are pulled to explore and feel open and alive. These circumstances call for effort and increased attention on your part.

5. **Hope:** Hope comes into play when things are not going well for you or there's considerable uncertainty about how things will turn out. Hope is sparked within the moments when despair is most likely. Hope contains the belief that things can and will change. It sustains you in these moments when your circumstances are dire. Hope energizes us to do as much as we can to make life good for ourselves and for others.

6. **Pride:** Pride is a self-conscious emotion. Any emotion can go too far, and pride gone too far can become negative. It is positive when tempered with humility. Visions of great achievements—especially socially valued ones—bring forth feelings of pride, which fosters the motivation to achieve.

7. **Amusement:** Amusement is a social emotion. True amusement spurs the urge to share laughter with others, signaling that you find your current situation a safe place to share lightheartedness and build connections with others.

8. **Inspiration:** Being inspired is attention-grabbing and heartwarming. Inspiration creates the desire to be at your highest and best. Along with gratitude and awe, inspiration is one of the self-transcendent emotions, pulling us out of ourselves into a broader world.

9. **Awe:** Awe is very closely related to inspiration. It is also a self-transcendent emotion. We are compelled to see ourselves as a part of something larger than ourselves. When in awe, we feel literally overwhelmed by greatness.

10. **Love:** Love encompasses all the positive emotions listed before it. Love is the most common positive emotion that people feel, and it has many facets. Feeling recurrent surges of love actually changes the inner chemistry of our bodies, creating biological responses linked with lifelong bonds, trust, and intimacy.

Each of these forms is backed by scientific research that speaks to the validity of her work. It is gratifying to know that her work supports our claim that authenticity is the bedrock of heartfelt positivity. Expressions of words that are positive without genuineness or authenticity as a base do more harm than good. These expressions are perceived as empty at best and manipulative at worst. So true belief in others is the mindset that underpins the positive statements we offer in coaching and feedback. "If we don't actually feel the positivity we express, we may actually be doing harm" (Fredrickson, 2009, p. 35).

Fredrickson's (2009) studies indicate that a benefit of positivity is that it builds *resilience* (pp. 97, 103). In study after study, researchers found that people who bounce back show more emotional complexity when facing stressors. Negativity does not disappear. Negativity sits side by side with positivity. The ability to tap into positivity allows one to reverse the course of a downward spiral and spring back more quickly. Positivity builds resilience (Fredrickson, 2009, pp. 97, 103).

Leaders who are nimble respond to and move through change quickly and effectively. They are emotionally responsive and quick to move on. They let go of the negativity and focus on solution rather than overanalyzing what might have gone wrong. Positivity is what makes them nimble. Resilience does not come with emotional disengagement. In fact, resilience is marked by emotional agility—the ability to bounce back quickly. Coaching's connection to neuroscience is further examined with regard to resiliency and additional examples in Chapter 2.

KEEP CALM AND CARRY ON! A STORY OF POSITIVITY AND RESILIENCE

Jennifer came to our coaching call with this question: "How can I maintain my composure when I am feeling emotionally drained and I seem to always be putting out fires—both figuratively and literally? I actually had to deal with a fire in the boy's restroom this week!"

After some exploration of her topic, she decided that she wanted to develop positive ways to calm herself in the midst of an often-chaotic high school environment. She wanted steps or a saying—her inner voice—something specific to call on to remind herself to stay proactive rather than reactive. She came up with this list for herself: breathe three times, count from 1 to 10, go to the beach and walk, have pictures in my office of calm scenes, stop taking things personally, imagine calm, pause before responding, give myself time to think rather than just react. She then separated her list into things to do in the moment (e.g., breathe, count to 10) and things to do outside the immediate setting (e.g., walk on the beach). Her two-pronged approach offered the opportunity to recognize her habitual response patterns as well as to bring more calmness into her overall thoughts, which now offer more resilient and respectful ways of responding in the short and long term.

Jennifer clearly realized that many of her anxiety-producing moments were out of her control. She *can* and *wants* to control her responses to such situations. She wants to be braver—to do things that "bring me back to proactive me."

Her vital commitment as a school leader to do everything she possibly can to ensure the engagement and success of her students and her staff is at the forefront for Jennifer at the beginning of a new school year. She recognizes that the way she shows up every day impacts the culture and climate of her school. She knows she must be intentional about being calm so she can be a mindful leader.

Fast forward to more than a year after this conversation. Jennifer is now principal of a large high school. When we talked earlier, she was a ninth-grade associate principal. At the end of her first year as a full-fledged principal, she was named administrator of the year for her district. Through positivity and resilience, she did the things that she wanted to do to "bring me back to proactive me."

KNOW THYSELF

We know ourselves in many ways. We see ourselves by reflecting on our thoughts, beliefs, and actions. We observe bits of ourselves through the eyes and ears of others. We employ or access a coach to assist us in seeing parts of ourselves that we may be unintentionally hiding or masking.

Assessments are ways to better know ourselves—especially our strengths. There are a number of assessments that can be accessed easily online that have been checked and rechecked for validity and reliability. Some have a brief version that is free and a more in-depth version available for a cost. **Here are three assessments based on strengths or core values that stand out as worthy of time and exploration for knowing thyself.**

VIA (VALUES IN ACTION) CHARACTER STRENGTHS

The purpose of the VIA Character Strengths survey is to empower people to discover what connects us to our best self and also to others. Character research shows that knowing and applying our unique character strength profile increases our life satisfaction and well-being. Knowing and developing your character strengths can have an impact on quality of life as well as a positive effect on relationships, work, and personal growth. A variety of VIA surveys are available online at www.viacharacter.org.

StrengthsFinder

Gallup created the science of strengths and continues to research and enhance knowledge and application of strengths-based knowledge and leadership. More than 50 years of research and books related to discovering and developing one's self through focusing on strengths vs. weaknesses have assisted many people in growing and developing their personal and leadership competencies. Each of us possesses a unique combination of strengths that come together to create the individual we are. The StrengthsFinder is available online at www.gallupstrengths center.com.

Core Values Index (CVI)

The Core Values Index (CVI), developed by Lynn Taylor, is a revolutionary human assessment that provides a description of the innate, unchanging nature of an individual, which is different from personality- and behavioral-based assessments. This unique instrument takes 10 minutes or less to complete and provides a highly accurate and reliable picture of the core motivational drivers of any person, with an instant report online. Those who experience the CVI frequently find validation and understanding of their own typical ways of responding and learn to access and apply additional values and strengths as situations call for different responses. Our greater understanding of ways we typically and naturally respond to specific tasks or challenges allows us to be mindful and intentional in our choices and responses. It is available at www.taylorprotocols.com.

Successful Leaders Set Specific, Written Goals for Improved Performance

Caroline Adams Miller, another pioneer in positive psychology, was among the first students accepted into the newly formed Masters of Applied Positive Psychology program at the University of Pennsylvania in 2005. She was one of the highly screened and carefully selected individuals who were accepted into this groundbreaking first cohort. Her book, *Creating Your Best Life*, is filled with research, success stories, and exercises and activities that bring to life the power of setting goals that give a sense of purpose and direction for our lives. She states that "clearly chosen goals that are anchored in our own values and the areas of life that matter to us give us an exciting feeling that others will recognize as zest and a can-do attitude" (Miller, 2009, p. 11).

Miller offers the following attributes for setting best goals:

- Specific and challenging
- Approach (exciting and magnetic) and not avoidance
- Value driven

- Create feelings of independence, connectedness, and competence
- Intrinsic and not extrinsic
- Measurable and have the opportunity to produce feedback
- Nonconflicting and leveraged
- Written
- Precommitment and accountability
- Capable of stimulating "flow"[1] states

Goals may be set for any area of our personal and professional lives. Assessments, such as the strengths, character strengths, and core values assessments described above, along with self-reflection on life-purpose, bucket lists, and desired legacy, offer abundant possibilities for goal setting.

Leaders Who Understand the Power of Engagement

A pervasive theme in education today is student engagement. The *Glossary of Education Reform* (n.d.) defines *student engagement* as follows:

> In education, student engagement refers to the degree of attention, curiosity, interest, optimism, and passion that students show when they are learning or being taught, which extends to the level of motivation they have to learn and progress in their education.

Numerous studies, articles, and strategies are available to teachers who are seeking to more fully engage students in their learning. Countless professional development opportunities are provided to teach teachers engagement techniques. So what is the missing piece? Gallup's 2009 study of more than 78,000 students in 160 schools found that teachers' engagement levels are directly related to those of their students, therefore to student achievement outcomes. Engaged teachers not only challenge students to grow, but they also trust, encourage, and engage their fellow teachers. A study commissioned by the Wallace Foundation (Seashore Lewis, Leithwood, Wahlstrom, & Anderson, 2010) found that adult relationships in a school indirectly affect student achievement. This study reinforces the importance of a community of professionals—a special environment in which teachers work together to improve their practice, therefore improve student learning.

It is imperative that school leaders model the type of engagement in our learning and work that we are striving to create and observe in our students. According to a recent Gallup poll including more than 7,200

---

[1]Mihaly Csikszentmihalyi (1990) describes flow as a state in which you lose track of time, and your emotions are somewhat neutral. It is defined as a time when you are completely engaged in the task at hand, without any feelings of worry, anxiety, or self-consciousness.

K–12 teachers, *nearly 70% of teachers are not engaged in their jobs* (Hastings & Agrawal, 2015). Approximately 31% are *engaged*, meaning they are involved in, enthusiastic about, and committed to their work and that they know the scope of their jobs and constantly look for new and better ways to achieve outcomes. Just over half (56%) are *not engaged*, meaning they may be satisfied with their jobs, but they are not emotionally connected to their workplaces and are unlikely to devote much discretionary effort to their work. About one in eight (13%) are *actively disengaged*, meaning they are dissatisfied with their workplaces and likely to be spreading negativity to their coworkers.

Teachers were dead last among occupational groups Gallup surveyed regarding their likelihood to say their opinions seem to count at work. They were also least likely of any profession surveyed on workforce engagement to respond positively to whether their supervisor creates an open and trusting environment.

What are possibilities for reversing this disturbing trend? The good news is that good teachers view their role as a *calling*. Many find at least someone at work who encourages their development. Great teachers are lifelong learners and want and need opportunities to take on new challenges. In light of the Gallup findings, school leaders must find a way to build in opportunities for collaboration among teachers and between teachers and administrators.

Coach leaders have the mindset and the skills to reverse this trend. They know the skills of committed listening, paraphrasing, presuming positive intent, and reflective feedback to engage teachers in thoughtful, reflective, and rigorous conversations. These are conversations that elevate status and create focus for the urgent results that are required. These are conversations where opinions matter; conversations where teachers are viewed as intelligent and competent professionals; conversations where teachers feel valued for the important part they have in impacting student learning; and conversations where they are trusted to make important decisions about their work. Conversations build collaboration, which eradicates the isolation and disempowerment teachers often feel. Environments of openness and trust are created and flourish at every level of the organization—classroom, school, or district.

Leaders Who Recognize and Appreciate Diversity

When leaders are inclusive of the diversity existing in today's workplace, employees are motivated and inspired to higher levels of performance, especially now that multiple generations are present in the workplace in increasing numbers. The Gallup surveys, as noted above, show a lack of engagement among a significant percentage of teachers in the workforce.

Today's leadership calls for understanding the varying needs of staff members who were born and reared during different eras. The significant events of the times and the environments of specific eras shape differences in value systems and worldviews. Inclusive leaders recognize that individuals born in different times than themselves likely hold mindsets that may vary significantly from their own. For example, people born in different economic and social times may define "work ethic" differently. Labels such as Baby Boomer, Gen X, and Millennial are often used to describe generalizations of similarities among individuals born during certain time spans.

For our purposes, these labels are offered as fodder for thoughtful reflection and not as hard-and-fast labels of any individual. Each individual is essentially a "culture of one" and may share certain characteristics with others of their generation but also share characteristics of individuals of different generations.

It's important to note that today's leaders do not gain motivation and influence simply because they have the title of leader. The old way of leading through command, control, and coercion no longer works. Nowadays people don't follow titles; they follow people. Generationally, the workforce is not as likely to be motivated by material compensation or by the threat of the lack of such reward. (See also Pink, 2011.) Instead, most of us are looking for connectivity, work-life balance, and a place where we feel supported and where we truly are making a difference. Robert B. Dilts captures this idea in the title of his 1996 book, *Visionary Leadership Skills: Creating a World to Which People Want to Belong*. People of all generations are seeking meaning in their work—a place that invites them to be engaged, be connected, and be a contributor to the workplace and beyond.

A superintendent who is at the cusp of the so-called young boomers and the older Gen-Xers remarked at the conclusion of one of our seminars that the Millennials will not be led for long in the traditional way of directing. They work best and are motivated best by serving a purpose higher than themselves, having a measure of autonomy, and being able to work toward their own personal mastery. Daniel Pink's (2011) work, *Drive: The Surprising Truth About What Motivates Us*, underscores the importance of these three elements as well.

Another consideration of diversity is apparent in one's stage of life. Those just entering the profession have very different mindset needs than those with several years of experience, those with many years of experience, and those close to retirement. Other life stages that impact mindset and thinking include professionals who are single, those with young families, those with nontraditional marriages or families, those who are empty nesters, and grandparents who may be raising their grandchildren.

How does one lead effectively in such diversity? How can one committed leader know everything there is to know about all the differences present in his or her arena of leadership? We are cognizant of the wide diversity that includes culture, ethnicity, language differences, and generational differences as we do our best to serve all children and communities in our increasingly diverse society. Entire movements are devoted to the study of understanding and leading in these broad areas of diversity.

The good news is that the effective leader is not necessarily the one with the most specific knowledge about any one topic or person. The most effective leader is the one who leads from the coach leader identity—listening without judgment, building or multiplying capacity in others, convening others for conversations, asking the questions that provoke thinking and innovation, and deciding how and when to take action as individual leadership is called for. There are essential skills critical for the enormous task. Committed listening, or listening to understand, is the first and best way to truly understand another, no matter how or when a person's worldview and values came into being.

Leading in a climate of diversity requires much more from the leader than directive leadership. The effective leader leads from a place of curiosity and openness regarding the thoughts, feelings, and values a diverse culture presents each day.

Leaders Who Hold Standards and Expectations

People often fail in the performance of their duties simply because they have no clear understanding of the standards and expectations of their job responsibilities and of their supervisor. Job descriptions are written every day, yet few are even read, reviewed, or used as the standard for performance of the position. Likewise, billions of dollars are spent writing, developing, and creating performance appraisals, but rarely are they used throughout the year to maintain the focus on the standard and expectation of the position. Once folks accept the job, we often just expect them to know what to do, yet without continual reminders of the targets, focus, and purpose of the positions, employees just start doing and lose sight of the what and why. Supervisors sometimes fall prey to the phenomenon of the "curse of knowledge" described by Chip and Dan Heath (2007) as "Once we know something, we find it hard to imagine what it was like not to know it. Our knowledge has 'cursed' us. And it becomes difficult for us to share our knowledge with others, because we can't readily re-create our listeners' state of mind" (p. 20). They just expect people to know and remember. It is just second nature, so everyone else must surely know. To mitigate this curse, coach leaders recognize the importance of clearly articulating standards and expectations and maintaining them in the forefront of all work.

Standards and expectations should be

- clear and articulated widely,
- frequently held up or discussed, and
- based on external or objective criteria.

Standards and expectations that meet these criteria are very often the missing link for achieving excellence.

One new principal, Eric, began his principalship by offering up the five standards and expectations he and his leadership team had selected as the main areas of focus for the school year. Even though the needs were great, Eric and his team knew that focus was important. At the first staff meeting of the new school year, Eric brought in a silver platter with five icons representing the selected areas of focus. These five areas were (1) working collaboratively in professional learning communities (PLCs), (2) building partnerships and trust with parents and community, (3) focusing on the writing process, (4) guided reading, and (5) small group instruction.

As Eric discussed each one, he held up the icon and described its meaning in detail. He then placed the silver platter with icons on the conference table in his office. Anyone looking in had a visual reminder of the year's focus. And anyone not meeting a particular standard had an opportunity to discuss with Eric the standard in question without feeling personally attacked. The standard was simply discussed as a reminder, and the individual receiving the reminder was given the opportunity to create a pathway toward meeting it. Eric exemplified coach leadership by maintaining status through listening, paraphrasing, asking questions, and offering positive feedback. This clarity of standards and expectations moved the entire staff forward, and as each was internalized, a new focus could emerge. Even though there was a lot to accomplish at Eric's school, teachers, staff, and students were not overwhelmed with uncertainty. Course corrections were determined along the way, and a new focus of standards and expectations could emerge to meet the very broad set of education standards and expectations that can seem overwhelming.

A STORY OF MAKING A DIFFERENCE THAT IMPACTED EVERYTHING

Many conversations with leaders focus on the energy and time it takes to create real change in attitudes—particularly when teachers balk at new expectations around such things as student interventions, working as PLCs, or using a new curriculum. A systems approach might include the way we hire for positions. There is a lot presumed when we hire staff. How might the system impact and increase the real requirements of teaching that are often out of alignment with general perceptions?

A leader we have worked with in Texas, Dr. Drew Watkins, is superintendent of a fast-growing district. He does not leave the understanding of standards and expectations to chance. Each year his practice is to meet individually with every new employee—and the number of new employees grows each year. His conversation serves one purpose: to confirm with the applicant that in taking a specific job in the district, the potential employee understands and agrees to the expectations. He reviews the required use of the curriculum, progress monitoring of each student, use of best practices, the norm of working collaboratively in teams to focus on success for all students, and partnering with parents in the education journey. Dr. Watkins asks for any clarity about the expectations, and then he offers the applicant the opportunity to change his or her mind or reconsider by saying, "Okay, this is your last chance to run if we are not the right match for you. There are many districts in the metro area and some hold different expectations that might be a better match for you. It's your final decision whether you accept the expectations of working in Prosper ISD."

Dr. Watkins reports that when new hires commit to him in the conversation, they want to live up to the expectations and don't want to let him down. He says he is committed to maintaining this practice regardless of the time it may take—even as his new hire numbers increase. The payoff is witnessed throughout his system. No conversations are needed to convince folks about what is expected to teach and get results in the district. A principal might only have to remind an employee of his or her commitment to the standard or ask if it might have changed. Energy and effort are focused on great teaching for great results for students. The data provide the evidence. Not only does the district enjoy the results of high student achievement, little to no turnover, and highly satisfied employees, but in 2015 they were also recognized in the Dallas/Fort Worth metroplex as one of the top 10 places to work—a rarity for any school district.

When leaders are intentional about the expectations that drive the focus of the work, maintain that focus, and continually identify the "what" we do and the "how" we do it of the position, people have clarity and certainty about what is expected to do great work. In the field of education, it is our work—to ensure the highest levels of learning for all students. How many ways are available to leaders to make systemic changes that dramatically and fundamentally change behaviors and practice for all students to succeed?

Leader as Convener

In his book *Community: The Structure of Belonging*, Peter Block (2009) asserts that community building requires a concept of the "leader as one who creates experiences for others—experiences that in themselves are examples of our desired future" (p. 86). This type of leadership has also been called *relational leadership*. The task of leader in this model is to provide context and produce engagement.

Leadership revolves around these three tasks:

1. Create a context that nurtures an alternative future, one based on gifts, generosity, accountability, and commitment.

2. Initiate and convene conversations that shift people's experience, which occurs through the way people are brought together and the nature of the questions used to engage them.

3. Listen and pay attention. Listening is critical to the role of leadership. In fact, "Listening may be the single most powerful action the leader can take" (Block, 2009, p. 88). This mindset speaks to the notion that listening is active, not passive. Listening without interpretation or judgment, listening to deeply understand the thoughts and feelings of another, listening to uncover what may be hidden even from oneself, listening to connect people, thoughts and ideas to each other, and listening for new possibilities are a few of the ways listening becomes transformative in our lives and our work.

Leader as Multiplier

Liz Wiseman's (2010) book *Multipliers: How the Best Leaders Make Everyone Smarter* examines leadership styles though analyzing data from 150 leaders. Her study describes "diminishers" and "multipliers." Multipliers fit hand in glove with the coach leader style of leadership. Multipliers are genius makers. It isn't how much the leader knows that is important. What matters is how much of another's intelligence can be accessed and put to use. Multipliers invoke each individual's unique intelligence and create an atmosphere in which innovation, productive effort, and collective intelligence may flourish.

Multipliers hold the belief that by investing resources and having confidence in other people and giving them the ownership of their success, they uncover the vast intelligence and capability that lies within. They invest in others in a way that builds independence to apply their full intelligence to the work at hand. Multipliers are more successful at getting more out of people.

Here are Wiseman's five disciplines of the multiplier:

1. Attracts talented people and uses them at their highest point of contribution

2. Creates an intense environment that requires people's best thinking and work

3. Defines an opportunity that causes people to stretch

4. Drives sound decisions through rigorous debate

5. Gives other people the ownership for results and invests in their success (p. 23)

Wiseman has also written a book specifically for schools, *The Multiplier Effect: Tapping the Genius Inside Our Schools*, published by Corwin Press in 2013.

SUMMARY

The demands of leadership are great. In today's complex society, the demands can at times be overwhelming. There is so much to know! And so much that is not yet known. Leaders must be able to operate at high levels of complexity, while broadening and building their own personal resilience and nimbleness. Great leaders lead themselves first, while intentionally building relationships that focus and build on strengths of others.

The coach leader mindset, by its nature, focuses on strengths. The work of Gallup, Seligman (2016), Fredrickson, Miller, and others offers validation of a strengths-based, positive psychology approach to human development. Knowing one's own innate strengths, character strengths, and unchanging core values assists the individual in self-growth and development. Knowledge and understanding of individual strengths inspire leaders as they partner with others to create awareness and thus the desire to embrace and use those strengths intentionally and with consistency. This coach leader mindset fuels personal and collective well-being and greater ability to achieve life goals, team goals, and goals of organizations and systems.

David Rock's (2009) work at the intersection of coaching and neuroscience further provides a solid foundation for thoughtful and deliberate advancement of individuals, groups, teams, and entire organizations. His SCARF model is a paragon of simplicity based on complexity that has broad cross-cultural and multiage application. As the coach leader brings the SCARF concept into his or her leadership identity, he or she experiences the positive transformation of individual and cultural transformation.

REFERENCES

Block, P. (2009). *Community: The structure of belonging*. Oakland, CA: Berrett-Koehler.

Csikszentmihalyi, M. (1990). *Flow: The psychology of optimal experience*. New York, NY: Harper & Row.

Dilts, R. (1996). *Visionary leadership skills: Creating a world to which people want to belong*. Capitola, CA: Meta.

Fredrickson, B. L. (2009). *Positivity*. New York, NY: Three Rivers Press.

Gallup. (2009). *The state of America's schools*. Washington, DC: Gallup World Headquarters.

Goldsmith, M., & Reiter, M. (2007). *What got you here won't get you there*. New York, NY: Hyperion.

Harvard Business Review, & Goleman, D. (2015). *HBR's 10 must reads: On emotional intelligence*. Boston, MA: HBS Publishing.

Hastings, M., & Agrawal, S. (2015, January 9). Lack of teacher engagement linked to 2.3 million missed workdays. Retrieved from http://www.gallup.com/poll/180455/lack-teacher-engagement-linked-million-missed-workdays.aspx

Heath, C., & Heath, D. (2007). *Made to stick*. New York, NY: Random House.

Kegan, R., & Lahey, L. (2009). *Immunity to change*. Boston, MA: Harvard Business Review Press.

Miller, C. A. (2009). *Creating your best life: The ultimate life list guide*. New York, NY: Sterling.

Pink, D. (2011). *Drive: The surprising truth about what motivates us*. New York, NY: Riverhead Books.

Rock, D. (2006). *Quiet leadership*. New York, NY: HarperCollins.

Rock, D., & Emde, M. J. (2012, April). Lead change with the brain in mind, NeuroLeadership Group, transform thinking and performance [Webinar].

Scott, S. (2009). *Fierce leadership: A bold alternative to the worst "best" business practices today*. New York, NY: Crown Business.

Seashore Lewis, K., Leithwood, K., Wahlstrom, K. L., & Anderson, S. E. (2010). *Investigating links to student learning: Final report of research findings*. Minneapolis: University of Minnesota. Retrieved from http://www.wallacefoundation.org/knowledge-center/Documents/Investigating-the-Links-to-Improved-Student-Learning.pdf

Seligman, M. (2016). Profile of Dr. Martin Seligman. Retrieved from https://www.authentichappiness.sas.upenn.edu/faculty-profile/profile-dr-martin-seligman

Student engagement. (n.d.). In *Glossary of Education Reform*. Retrieved June 8, 2015, from http://www.edglossary.org/student-engagement

Wiseman, L. (2010). *Multipliers: How the best leaders make everyone smarter*. New York, NY: HarperCollins.

2

Leading With the Brain in Mind

Human behavior flows from three main sources: desire, emotion, and knowledge.

Plato

In this chapter, we offer convincing reasons why successful leaders of today know and use key findings about the brain to better lead themselves and others to extraordinary results. We explain important facts about the workings of the brain and show practical ways to put the knowledge into specific leadership actions. We describe how leading is a matter of the head and the heart and emphasize the importance of creating a culture of respect, where working with emotions is a given rather than a rarity. We provide examples throughout the chapter and invite you to engage in practice so that you are ready to put your learning into immediate actions.

THE CALL FROM LEADERS

Since the publication of our first book, *Results Coaching: The New Essential for School Leaders*, there is a growing message—an undeniable force that cannot be ignored. That message is that leaders are hungry. They are searching for ways to motivate others to do the hard work that is called for in today's schools and businesses and to do it in such a way that people are attracted to the cause and resolved to accomplish it together as a unified team. They are asking for support in this area—one that most likely did not take a priority position in their earlier leadership training.

We speak from personal experience here. It was when we began to work in the field of coaching, long after receiving our leadership credentials, that we knew—and has since been supported by research—there are certain relational skills that can no longer be ignored or thought of as "soft" when one is determined to successfully fill the role of leader. Regarding the role of leader today, it includes anyone who has the opportunity and desire to influence, inspire, and facilitate growth and change in another person or a group of people.

Successful leaders understand that for a team, organization, or company to succeed at high levels of performance, it is necessary to build and foster a collegial culture of trust and respect intertwined with challenging and specific, articulated standards for thinking, performing, and achieving. In today's world, leaders must hold, and expect and support others to hold, thought-provoking conversations that focus on important topics designed to bring clarity, insights, and impetus for change demonstrated through specific actions.

Leaders are called to lead others and themselves toward extraordinary results—as individuals and as a united team. This is why the term *coach leader* has risen to a prominent position in leadership behaviors of today. Leaders are charged to elevate the thinking of every member of the organization, both as individuals and as a team, to accomplish growth and change within the organization. This best happens when leaders lead with their head and their heart, when thinking is combined with feeling.

How does one best do this? How do leaders of today motivate and engage others to think, perform, and accomplish at high levels? How do they inspire and influence those they lead to do the expected work and do it at exceptional levels while also feeling connected to each other and part of the greater purpose or higher mission associated with the work? And how do leaders tend to their own motivational and inspirational needs to lead others in ways they desire and deserve?

To answer these and many other leadership questions we are called to examine current research related to the inner workings of the brain. Through these findings we will better understand the theory of motivation, inspiration, engagement, and results. Leaders of today lead with an understanding of the brain in mind as they move toward desired growth and positive changes.

While there is no need to comprehend the design and workings of the brain at near the level of brain scientists, we can certainly take what they are learning and put it into practical application while gathering data on the differences it makes to us and to the people with whom we lead and interact.

IMPORTANT FACTS ABOUT THE BRAIN

Let's begin with some basic information about each of us. For this, we turn to the work of experts like Jill Bolte Taylor, a neuroanatomist, who suffered a massive stroke at the age of 37. In *My Stroke of Insight: A Brain Scientist's Personal Journey*, Bolte Taylor (2006) shares the story of her miraculous and inspirational recovery, with part of her book providing simple and easy–to–understand information about the basic functions of the brain.

While it's a given that every human being in the world is unique, with no one sharing another's exact DNA, there are many ways in which we are all very similar to one another. According to Bolte Taylor (2006), "As members of the same human species, you and I share all but 0.01% or 1/100th % of identical genetic sequence. So, as a species, we are virtually identical to one another at the level of our genes (99.9%)," yet we are distinctively different (p. 15). The 0.01% in which we are different shows up in how we think, look, and behave—and that is where it gets interesting. How do we best deal with the 0.01% difference in the people we are called to lead? While that percentage seems minute, the differences are significant. This is where we move in closer toward the science of the brain to better understand how to effectively lead others who, while similar in multiple ways, are also uniquely different.

Our brain is one of the most wondrous and complex organs in our body. It controls our breathing, nervous system, and muscles while providing numerous other functions. It is the part of our body through which we make sense of our world. Serving somewhat as a living scanner, it takes in information from all our senses, filters the information, and sends off signals on how best to respond to this data.

The outer portion of our brain, the cerebral cortex, is divided into two major hemispheres, each complementing the other (Bolte Taylor, 2006). These two hemispheres communicate with each other through a highway for information transfer, the corpus callosum. While each hemisphere is unique in the specific types of information it processes, when connected and working together, they generate a single seamless perception of the world. And as we know from personal experiences, perceptions differ from individual to individual. You read a book and think it is wonderful. You tell your friend about the book. She reads it and likes it to some degree, yet she does not experience the same level of enjoyment from reading the book as you did.

Or you make a statement to your staff as a means to inform. For example, "Our test results are the lowest in the district. We have to make a change," and your highest-performing staff member takes that comment as a personal attack against her hard work, resulting in a flow of tears and a dramatic exit from the meeting, which in turn increases your own anxiety. How does that happen? You were about to say that those scores are in the process of changing because of the staff's hard work and focus on

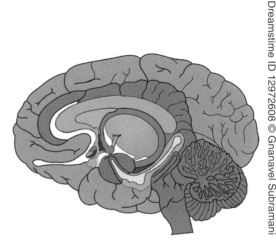

Cerebral cortex, human brain

Corpus callosum, the highway for information transfer

higher results, which she would have heard if she had just given you a few seconds to complete your message.

It's that 0.01% difference. While our brains are closely comparable in looks, structure, and functions, causing us to be capable of thinking and feeling in similar ways, there are still extreme differences in how we see and move through the world. Variation, not exception, is the rule of the way the cerebral cortices are finely wired, and these variations contribute to our individual preferences and personalities.

The outermost layers of the cortex, which we look at as the external surface of the brain, are filled with neurons that are believed to be uniquely human. It is at this level that we create circuits that produce our ability to think linearly, as in complex language while also thinking abstractly and symbolically. This is the area where we reason and understand. Going deeper within the cortex, we find cells that compose the limbic system, an area that influences our thinking.

Our limbic system receives stimuli streaming in through our senses and places an affect or emotion on them. The limbic system is often referred to as the *reptilian brain* because we share this portion of the brain with other creatures. It's also referred to as the *emotional brain*. It is here that emotions come forward in response to what we are sensing, and those emotions send

Singulate Gyrus

Septum

Olfactory Bulb

Hypothalamus

Hippocampus

Amygdala

Mammillary Body

Limbic system structures

messages to our cerebral cortex, influencing the way in which we think about a given situation. In other words, by the time the area of the brain where we do higher-level thinking receives incoming stimuli, it arrives wrapped in "feelings" associated with whether we sense the situation as pain or pleasure.

Bolte Taylor (2006) says, "Although many of us may think of ourselves as thinking creatures that feel, biologically we are feeling creatures that think" (p. 19). That is important for us to remember in relation to our own thinking and the thinking of those we lead. Feelings matter! Successful leaders of today demonstrate an understanding of emotions—their own and those of others.

EMOTIONAL INTELLIGENCE

Daniel Goleman, well known for his work in the area of emotional intelligence (1998), says that it is in the limbic system that our emotional intelligence is born (2015). Given that emotional intelligence is the combination of self-management and our ability to relate to others, Goleman says, "Emotional intelligence is born largely in the neurotransmitters of the brain's limbic system, which governs feelings, impulses, and drives. Research indicates that the limbic system learns best through motivation, extended practice, and feedback" (2015, p. 148). Goleman goes on to say that there is a need for leaders to have training on the limbic system, because once we understand how it works, we are better prepared and committed to break old habits and establish new ones. In other words, we want the emotional part of our brain to work in harmony with the reasoning part of our brain so that the choices we make include both our feelings and our thinking, which in combination lead us to more productive responses. Likewise, we want those we lead to continually build their own skills in emotional intelligence, where thinking and feeling meet together in productive ways. This happens as we understand how the brain works as individuals and as an organization. After all, every person you lead or with whom you are interacting is constantly scanning you, via their limbic system, to determine if what you are saying, or how you are behaving, is conveying a sense of trust or a feeling of distrust within their own brain.

Interestingly, as newborns, the cells in our limbic system begin to become wired together in response to sensory stimulations. And while most cells in our body are reproductive in nature, the limbic system cells function the same throughout our lifetime, never maturing. As a result, when our "emotional buttons" are pushed, as they were in the example given for the teacher who left the meeting in tears, "we retain the ability to react to incoming stimulation as though we were a two year old, even when we are adults" (Bolte Taylor, 2006, p. 18). Thus, there appears to be truth to the fact that some adults act like two year olds when they are under stress. They do and we do, unless we all develop more intentional and advanced methods of response. We have the innate ability to do just this. It's all related to how our brain senses safety or pleasure connected to incoming stimuli, followed by our response choices. Response choices seem to happen either in an automatic and spontaneous way or in a controlled manner as we engage in more thoughtful and intentional approaches to incoming stimuli.

The brain wants to feel safe with a sense of familiarity. It wants a positive affective experience. When it *feels* safe, the brain is in a calm state, capable of listening, learning, and producing. The moment the brain feels threatened or attacked, by something as simple as being corrected in front of others, or devalued through language, voice tones, or physical gestures used by another, anxieties rise and the brain moves into a state of protection, or survival mode. When that happens, it is hard to think about anything other than protecting ourselves.

EMOTIONAL REACTIONS

In fact, Dr. Stephen Porges (2013), a neuroscientist at the University of North Carolina at Chapel Hill, Department of Psychiatry, says that there is a visceral reaction (in lay terms—a physical reaction between the head and the heart) when someone uses a tone that sounds threatening or turns away from the person speaking. He says that you can see it in the face of the person who is the receiver of the negative voice intonations or physical movements and that in turn produces a fight-or-flight type of behavior. "When you feel safe, you can do lots of interesting things. When your nervous system detects risk and fear, you can't even sit in a room without being hyper vigilant about what is going on behind you" (Porges, 2013). When fear is removed, it is empowering. Voice tones matter. Language matters. Physical cues matter. While someone is speaking, the listener is cuing. "When people feel comfortable, their nervous system is triggering an inhibitor to their sympathetic nervous system and this in turn facilitates health, growth and restoration through social interactions" (Porges, 2013). However, Porges further explains, when we hear a voice tone that is perceived as a threat, our nervous system has well-defined receptors that can turn on and off defensive behaviors impacting *your* nervous system which has well-identifying receptors that turn on and off defensive behaviors on our part.

At one point or another, most if not all of us, have experienced the surge of emotions that flow through us when someone speaks to us in a tone that leaves us feeling devalued (even if the tone comes via e-mail), does not make eye contact with us as we speak face-to-face, or even walks away from us as we are speaking. When that happens, we are experiencing an automatic fight-or-flight response, associated with feelings of pain or threat. Understanding this reaction helps us make the best choice possible for the situation at hand.

Just as with our ancestors, when in a perceived harmful situation where we feel threatened or attacked, we instinctively move into a survival mode where our nervous system goes into high alert to protect us. Thus, the idea of "survival of the fittest," first coined by Herbert Spencer after reading Charles Darwin's *On the Origin of Species* in his *Principles of Biology* (1864). Or, as first described by Walter Bradford Cannon, when under a state of threat, we move into the fight-or-flight-response (1932), in which our adrenalin glands go into high production, releasing increased amounts of stress hormones. Out of a sense of protection, when we are stressed or feel threat, we will defend ourselves (fight), remove ourselves (flee), or stay very still and do nothing (freeze). Our response tends to be spontaneous, or automatic. Sometimes those responses or actions are spot on for our safety and the safety of others. At other times, typically surfacing after the event when we have had time to calm down, there is a sense of regret associated with our immediate response.

RESPONSE REGRETS

Most likely, once the teary teacher had a chance to calm down and reassess the situation, she may have regretted walking out of the meeting. Also, had the principal begun his statement with language and intonations aligned with safety and assurance, something like, "We can all be very proud of the work we have done this year. While our test results from last year were at the lowest range, we are about to set a new record for our district as we head toward the top!" the teacher may have never felt the urge to walk out of the meeting and the principal may never have experienced his own increased level of anxiety by the teacher's exit.

We can reduce the number of response regrets we have when we develop patterns of behavior focused on choices aligned with our desired way of being rather than giving in to a rush of emotions surging through our bodies as a result of sensing threat. This happens as we activate the cerebral cortex, the portion of the brain that reasons and thinks, to work in conjunction with the emotions flowing from our limbic system.

One approach in reducing regret responses is to have a clear picture of who we are when we are at our very best. This way we can figuratively reach out or move toward that best self during those challenging times, when our emotions are trying to pull us in a different direction that we may later regret—a regret behavior that is sometimes described as *going limbic*.

When an unexpected event happens that arouses our automatic fight-or-flight response, it's helpful to have a visual of our best self as we move through the challenging situation. The visualization benefit, supported by brain research, affirms that when we imagine something in detail, we ignite the same brain cells that are actually involved when doing it.

Visualization strengthens connections, even when we just repeat the sequence in our minds (Goleman, Boyatiz, McKee, & Finkelstein, 2015, p. 703 of 2987 electronic book). This is why rehearsal is a powerful tool in coaching. Think about yourself. What are words that describe your state of being when you are at your best, even when you are working under intense pressure?

Quickly moving toward our best self when emotions are about to hijack us is critical. It appears that we have a limited time to restrain our emotions from taking control of our cognitive reasoning. David Rock (2015), whom we reference throughout our book, explains the limited time to his children through the metaphor of stopping a motorcycle once it begins to move. When sitting on a motorcycle—right as it slowly begins to take off, you can put your foot down and stop it. However, once the motorcycle is moving, you cannot stop it by putting your foot down on the ground. Hence, there appears to be increased support in favor of the ancient words of wisdom to "think before you speak or act."

Bolte Taylor (2006) offers the 90-second rule, as a way for us to understand our reactions to threatening situations. When we are faced with a situation where we feel a sense of threat, as danger approaches—which can happen when someone speaks to us using a tone that appears angry or disrespectful, or when we feel overcome with anxiousness or heightened levels of nervousness or stress—our body reacts with a chemical response. In other words, at times we can have an automatic and physiological reaction to a given situation of threat that impacts our state of being, which in turns influences what we do and how we behave. However, this physiological reaction only lasts for 90 seconds or less before it has moved through our body. Whenever we stay angry or upset with someone based on our response to his or her behavior, or we let our emotions overtake us, it is a choice that we have made, says Bolte Taylor. Or perhaps it is because of a choice we did not make when we gave in to the emotions. One way or another, a decision is made, either automatically or after controlled thinking—let's call it *mindfulness*—that keeps us from jumping to an automatic response that we later regret.

NEW PATHWAYS

In other words, every response we make is based on conscious or unconscious choices. The brain wants to operate on automatic pilot to conserve energy. It's up to us to choose the form of automatic response we want to develop when dealing with challenging situations and then to stay focused on that choice. It includes more than just restraining impulsive behaviors. It means building new pathways for dealing with challenging, a.k.a. threatening, situations before they get the best of us. And, as we all know from experience, some pathways are built rather quickly while others take more focused choices, especially when dealing with stressful situations. It's helpful to remember that most changes in behaviors are based on decisions to give that desired behavior dedicated time, attention, repetition, and positive feedback (TARP as defined by David Rock, 2006b).

Consider the power behind leaders and entire teams that commit to learn, develop, and use behaviors associated with higher levels of emotional intelligence. After all, we now have research findings that support the importance of leaders strengthening their ability to make decisions based on both intelligence and emotions. In the long run, slips in emotions over slips in intelligence usually make it harder for leaders to experience the results they want to achieve. In fact, the emotional skills seem to determine if leaders are promoted in their work or fired (Ringleb, Rock, & Ancona, 2015, p. 17). Or, as sometimes expressed, emotions determine whether a person is shown the elevator up for advancements or out the front door for terminations. One slip does not typically bring about the downfall of a leader, but multiple slips might, similarly to Susan Scott's (2009) response to the question, "How did we get here?" Her answer, "Gradually then suddenly."

This is one of the powerful reasons for humans to reflect and think through situations before responding to make the most informed decision. This also provides critical data about the importance of having a safe and respected environment for thinking. *When we are in elevated states of stress, it takes added, even extreme energy to think and act in thoughtful and intentional ways.*

We have the ability, as our cortical cells mature and become integrated in complex networks with our neurons, to create a new view of or reframe the present moment. By using a process of reassessing the current situation with the new information of our thinking mind, we can purposely choose a more mature response. This calls for us to slow down and think through a situation before we rush to a response, unless it has proved to be a response that has worked well in past uses.

It becomes easier and more habitual to make mature responses under stress when we dedicate concentrated time and energy to building our skills in nonstressful situations. And to build our leadership skills in non-stressful situations, we must take into account the way in which others receive our words and actions. Flourishing leaders know that it is vital to expend time and effort on attending to the individual differences of the people they lead by developing skills of empathy intertwined with language and behaviors that demonstrate respect and personal regard. This is why behaviors of committed listening are so critical for leaders to develop and use. Listen to understand from the perspective of the other person. Ask questions that demonstrate respect and empathy—even when you are called to make decisions that impact the other person in ways that may not be aligned with what they want.

THE POWER OF EMPATHY

Dr. Dan Siegel (2015), executive director of the Mindsight Institute and Clinical Professor of Psychiatry at the UCLA School of Medicine, shares a personal story about empathy that had a big impact on his career, which now focuses on empathy for the inner world of another, or what he calls *mindsight*. Back in the late 1970s, he was a medical student at Harvard. At that time, there was little or no focus on the emotional well-being of the patient as doctors dealt with the physical ailments. Siegel said that after receiving the lab data, the attending physician would walk into the patient's room, deliver the results, for example sharing that the patient had an inoperable disease and had only a few months to live, and then would walk out. Siegel was troubled by this method and asked about the need to talk to the patient about how he or she felt. The attending physician would respond saying, "I've tested them and given them the information. There is nothing more I can do." Siegel dropped out of medical school as a result of many such experiences. Fast-forward 25-plus years and Dr. Siegel was giving the keynote address at Harvard Medical School to a series on neuroscience and medicine. The topic was "The Importance of Emotions and Narrative in Medicine." See Dr. Siegel's (2015) video presentation on interpersonal connections at his website.

Siegel cites a double blind research study supporting the impact of physician empathy on patients. In a study of college students with a common cold, one group had a physician who focused only on the patient's physical ailments. A physician with the same level of medical qualifications attended the other group. However, this physician attended to both the physical and personal component of the patient saying things like, "Aren't you a student at the college? This must be a really tough time for you to have a cold and be studying for your final exams." The empathy group got over their cold a day sooner, and their immune function was much more robust.

Not only does it appear that empathy promotes health, it also appears to provide support for leaders offering empathy to those they lead, which in turn can increase health of the organization and decrease an employee's possible fight-or-flight response. Consider these two actual examples from our coaching experience. Two high-performing educators, Mary and Jane, unknown to each other and working in different school districts, were both dealing with tough situations in their personal lives. Mary, a teacher, was going through a divorce, and it was evident that it was a very difficult time for her. Her principal met with Mary privately and demonstrated care and concern (empathy) for her and emphasized that Mary take care of herself during this stressful time. Mary did move through that hard time and came out on the other end victoriously, while never neglecting the needs of her students. She greatly appreciated the fact that her principal understood her situation and used language and behaviors that showed that she understood and genuinely cared. Mary continues to be a high-performing teacher at her school and demonstrates her ability to be resilient, inclusive of her own determination and support of her supervisor.

Jane, a principal, did not share the same experience. Jane's husband was extremely ill and was progressing through the last stages of his life. This caused Jane to miss a great deal of school to be with her husband during that final time. There was little or no empathy demonstrated by Jane's supervisor, an area director. When Jane returned to work after the death of her husband, she was placed on a growth plan, with no attention given to the affective component of Jane's personal loss. The relationship between Jane and the area superintendent was severed. Jane, demonstrating resilience when dealing with personal loss and lack of support at work during a highly emotional time, left the district, regained her energy and focus, and is now working as a principal in a different district under a different leader and is again performing at high levels.

Using language as simple as "This must be a really hard time for you" can go a long way to calm anxieties (the fight-or-flight response) associated with uncertainties about upcoming situations or events. Take for example the situation that happened with one of our clients, a principal, Carolyn, who was in the process of leaving her district at the same time that big changes were happening within the district. The staff had recently been told that their highly respected principal was leaving at the end of the year for personal reasons. Staff members were still processing that announcement when the new superintendent came to a faculty meeting to share information about upcoming changes for the school that were to take place prior to the beginning of the next school year. The superintendent's intent was to share a status report in an informative and matter-of-fact way. However, the staff's response to the information was demonstrated through heightened levels of anxiousness, because their limbic systems were engaged. They asked multiple questions for which the superintendent was not ready to answer in detail. The meeting ended with increased levels of anxiety as observed by Carolyn who was part of the meeting. The next day she called the staff together and demonstrated a strong focus on empathy, saying words like, "I know this is a very anxious time for you. There are lots of unanswered questions as of today. The superintendent cares and wants you to know that as soon as we know more information about where people will be next year, we will share the information with you. Remember, you are very qualified teachers and you will do well this next year, regardless of the changes that come your way." This simple yet empathetic, reassuring response helped bring a sense of calmness over the group. We all want to feel valued and given information that impacts us as soon as possible. We also seek certainty, which we discuss in more detail later in this chapter.

WHEN WE THINK WE CAN

Environmental conditions do matter. A study recently cited in *Time Magazine* (Kluger, 2015) reminds us of the landmark "counterclockwise" study conducted by Ellen Langer, who was just beginning her Harvard teaching career. She recruited a group of eight men in their 70s for a 5-day stay at a retreat in New Hampshire. The men were identified as age-appropriate related to health. They were neither in good nor bad health. They tended to be slow, bent, and easy to fatigue. Langer was determined to change that. The retreat took place at a former monastery, designed to look as the world did to the men in 1959. Vintage programs played on the TVs, and midcentury music played on midcentury radios. The men were treated as they would have been treated in 1959. They carried their own luggage, and no one offered to help them with their bags or fetch blankets. They kept their conversations to those discussed in 1959: ballgames, the workings of President Eisenhower, and so on. All mirrors were removed from the space. Langer administrated a series of pre- and post-physical and cognitive aptitude tests to the men. On virtually every metric, their performance improved dramatically, and in many cases it was closer to what would be expected for men a decade or two younger.

Langer conducted another impressive study related to the mind-body connection with hotel maids who were battling their weight. She told half the sample that the work they did was vigorous enough to represent calorie-burning exercise. The other group was given no such information. Both groups did the same work. At the end of the study, the women who believed that their work was a workout lost more weight than those in the other group.

What do these studies mean for leaders of today? It certainly gives support to the idea that the way in which people think and are treated (i.e., with respect and emphasizing that they bring value to the work) has the opportunity to increase the likelihood that people will rise to the occasion. If we think we can, we are more likely to accomplish the compelling expectations of today.

One other fact that Bolte Taylor (2006) brings up in *My Stroke of Insight*, and that we find interesting and fun to know, has to do with the cells in our brain and the way in which they do not regenerate weekly or monthly as do the cells in other parts of our body.

> The primary cells of the nervous system, our neurons, do not multiply after we are born. This means that the majority of the neurons in your brain today are as old as you are. This longevity of neurons is associated with why we feel on the inside at the age of 40 or 70 as we did when we were 10 or 12. The cells in our brain are the same, but over time their connections change based upon their/our experiences. (p. 13)

In other words, your experiences have a significant impact on the way you see and respond to the world. Thankfully, people well beyond the median age still have the ability to think and function as "young" in attitude and actions.

PRACTICAL USES

Let's move to some practical examples of what we are learning. You are in a meeting with a group that you lead. For this example, let's say that you have 25 people in the room. You understand that each person in the room is unique based on their individual DNA composition and structure, as well as their past experiences and trainings. You also know that they are like-minded people who have been selected and have confirmed a personal commitment (via their signed contract) to the mission and purpose of the work that all are called to accomplish as individuals and as a team.

Because you are a leader committed to understanding and using motivational techniques that inspire and influence others, you know that words and actions matter. You understand that every person in that room is receiving your words and your physical gestures via their senses and are attaching an emotion to those words and gestures. They are scanning to determine the level of safety for themselves and others. The brain feels safety in much the same way as it feels pleasure or reward. If it feels safe and worthy of their energy and time, they will continue to engage with you. If however, the brain's level of anxiety increases and there is a sense of threat, or another negative feeling, like disrespect, boredom, anger, and so on, the brain's focus will move to the immediate situation to self-protect and disengage. As the brain moves into self-protection behaviors (fight, flight, freeze), the stress level increases, resulting in an *away from* state rather than a *toward* state. A feeling of safety brings trust. A feeling of fear brings distrust.

This is why you choose your words carefully when you communicate with the team. For your team to buy in to and be fully engaged in the work, there is a great need for them to feel safe, respected, connected, and involved in decisions and actions to be made. You want their limbic systems to be highly engaged in positive feelings associated with the work. And by positive feelings we are not talking about everyone always hugging, smiling, and singing "Kumbaya" together. We mean attitudes that are focused on solutions rather than problems, behaviors that are constructive, supportive, and forward moving rather than destructive, exclusive, and draining. These constructive, supportive, and forward-moving behaviors and attitudes increase our possibilities for reaching extraordinary results. When people engage in positive feelings, there are added levels of energy, which increases our ability to think creatively and solve problems. Positive feelings give us added levels of energy to do the hard tasks associated with work and personal lives. This state of being is often referred to as *a state of well-being*.

Example 1

Back to the meeting you are leading. Based on what you know about the brain, which statement below do you think will have a stronger possibility of being received by the team through the filter of positive intent and safety, thus resulting in active engagement by the team?

> Ladies and gentlemen, let's don't waste time here. We are all tired and ready for a break, but we have things that have to be accomplished before anyone can leave. So let's suck it up and get with it! We are expected to have this meeting and to decide on a plan for our parent conference. Does anyone have an idea?

OR

> Thanks for being here on time. It's a given that after a full day with our students, we have limited supplies of energy remaining for work, and we want to make the most of that energy. We have been asked to meet and to identify new or additional ways to engage parents in a goal-setting conference that demonstrates our desire to work as partners in support of the academic and emotional growth of every student we teach. Everyone's thinking is invited and valued. In the next 20 minutes that we have dedicated to this subject, what ideas are already beginning to form for each of you?
>
> If you were a parent coming to our conference, how would you want to be treated and what are ways that you would like to be engaged in the goal-setting process? Take a few minutes to write down your ideas and then we will hear from each person, with no feedback from the group while ideas are being expressed. Then, we will come back and have a brief discussion and selection on our top three choices. How does that sound to everyone?

Clearly, the second example offers a stronger possibility of motivating team members to become engaged in the thinking. The language used is said in a respectful tone, which increases the likelihood that the brains of team members will receive it as safety. Unlike the first example, there is not an indication of complaining or dread being offered through the leader's language. While it may not be the desire of every team member to spend their time on this topic, they are much more likely to engage when they feel that they are respected and their ideas are valued (status). They also know that they have a specific amount of time that has been dedicated to this topic. They also have more information about the purpose and desired outcome of the meeting and know that everyone will have an opportunity to contribute ideas with the final decision reflecting the work of the group (certainty).

The leader of the second example has been intentionally working with her leadership coach. Here are some of the areas that were discussed during her coaching conversations:

- Identifying ways to positively influence and inspire the team to engage in productive and forward-moving work
- Reflecting, visualizing, and creating a plan for what the leader wanted to say to the group, including how to begin and frame the purpose and outcome of the meeting
- Selecting a process to involve all in the meeting task in a timely manner
- Predicting possibly ways the conversation might be derailed and creating best approach methods to prevent derailments

In the first example, there appears to be a lower level of understanding or care for how the team will receive the message and the lasting impact it will have on the way in which the members view the leader. Yes, people may get involved to "get it done and get out of there," as presented by the leader. But what is the overall value-add to the experience, and in what ways is this experience impacting the overall commitment of the team to intentionally work toward a stronger parent-teacher partnership (the bigger purpose)?

Also, if this team is composed of people who are ready to move into a fight approach at the drop of a pin, the first example holds the possibility of having someone go into a complaining mode that will eat up time dedicated to the work at hand and suck the energy right out of the group. The second example holds greater possibilities that people will turn their energies toward the work and away from resistance.

NEUROLEADERSHIP INSTITUTE INFLUENCES

This leads us to the work of David Rock and the NeuroLeadership Institute. Rock has spent years studying the science of leadership and has worked diligently with neuroscientists to better understand the brain's functions to support leaders in increasing thinking levels for themselves and for those they lead so that together they reach expanded results in ways that increase motivation, trust, and job satisfaction. His work has had a significant impact on the work of Results Coaching Global as well as that of other leaders throughout the world. We highly recommend his books *Quiet Leadership* (2006b) and *Your Brain at Work* (2009). As we discussed in the introduction, he created the concept of the SCARF Model that holds a place of respect and importance in the work that we do, including the seminars we provide to organizations and individuals.

Rock has been influential in supporting reasons for leaders to restrain impulsive behaviors that could be received by others as threatening and demeaning, while forming and practicing intentional behaviors that increase motivation and impetus for change. His work focuses on ways to reduce threat and increase rewards. He has taken research about how the brain reacts to threats and rewards and framed them as either a *toward* or *away from* state. A toward state is associated with pleasure or rewards while an away from state is connected to threats or pain.

The research-based SCARF Model (2008, 2012) offers a succinct way of thinking about the ways in which a leader's behavior and a team's dynamics can activate strong feelings of threat or reward responses from others. The model suggests five domains of experiences that encompass a wide range of human emotions, all strongly connected to the social processing in the brain. These domains are Status, Certainty, Autonomy, Relatedness, and Fairness, referred to as SCARF for an easy mnemonic. Rock (2008, 2012) explains that when leaders understand and use the SCARF Model as they communicate with others, they strengthen the possibilities of influencing the levels of thinking and performance of individuals and teams as they elevate a sense of reward and reduce the sensation of threat. Having the language of SCARF increases our ability to label or reappraise our emotions, thus increasing our ability to regulate social threats and rewards (Ochsner, 2008). In fact, Rock (2008, 2012) says that when people hold the SCARF Model in mind as they interact with others, they increase the possibilities for improved interactions with colleagues, friends, or family. Who would not want that?

Status refers to one's sense of importance relative to others (e.g., you the leader, a fellow peer, a family member). We define status as "What I think you think about me" or, at times, "How I feel when I'm around you." Remember, people are scanning for cues that support safety and pleasure as they interact with you. When we call people by name, or ask them what they think, or request that they serve on a committee, we increase the likelihood of elevating their sense of status. When we give positive feedback around the work they do, we increase the potential for elevated status, as does giving others public or private recognition for a job well done. When people feel they are learning and improving and attention is paid to the improvements, there is an increase in status. However, when we use a tone that is harsh or rude as we talk with others, we lower their sense of status. When we do not give others our full attention as they talk, we lower their sense of status, which increases a sense of threat in their brain.

Certainty, which is craved by the brain, is about a need to have clarity and make predictions about the future. Having just a little certainty helps.

Without certainty, the brain exercises more energy in the prefrontal cortex to process moment by moment. Having just a small amount of uncertainty can generate an error response in our orbital frontal cortex, and as Rock explains, this is somewhat like having a flashing light on a printer indicating a paper jam. Until that jam is cleared up, it's hard to focus on the other work at hand. When we do not have certainty about what is expected in our job, or overall job security, it can be debilitating. Any big change brings uncertainty. When we feel a sense of certainty, our brain can calm down and focus on thinking and the tasks at hand. Establishing a time frame for a meeting, having a written agenda articulated before or as the meeting begins, stating clear expectations for processes and outcomes, and then following through as articulated offers feelings of certainty to situations. When others know that there is a sense of certainty around how the leader deals with people or situations, it holds the potential to reduce stress and increase productivity. For example, "I know that John will listen to me when I go to talk with him, and he will not make rash judgments" versus "Don't tell John about this because he will go ballistic. He just can't handle conflict."

Autonomy is about having a sense of control over a given situation and feeling that one's behavior has an impact on the outcome of a situation. When we give people choices within the boundaries of their work, they feel more in control, and this holds the potential to lower their levels of stress. When we micromanage or continually tell others what to do, we increase stress levels and lower their sense of autonomy. Daniel Pink (2009) offers a wealth of information on the importance of autonomy, in his book *Drive: The Surprising Truth About What Motivates Us*, which we discuss in more detail in Chapter 4.

Relatedness is about ways in which others have a sense of connectedness to and trust in the other person (it's the friend or foe feeling). The decision about whether another person is a friend, part of the in-group, or a foe, part of the out-group, happens quickly and impacts the way in which the brain functions. Information from someone considered to be a friend is processed differently than information from foes. People want to feel they are part of the group and that they share clearly defined and articulated goals. We trust those with whom we share common goals and process their information using the same circuits we use to process our own thoughts. Different circuits are used to process information from foes, meaning we don't let that information in as we do from someone in our in-group. When people feel they are in an unfamiliar social situation (like the new member of a team), there is an increased sense of threat and feelings of being lonely. Simple introductions or handshakes when someone is new to the team lower feelings of threat and increase feelings of trust and connections of empathy. Forming teams and sharing personal stories and photos increase feelings of relatedness. Having shared experiences does not necessarily strengthen feelings of relatedness. However,

when teams share goals there are greater possibilities for a strong emphasis on elevated levels of relatedness.

Fairness refers to a just and nonbiased exchange between people (e.g.,
equal pay for equal work, sharing a treat with everyone, spending equal
time with members of the team). Increasing transparency, providing information to the team, and following through on your word increases a sense
of fairness. Having clear and articulated expectations increases fairness.
Having teams establish their own norms within the broader norms of the
entire organization elevates a sense of fairness. When there are unclear
ground rules or expectations, the sense of fairness is lowered.

From a national perspective, in 2015 the U.S. women's soccer team won
the World Cup Championship. Notice the difference in the size of the wom-
en's trophy as compared to the size of the trophy given to the winner of the
men's competition. NBC News reported after the event, "Despite on-field
success, female players in the United States face an uphill battle to catch up
to the financial success of men's soccer" (Pramuk, CNBC, & CNBC, 2015).
Was this fair? Certainly our history books and even current news reports offer
many other examples of ways in which our country has sought to increase
fairness in social situations, encounters, schools, and the workplace.

Notice that within the explanation of the SCARF Model, the description "sense of" is used multiple times. When people have even a small
sense of positive connections to SCARF, they can relax and get down to the
business of working in a productive manner.

Being knowledgeable about and skilled in the use of the SCARF Model
when leading and interacting with others holds strong possibilities to positively impact emotions, trust levels, and overall results. Rock emphasizes
that it is important for leaders to harness and regulate their emotions and
the emotions of those they lead (see Ringleb et al., 2015). Think of the
impact an organization can have on all those involved when everyone har-
nesses and regulates emotions.

If an outsider were to come into your school or organization and
observe you leading, or individuals and teams interacting, what ratings do
you think each group would receive as it relates to awareness and use of
the components of the SCARF Model? How would you rate yourself on
the use of the SCARF Model components?

Jonathan Haidt (2006), author of *The Happiness Hypothesis*, connects to
the ideas of harness and regulate when he describes the emotional or affective part of our brain as a big elephant with a rider, representing our reasoning or cognitive part of the brain, sitting on top of the elephant. This
metaphor certainly helps us understand the power of our emotions and
that no rider can overpower an elephant that is out of control with fear.
The only real hope for the rider is to train the elephant on what to do when
it comes across threatening situations. As we feel threat approaching, we
begin to harness and regulate our emotions so they don't carry us away in
a direction we do not want to travel.

PRACTICAL USES

Self-Monitoring and Reflecting With a Coach

As we have stressed in this chapter, it's a given that self-monitoring is a must for any leader. There is an added benefit when leaders reflect with a coach. Reflecting with another "can make a tremendous difference to other people's thinking by helping them clearly identify the insights they would like to hardwire, and over time reminding them about the insights" (Rock, 2009, p. 25).

David Rock says (2006a), "Change requires more than just scant thought; it requires ongoing attention and a significant effort of the will. There are several reasons why change is so hard, and they point to the need to provide additional resources to an individual who wants to successfully change in any way. Hence, brains need coaching" (p. 3).

Example 2

The example below offers possibilities for self-monitoring privately or with an experienced coach. In what ways did the coach in the following example support a deeper level of thinking and responding on the part of the principal? What connections are you making from your own experience?

- As the leader, you find yourself becoming more and more annoyed with a staff member who is not living up to her responsibilities and expectations as articulated in her contract and by you. She comes in late at least three times each month, impacting the administrative staff and her teammates who must cover her class. She also leaves early, affecting collaborative work with her team. This behavior has gone on for the last 2 months. In no way has she offered to you or the team an explanation for her behavior. Your emotions are in an elevated state (*fight*) and you decide, "I'm just going to write her up!"
- You share those thoughts and emotions with your coach who certainly witnesses your emotions or state of being, or struggle (*empathy*), and also asks you how helpful it might be to think through exactly what you want to do before you "write her up" (*harness emotions*). You agree, and as you have time to calm down, take some deep breaths, and reduce your elevated level of stress, you begin to think in a more rational way, while also staying connected to your emotions. You begin to take a different perspective to the situation (*regulate emotions; reframe*).
- You respond, "Something must be going on in the life of this teacher. This is not the behavior that I saw last year." Your coach asks you, "What are you thinking will be the best way for you to

get clarity on the situation so that you better understand how you want to move forward?" You reply, "Clearly I need to have a calm conversation with her and ask what is going on in her life that is distracting her commitment to be on time and stay focused at the end of the day. That is how I would want to be treated if I found myself in a similar situation. I would want and expect my leader to presume positive intent on my behalf until and unless I demonstrate otherwise (*create a new pathway for thinking*). Thanks for helping me think through this and not let my emotions overtake me and lead me in a direction I might later regret. I do care about her, and I want to walk the walk that I say aligns with who I am as a leader."

Regulating and Reappraising Your Emotions

Consider the last example. Something has happened that has elevated your level of stress, and as a result you feel anxious, uncertain, and angry! What are some quick steps that you can take to deescalate the emotions and limit the level of regret you may later have based on your reactions to the event?

Here are three steps that are offered as ways to stay cool when under pressure. These are steps that are consistently used when coaching someone who is dealing with their own strong emotions over an event as it occurs.

Three Steps for Regulating Your Emotions and Staying Cool Under Pressure

1. **Label your emotion.** This simple act has a calming impact on your emotions. By naming the emotion, you slow down the fight-or-flight response. When we connect words with the emotional state, we tend to revert the stress response. This does not mean talking on and on about how you are feeling. Rather, just describe how you are feeling in a few words and then move on. Giving the emotion a name and figuratively setting it aside helps you to be able to move on.

2. **Slow down your breathing.** Take some deep breaths to bring more oxygen into your lungs and your bloodstream, which is the opposite effect of what is happening during a flight-or-fight response. Breathe in to the count of four and out to the count of eight and repeat multiple times. This offers the opportunity for you to regain mindfulness around what you really want.

3. **Reappraise your emotions.** This is where you look at the situation from a different perspective and reinterpret or reassess what is

Table 2.1   Reappraising Your Emotions

From Negative Emotion	Toward a More Productive Emotion
Feeling anxious about the upcoming meeting.	Focusing on the possibilities that can come as a result of the group working together on the goal of the meeting.
Feeling disappointed over the comments of a parent.	Looking beyond what the parent said and thinking about what the parent really wants on behalf of his or her child.
Worrying about an upcoming meeting.	Focusing on how to move through the meeting in a careful manner so as to stay calm if possible conflict arises. Looking for ways to celebrate the small accomplishments.
Feeling frustrated over what seems to be the never-ending comments of a staff member.	Offering respect and personal attention to the staff member while remaining calm.
Feeling pressured over the demands of the work.	Intentionally looking for small successes and reminding yourself that small steps lead to big accomplishments.
Feeling resentful of a team member who appears bored during a team meeting.	Thinking that something must be going on in the personal life of the team member that has drained his or her energy and perhaps kept him or her awake during the night while you remember that the team member is committed to the goals of the work.

happening, giving your emotions a different label and a different impact. The intent is to move away from the negative emotion and toward a more productive emotion, while not downplaying how you originally felt. It's ok to feel angry. However, how do you best want to move away from the anger and toward a resolution that represents you at your best as you deal with challenging situations? Table 2.1 suggests ways that you can move from a negative emotion and turn it around to a more positive and productive frame of mind.

Example 3

During stressful situations, negative feelings become stronger than positive feelings (it's the fight-or-flight mode). In fact, overall, negative feelings are stronger than positive feelings, and now we better understand why. It's all in an effort to protect.

Consider that you are sitting quietly thinking about something you plan to do later in the day. All of a sudden, with no warning or indication, someone walks up to you and yells, "Hey!" Your brain quickly receives this as a threat, and before you can think logically about what is happening, you gasp for air and jump up. You automatically respond to the situation as fear—when in fact it was someone playing an unfortunate joke on you. You love the person, but for a moment you were ready to go over and give them a hard shake.

Or let's say that you are sitting in your office or work area, deep in thought. This time, Helen, a colleague who tends to only approach you in private when she is upset, sticks her head inside your office with what appears to be a scowl on her face. You immediately feel your heart rate increase, a negative reaction that happens when you see Helen. Once again, you respond automatically to a possible threat. Remember, negative is stronger than positive. However, remember that you have the ability to tame or restrain your elephant and regulate how you respond. This takes practice and focus on what you want and how you want to be.

POSITIVE PSYCHOLOGY

Negative feelings tend to drain us of energy and block our creative and problem-solving behaviors. We know from personal experience what it feels like to be drained of energy as we face the demands of a job and everyday life. And, as professional and executive coaches with more than 150 years of combined experience in this field, we understand the importance of facing a problem or situation from the perspective of how to move through or around it and beyond it. Thus, we turn to the work of positive psychology, which began to find its place in science and leadership in 1998, when Dr. Martin Seligman (2011) chose the theme for his term as the president of the American Psychological Association. Seligman, who spent the first part of his career focused on ways to treat mental illness, now is dedicated to ways to promote mental health. He is often referred to as the father of positive psychology and has written multiple books on this topic. We highly recommend his latest book, *Flourish: A Visionary New Understanding of Happiness and Well-Being*.

Positive psychology is rooted in scientific evidence and centers on developing states of well-being. Seligman explains that well-being is composed of five elements working together. These five elements are positive emotion, engagement, meaning, positive relationships, and accomplishment. He gives specific examples of ways that organizations, our armed forces, and schools are intentionally using strategies focused on positive psychology to have a strong and positive impact on people's lives and students' academic performance.

While we understand that negative ways of thinking are a part of our DNA, let's remember that groundbreaking work has been done in the area of reducing negative feelings and building greater states of well-being. As was mentioned in Chapter 1, Barbara Fredrickson (2009) has done much work on measuring the impact of negativity within organizations. She provided us with a ratio, meaning the frequency of positivity over a given time span, divided by the frequency of negativity over that same time span, and has come up with a 3:1 ratio for healthy and productive organizations. In other words, for every negative comment, healthy and high-performing businesses offset it with three positive comments. You can find out more about the details of her findings in her easy-to-read book *Positivity: Groundbreaking Research Reveals How to Embrace the Hidden Strength of Positive Emotions, Overcome Negativity, and Thrive.*

The work from Seligman, Fredrickson, and other positive psychology experts supports the need for a strong focus on using language and processes that are designed to *keep the negative emotions tamed* while we spend greater energy on producing positive emotions. In Chapter 3, you will see the ways in which we focus on positive intent and positive behaviors to greatly improve creative thinking.

SUMMARY

Leaders of today lead with a deep understanding of how the brain works. They understand that their words, actions, and behaviors influence states of safety or threat in those they lead.

- States of safety or threat impact thinking and overall performance and results.
- When the emotional part of brain works in conjunction with the rational part of the brain, better decisions are made for both individuals and teams.
- Emotional intelligence or lack of emotional intelligence is a strong determining factor in the success of a leader.
- Learning to reduce regret responses is an important skill for individual and teams. This happens when we think before we act and as we build behaviors that are aligned with best-self approaches.
- Demonstrating empathy is a must for successful leaders.

REFERENCES

Bolte Taylor, J. (2006). *My stroke of insight: A brain scientist's personal journey.* New York, NY: Penguin.

Cannon, W. B. (1932). *The wisdom of the body.* New York, NY: W. W. Norton.

Fredrickson, B. (2009). *Positivity: Groundbreaking research reveals how to embrace the hidden strength of positive emotions, overcome negativity, and thrive* [Kindle edition]. New York, NY: Three Rivers Press.

Goleman, D. (1998). *Working with emotional intelligence.* New York, NY: Bantam Books.

Goleman, D. (2015). What makes a leader? In D. Goleman, R. Boyatzis, A. McKee, & S. Finkelstein (Eds.), *HBR's 10 must reads: On emotional intelligence* [Kindle edition]. Cambridge, MA: Harvard Business School.

Goleman, D., Boyatzis, R., McKee, A., & Finkelstein, S. (Eds.). (2015). *HBR's 10 must reads: On emotional intelligence* [Kindle edition]. Cambridge, MA: Harvard Business School.

Haidt, J. (2006). *The happiness hypothesis: Finding modern truth in ancient wisdom.* New York, NY: Basic Books.

Kluger, J. (2015, February 23). The antiaging power of a positive attitude. *Time, 185*(6).

Ochsner, K. (2008). Staying cool under pressure: Insights from social cognitive neuroscience and their implications for self and society. *NeuroLeadership Journal, 1,* 26–32.

Porges, S. (2013, May 15). The polyvagal theory. [Video file]. Retrieved from https://www.youtube.com/watch?v=8tz146HQotY

Pramuk, J., CNBC, & CNBC.com. (2015, July 6). For U.S. soccer women, success won't bring compensation equality. *NBC News,* Business Section. Retrieved from http://www.nbcnews.com/business/business-news/u-s-soccer-women-success-wont-bring-compensation-equality-n387566

Ringleb, A. H., Rock, D., & Ancona, C. (2015). Neuroleadership in 2014. *NeuroLeadership Journal, 9.*

Rock, D. (2006a). A brain-based approach to coaching: David Rock. Based on an interview with Jeffrey M. Schwartz, MD. Retrieved from http://web.archive.org/web/20100414164238/http://www.workplacecoaching.com/pdf/CoachingTheBrainIJCO.pdf

Rock, D. (2006b). *Quiet leadership.* New York, NY: HarperCollins.

Rock, D. (2008). SCARF: A brain-based model for collaborating with and influencing others. *NeuroLeadership Journal, 1.*

Rock, D. (2009). *Your brain at work.* New York, NY: Harper Business.

Rock, D. (2015).YouTube presentation published on March 18, 2015; David Rock speaks to DSI students about neuroleadership as part of the Spring 2015 Global Guest Lecture Series.

Rock, D., & Cox, C. (2012). *SCARF in 2012: Updating the social neuroscience of collaborating with others.* New York, NY: NeuroLeadership Institute.

Scott, S. (2009). *Fierce leadership: A bold alternative to the worst "best" business practices today.* New York, NY: Crown Business.

Seligman, M. (2011). *Flourish: A visionary new understanding of happiness and well-being* [Kindle edition]. New York, NY: Atria Books.

Siegel, D. (2015). Interpersonal connections [Video]. Retrieved from http://www.drdansiegel.com/resources/video_clips/

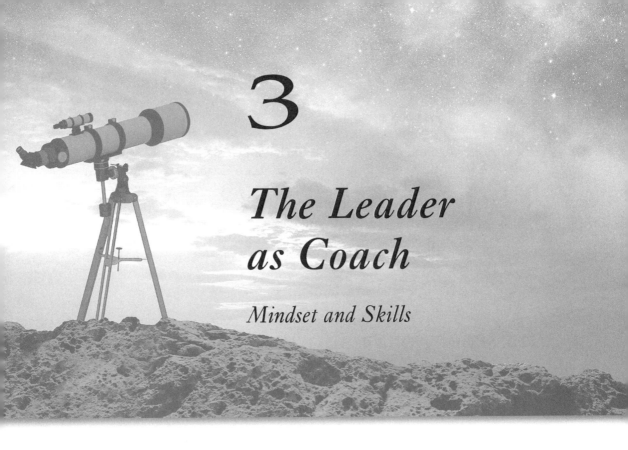

3

The Leader as Coach

Mindset and Skills

Being a coach leader is a key competency, a new identity, for anyone in the business of building capacity in teachers, staff, and students.

Kee, Anderson, Dearing, Harris, and Shuster (2010)

Our most effective coach leaders are those who have fully embraced the mindset of being a coach leader. These leaders have transformed their mindset from coaching being something you *do* to something you *are*. Coaching has become the core of their being. They have made what Ronald Heifetz (1998) calls an adaptive change over a technical change.

A *technical* change challenge involves a skill set that is well known, even if complicated to perform such as the work of a brain surgeon, the technical skills of an Olympic ice skater, or the strongly embedded pedagogy that supports the work of a master teacher.

On the other hand, an *adaptive* change challenge can only be met by transforming one's mindset, by advancing to a more sophisticated level of mental development. It is how one thinks about something—what one holds to be true about something.

Heifetz (1998) says our greatest change challenge is application of a technical approach to an adaptive change challenge. This error becomes self-sabotage, which keeps us from getting what we say we want. The leaders who have been most successful with deep internalization of the competencies and skills of coaching are those who have recognized it is first a mindset change supported by the technical skill set of coaching.

These leaders are applying the International Coach Federation definition of coaching to a new way of leading in our schools: "Coaching is partnering with clients in a thought-provoking and creative process that inspires them to maximize their personal and professional potential." In other words, they have moved from conversations that are directing and telling to conversations that are motivating and inspiring; conversations that actively engage people in creative and thought-provoking dialogue toward the accomplishment of desired results.

THE SEDUCTION OF ADVISING OR TELLING

Admittedly, one of the first major changes school leaders have attested to making is the move from a leader who offers advice to one who provokes thinking—an adaptive change. They are driven by the work of David Rock (2006) who, in *Quiet Leadership*, says the best way to improve the performance of another is to improve his or her thinking. Easy to say . . . *hard* to do!

At the same time we hear "this is hard to do," we hear "the payoff is so huge!" Why? Why would such a change have such potential for impact? Here are a few possibilities we have heard from you.

- People grow by developing their own thinking.
- Their learning is self-directed and multiplies the potential for action. They buy in when it's their idea rather than ours.
- Change only occurs when people see the need and benefit of the change for themselves. We know that one person cannot change another.
- When we give advice, we send an underlying message that people cannot think for themselves and that we have a better solution than they do. In other words, we diminish their status.

Now back to why this is so difficult. **Number 1—It feeds our own status.** When a person says, "Just tell me what to do," it kicks in the seduction factor. They believe I know, so I can't let them down, so I tell them what I would do. This usually results in inaction because they do not own it, or they try it, it fails, and you get the blame. "Ok, smarty pants, what should I do now?" Thus the cycle of dysfunction begins. The swinging door gets some WD-40, which keeps them coming back to you for thinking and problem solving.

A perfect illustration of this was shared by a participant in one of our seminars. Between Days 1 and 2 of the 4-day session, a district curriculum person decided to approach a teacher with whom she had been working all year from a coach leader perspective over her usual way of offering strategy after strategy.

> All year I have been working with this teacher to get her to use literacy strategies in her classroom. Every time I go, I offer ideas for what she *should* do—small group instruction, word wall, leveled reading books, and so on. To date, she has incorporated none of my suggestions. So I decided to try this *"coaching thing,"* and I greeted her by asking something about her daughter who I knew was important to her. Then I stated the purpose of our meeting—to talk about literacy strategies for her classroom. Next, I said, "Knowing we have discussed a variety of options for building a literacy classroom, where are you thinking you want to begin?" To my surprise, she talked about everything we had discussed so far during the year. What was different was *her decision* to begin with word wall. We were off and running in the very direction I wanted her to go. Nothing had changed but me!

Different mindset; different result. After giving the teacher status by asking about her daughter, the curriculum coordinator, Suzie, offered certainty by stating the purpose of the meeting. Suzie's presumption that the teacher wanted a literacy classroom even though she hadn't yet begun resulted in forward movement and commitment to action. Suzie's words demonstrated belief in the teacher to do what she could do for herself. And thinking shifted from the coordinator doing the heavy lifting to the teacher being the expert in her own life.

So Suzie's final comment was, "This *coaching thing* really works!"

A second reason that avoiding advice or telling others what to do is so difficult: We fall into the trap of giving advice is *the myth that it saves time.* Perhaps in the short term it does; however, for long term, NO. It is the difference between a Band-Aid vs. long-term capacity building. Telling people what to do teaches them to rely on us for the answers and reduces their sense of status and ability to look beyond themselves for options and possibilities. It feeds our status and keeps the codependence going. Instead of investing in your capacity to think and find solutions, I am spending my time over and over again telling you what to do. Imagine a school where the mindset is that the principal has all the answers. What happens when he or she is absent? What happens to the overall thinking capacity in the school? This also applies to the classroom—a teacher who constantly tells his or her students what to do misses the opportunity to develop independent thinkers.

So what do we do when someone says, "Just tell me what to do"? Our role as a coach leader is to provide ways of thinking through many options and pathways or to reconnect them to an existing standard or expectation.

Once that has been done, the person determines his or her own best decision. This helps the individual grow in confidence and ability to think and process independently in more effective ways. When a leader replaces the idea of giving advice to "offering an option" among many, it builds an individual's capacity for action while it maintains his or her sense of status and offers autonomy. If the option someone has initially chosen is not successful, there are plenty of possibilities for what might be chosen next.

Offering an option is like taking a friend to a restaurant for the first time. You point out what you have tried but ultimately your friend chooses what he or she prefers to eat. In the same way, you can avoid giving advice by

- generating options and possibilities including your own,
- reconnecting them to a standard or expectation, *then*
- asking them to narrow the options and select the *best* one for their situation.

By structuring our support of others using the language of multiple options, we facilitate the confidence and belief in other people's ability to make their own best choices. Our success as coach leaders is not a reflection of our expertise and knowledge but rather a reflection of the insight and wisdom generated within others. As a result, we derive a two-for-one benefit, an increase in our status through the success of another, which increases their status.

While successful coach leaders have made the mindset change that transitions them from telling to coaching, it is use of the essential skills that ensures alignment between what they believe and the language that demonstrates that belief. Simply, it's a strong message of "walking the talk." It is one thing to say I believe in your capacity to solve your own problems followed by the companion language, "What steps are you considering?," vs. the language, "Have you thought about . . . ,?" which sends the hidden message that I don't believe you have thought about it.

THE ESSENTIAL SKILLS—LESSONS LEARNED

So what have we learned about the essential skills of being a coach leader since we wrote the first book? You have taught us so much. You have reinforced that they are the essential bundle that positions us to be coach leaders. Certainly, there are layers of other skills and competencies but these are the essentials.

- Committed listening
- Paraphrasing
- Questions that presume positive intent
- Reflective feedback

Our intent in this book is to share new understandings about the essential skills. It is a companion to the first and in no way is intended to replace what is taught there with regard to these skills. To support your journey and growth as a coach leader, a Mindset/Skill Self-Assessment is included in the Resource Section of this book. This tool is for monitoring your progress toward the standard of being a coach leader.

ESSENTIAL SKILL #1:
THE POWER OF LISTENING

Current literature offers plenty of evidence of the importance of listening in communication. Here are a few:

- Jenny Rogers (2012b), an executive coach from the UK, says this about listening, "The most fundamental coaching skill is listening. Listening is not the passive process it seems because it involves dedicated attention to the other person and exquisite attention to the language they are using" (p. 91).
- Stephen Covey (2006) says, "Listening is the psychological equivalent of air."
- Mark Goulston (2010), trainer of FBI and police hostage negotiators, titles his most recent book, *Just Listen*. His work as a psychiatrist and business coach has taught him that listening breaks down the natural obstacles that keep us from relating to and supporting another person when productive communication seems impossible.
- David Rock (2006) states, "When a quality listener listens, they listen to people and believe in others completely. They encourage and support others in being the best they can be, just in how they listen, without saying a word" (p. 76).
- Suzette Haden Elgin (2000) offered evidence from 1984 of the need for doctors to increase the time they listen to patients. Elgin reported on a study where doctors listened to patients for an average of 18 seconds before they interrupted. These doctors, who knew they were being studied for their willingness to listen, were surprised with the results and responded in two ways:
  - They insisted they had let the patients talk for much longer.
  - They also conveyed that, "If they listened to patients without interruption then they would never get anything done because the patients would talk on and on, endlessly." (Location 1067)

In a follow-up study to see if it were true that patients would talk on and on, Beckman and Frankel (Haden Elgin, 2000) found that when patients were allowed to talk as long as they wanted, without interruption from the doctors, no patient talked longer than for 90 seconds and most talked for only about 30 seconds. Also interesting was when doctors were asked to indicate, without looking at a watch or clock, when they thought 1 minute had gone by, the "nows" started at about 20 seconds and sometimes even sooner.

The study concluded that the handful of minutes saved when not listening to patients over the day as compared to the many hours spent dealing with potential and actual malpractice suits caused by communication breakdowns is a significant difference.

Further, in Malcolm Gladwell's (2007) *Blink: The Power of Thinking Without Thinking*, the medical research related to listening conducted by Wendy Levinson who recorded hundreds of conversations between a group of physicians and their patients was reported. About half these doctors had never been sued, while the other half had been sued at least twice. The surgeons who had never been sued spent more than 3 minutes longer with each patient than did the doctors who had been sued (18.3 minutes vs. 15 minutes). The non-sued doctors invited more talking by their patients, saying "Go on, say more about that," and also were more likely to laugh and be funny during the visit. While there was no difference in the quality of information given to the patients, how the doctors talked with the patients was the defining difference.

As if this were not enough to persuade us of the importance of listening, the most recent studies in neuroscience provide the scientific support for the significance of listening. Through technology, now that we can see the workings of the brain in real time, we can see that the prefrontal cortex fires in a different way when a person has a committed listener than when the same conversation occurs with the self.

We agree 100% with these statements and findings. In fact, we teach that without full presence while listening, the other skills have a diminished effect. Most people think they are a good listener until they assess, learn more about the attributes of committed listening, and actually practice the art of committed listening without speaking.

One of the principles of listening taught in our seminar is that committed listening lays the path for building responses and solutions. Some learners are skeptical, at best, because of the stated distraction of worry about "what I'm going to say next." With intentional practice focused on full presence without saying a word, the light bulb begins to turn on. Then, with the request to practice this kind of listening in their lives, testimonies come back, "When I stopped thinking about what I was going to say next or what brilliant question I was going to ask and decided to just listen, I knew what to say when it was time to speak. And because I was truly listening, what I said was more relevant to what the person was sharing." This demonstrates that when we trust the process of coaching *and* get out of our heads and just listen, we will know what to say when it is time to speak.

Another potential self-distraction can be avoided by asking ourselves the question, "How are we listening?" Are we listening as if the person is capable, strong, and fully able to come up with great ideas and solutions *or* as if someone is in difficulty who needs our help? Does the person need help, or does he or she have the answers inside? The very language we use, help vs. support or expert vs. thinking partner, impacts the results of our conversations. Our mindset choice impacts the outcome of the conversation.

In our decade of work, another lesson has become crystal clear with regard to listening. When we reframe our listening from *listening to* to *listening for*, the results are astounding. This adaptive change becomes the bridge to the second skill of paraphrasing and takes the language from a literal translation to something much deeper. Examples of this are in the next section on listening and paraphrasing. Our purpose here is to consider what *listening for* means.

From "Listen To" to "Listen For"

We spend a lot of time listening to details. *Listening for* requires staying out of the details. We keep the big picture while noticing the nuances in front of us. Listening in this way takes the conversation to a deeper level. So what does one *listen for*?

- **What the person wants**—This question runs throughout the conversation. Listening for what another wants cuts through the detail and takes us to the heart of the conversation. Some call it bottom line, others call it essence. Ultimately, it is what the person cares deeply about.
- **Emotion**—Listening for emotion offers a barometer for the strength of how the person is feeling about something. Frequently, the entire conversation is about emotion over the content of the words the person is using. Emerging brain research and emotional intelligence speak to the significance of emotion in our lives. While often suppressed, we are learning that it is the mass under the tip of the iceberg. Naming the emotion does two things. It diffuses its power over us and sends the message that another understands what we are feeling. More about this idea is explored in Chapters 1 and 2.
- **Passion**—Listening for my passion lifts up what is really important to me. Your recognition of what I have deep passion about connects us and shows that you care enough to hear what I love or care about.
- **Options, possibilities, potential**—Surfacing options and possibilities from my language promotes my thinking and plants me in the present or prepares me for the future. This might also be called *listening for potential*. This kind of listening hears where I am heading rather than what might not be working. Judgment is absent.

Filters, if any, are transparent. You see me for who I am, what I care about, and where I want to go.

- **What is already working**—We grow from our successes and strengths, and sometimes people are so focused on what is not working that they forget that many things are working.

Listening for Reframes

In addition to the "listen fors" noted above, our continuous study of coaching introduced us to authors who have strongly influenced our thinking with regard to listening. A few of those are Orem, Binkert, and Clancy's (2007) *Appreciative Coaching* and Kegan and Lahey's (2002) work in *How the Way We Talk Can Change the Way We Work* followed by their (2009) book, *Immunity to Change*. This learning combined with our conversations with you, resulted in the notion of "listening for" opportunities for reframing:

- From negative to positive
- From problem to solution
- From complaint to commitment

From Negative to Positive

Visit any bookstore and you will see shelves devoted to the power of positivity. Longer life, greater joy, and increased happiness are a few of the benefits noted in the literature. One side effect of our work is our almost insane attention to language. What we notice is that negativity permeates our language. Therefore, we have embraced the opportunity to create awareness around the choices we make with our language. In fact, presumption of positive intent is our standard and expectation for how we work. We have seen the power potential in our own work, and we practice it even when we are not with you.

Barbara Fredrickson (2013), positive psychology researcher and author of *Positivity*, states, "Daily experiences of positive emotions forecast and produce growth in personal resources such as competence (e.g., environmental mastery), meaning (e.g., purpose in life), optimism (e.g., pathways thinking), resilience, self-acceptance, positive relationships, as well as physical health"(p. 12). We reference her work in our goal to encourage a ratio of three positive comments to one negative comment to foster growth and resilience. *And* we are not the ones offering negative comments. Our aim is to counteract the negative comments still prevalent in many of our workplaces and other environments.

From Problem to Solution

Because language matters, our attention to it is critically important. When we share this chart (see Figure 3.1) with our seminar participants, little more is required because it carries the message so clearly.

Figure 3.1   Changing a Conversation From Problem Focused to Solution Focused

Problem Focused		Solution Focused
Why didn't you hit the target?	vs.	What are you planning to do next time to hit the target?
Why did this happen?	vs.	What do you want to achieve here?
When or where did it all start to go wrong?	vs.	How do you want to move this forward?
Why do you think you are not good at this?	vs.	What are ways you want to develop strength in this area?
What's wrong with your team?	vs.	What strategies are you putting in place for your team to succeed?
Why did you do that?	vs.	What are you thinking you want to do now?
Who's responsible for this?	vs.	How shall we best achieve this?
Why isn't this working?	vs.	What steps do we want to put in place to make this work?

SOURCE: Adapted from Rock, D. (2006). *Quiet leadership*. New York, NY: HarperCollins. ©HarperCollins.

What observations are you making with regard to the impact of the words chosen and the emotion it evokes?

_____

_____

Because the learning in our sessions has placed emphasis on presumption of positive intent, the most frequent response to the chart is, "The left side does *not* presume positive intent." We also hear there is blame and finger pointing that accompanies the comments on the left-hand side. On the right-hand side, comments include presumption of positive intent, believing in the person to find their own solutions, and a focus on the present or future rather than the past.

_____

In one of our recent seminars, a participant spoke up, saying, "These questions are in the present progressive tense!" She then laughed about always being sent to the principal's office as a student because she was constantly correcting her teachers. The verbalization of her "Aha!" moment provided clarity to us, along with another way to speak about the language of coaching. The present progressive tense indicates continuing action—something happening now or what will happen in the future. Present progressive language keeps us in the present and future rather than moving us backward or keeping us mired in the past.

Focusing on the problem makes the problem larger, deeper, and stickier. Reframing the problem to a solution surfaces options, possibilities, and the promise of resolution.

From Complaint to Commitment

One of our most profound insights came with the study of Kegan and Lahey's (2002) work. This quote alone shifted our thinking in significant ways.

> We believe that people wouldn't complain about anything unless they cared about something. Underneath the surface torrent of complaints and cynical humor and eye-rolling, there is a hidden river of passion and commitment which is the reason the complaints even exist. (p. 20)

Kegan's quote represents a *game changer* because it rewires our brain to listen for what the person really cares about instead of what they are complaining about. Second, it offers a potential shift to the thinking of the other person when we reframe what they have said.

What makes these reframes important? In coaching, a reframe holds the potential for a cognitive shift that opens up new thinking, new directions, and an enhanced emotion. Moving from "can't do" to "I've got this" or "I'm on my way to getting it" aligns the energy and emotion for action, creating awareness for the person about what they really want.

Listen for . . . Second Dimension

In our quest to be the best coaches we can be, we dedicated our professional learning this year to the reexamination of the core competencies under the guidance of our mentor coach, Dr. Francine Campone, MCC (Master Certified Coach). In our study of the competency of active listening, we added four new "listen fors" to our growing list.

1. Story

2. Metaphor

3. Contradictions

4. Limiting beliefs

A key idea accompanying "listen fors" is the notion of "clean language," which Jenny Rogers (2012b) attributes to the work of the late New Zealand therapist, David Grove. In *Manager as Coach*, she states, "The phrase 'clean language' means you notice and then explore the language of the other person never assuming you know what such language means." As well, you are keenly aware of and think about any nonverbal cues from the person such as a furrowed brow, a tear in the eye, finger tapping, and so on. In the second dimension of *listen for*, we take it all in—verbal and nonverbal cues. We check for cues throughout the conversation to ensure understanding and clarity on the part of the other person without interpretation or filtering on our part. Whether it's a story, a metaphor, a contradiction, or a limiting belief, coach leaders note the language and make it explicit from the other person's perspective.

Story

Active listening puts us in a place to listen for the person's story. It's not fact; it's the truth as they see it. When we listen for the story, we get data about who, what, when, and why. The words chosen tell us volumes about the person's point of view. Our language betrays what we are thinking and feeling unconsciously. Listening for the language of the person begins to give us insight about what is working at an unconscious level. For example, the speaker may say, "I felt isolated," which indicates they are standing alone as they face the situation. Language cues provide a sense of how a person positions themselves in the story. They might be a victim, a hero, a martyr, and so on. For example, when a coach heard a person say, "I see myself as her protector," the coach used the story later in the conversation to ask, "How is your message protecting her?"

Not only do we get impressions of how the people see themselves; we get information about how they position themselves with regard to others. For example, when someone is complaining about another person, listening for the character he or she is taking in the story can be manifested in a question such as, "What character are you in this story?" Another strategy for moving a person from the details of a story is to shift the focus onto the effect or the impact of an event rather than the he said-she said from the event.

Metaphor

Because language is so important, by listening for the metaphors used by the person, a committed listener may gain insight into the speaker's thinking and feeling. For example, when a person says, "I've reached a turning point," our committed listening hears this as significant. It informs our paraphrase and possibly a follow-up question. We might say, "Something has happened—a turning point—and you see it. What exactly do you mean by turning point?" or "What are you turning from . . . to?" The person is finding meaning through the use of metaphor, either implicitly or explicitly. When we listen for and "lift up" these nuances, we open the door for deeper meaning by gaining clarity of the language for the person. We remember the strong metaphors that they use and see the possibility for how it may open the door as a pathway to what they want. Metaphors are powerful in that they replace abstract thinking with concrete examples. When a coach uses metaphors, it holds the potential for accelerating thinking or action in the direction of desired results. Skilled coaches know how to take a negative metaphor used by the speaker and weave it toward a positive approach. "Climbing over a brick wall" shifts a barrier into the possibility for action, for planning, for power. The metaphor reframe from negative to positive connects to a deeper meaning increasing self-understanding of the power one has to overcome barriers.

Metaphors may show up in different forms such as the following:

- Color metaphors: "I'm feeling like I'm in the pink."
- Architectural metaphors: "I feel like I've hit a brick wall." Or "I want us to build a stronger organization."
- Dimension metaphors: "I'm feeling like I am getting smaller."

Contradiction

As coaches, we also listen for consistencies and inconsistencies in the story, in the metaphor, or in the language or emotion of the person. One example is someone who is "telling and retelling a story" about an evaluation that was less than stellar, and the words to you are, "I'm okay." Clearly, they are not. Holding up this contradiction is our work as a coach. "Your words say you are okay, and yet you keep telling me the same story as if it is not okay. What do you want to say about that?" Another example is a person in the position of being a leader who continues to put themselves in the victim mode in the story. Holding up the contradiction might sound like, "You are a leader who has enjoyed success in this arena before. Now your words seem to release your power as a leader—even to give it away to others. How do you want to reconcile this difference?"

Limiting Beliefs

We learn about the potentially negative impact of limiting beliefs through Cognitive Behavioral Therapy. Within cognitive psychology, a schema is an abstract plan that guides an individual's thinking and responses. In coaching, a schema is a broad mental guideline for interpreting a situation and how to respond to the situation. Schemas lead to sets of behaviors that are coping styles, which may or may not be productive. We observe limiting beliefs as behavior patterns and language patterns in others. We listen for language or descriptions of behaviors that indicate schemas that lead to helpful or unhelpful coping strategies (Auerback, 2006).

Limiting beliefs show up in language people use to describe themselves. "I'm a klutz!" Or, as we have heard in our seminars, "I'm a real jerk (or worse)." David Rock (2009) reports that the amount of self-criticism, when tallied in hours is remarkable, ranging from 500 hours a year to as high as over 2,000 hours a year. It also shows up in the way people view their world. "I'll never be able to get that job," or "This child is the type that you can never really reach."

Jenny Rogers (2012a) asserts that we all have beliefs that limit us and limit how we can be coached because they are irrational. We have developed flawed schema or thinking patterns that are unhelpful distortions or reality that often cause misery or ineffective behaviors. Some examples from Rogers are:

- The pessimist
- It's all my fault
- Other people can make me happy or sad
- My past defines me
- Super-competent-me
- No-such-thing-as-grey
- It's not fair
- I can change people
- The disciplined perfectionist
- The self-sacrificer/compulsive carer
- Everything should be peaceful and harmonious
- You have to be tough
- The narcissist

Other examples:

- All or nothing thinking
- "Should" statements
- Emotional reasoning
- Control fallacies
- Personalization and blame
- Jumping to conclusions
- Catastrophizing
- Overgeneralization
- Mental filter (pp. 172–173)

For example, "should" statements are a pattern of belief that things must be done in a certain way—either by you or by others. "I should have anticipated that the conversation would turn out badly." A coach's response might be, "You are disappointed in the outcome, and you are looking for a way to continue the conversation with a goal of win-win." Or "The teachers should be doing better at guided reading instruction by now. They have had countless workshops and professional learning community (PLC) conversations devoted to guided reading! How can I get them to do what they know they should be doing?" A possible coach's response, "You have clearly set the stage for teacher success with guided reading. What are some things you are thinking you want to do as next steps to continue the focus on implementation with those who are still in the beginning stages?"

Additional options for challenging limiting beliefs are the following:

- As in all other coaching interactions, believe in the other person and presume positive intent.
- Name or ask for the thinking pattern.
- Reframe in a paraphrase.
- Challenge the generalization that lies beneath the pattern.
- Introduce the client to greater flexibility in thinking using the language of possibility.

Questions that may support your efforts to challenge limiting beliefs include:

- What is the evidence?
- What other explanations could there be?
- What would it be like if the opposite were true?
- What would you like instead?
- How might you expand your thinking to include additional possibilities?

Reframe Example

Recently, a school principal lost her right-hand assistant principal to another school. This was a reassignment from the central office that broke the strong bond she had in her administrative team. She felt trust had been violated, and the words she kept repeating throughout the conversation were, "It's hard. It's just so hard." The coach listened to this story and the language being used. The who, what, when, and how of the story were placing a usually confident leader into the victim mode. She had given her power away.

After at least three repetitions, the coach said, "Your strength as a leader is evident every day as you work to move this school to new levels of performance. Here is an obstacle that is very hard to comprehend. Knowing that what you say repeatedly is a message to your brain, how might tweaking the message to your brain from 'It's hard. It's so hard' to 'It's hard. It's so hard *and* I can do it!' influence your results?" At the conclusion of this conversation, the principal indicated that the most valuable part of the conversation was when the coach held up this contradiction in the situation. She said, "You helped me move out of my negativity back into my power as a leader." This was a cognitive shift for her and changed the course of her actions. She took her power back, held a fierce conversation with central office, and is currently celebrating a new position in another system.

Another Reframe

There is a sense of uncertainty, let's call it being vulnerable, when we hear another person using language that is out of alignment with who we know they are, and we feel compelled to hold the language they are using up to them. We do this not to make them feel bad, but rather to offer new awareness of the language they are using to clarify that it aligns with what they really want. For example, during a coaching conversation a few years back, Wanda, a district level leader, was expressing her deep feelings and disappointment about the way she was being viewed and treated by her direct report, Jim.

Jim was not pleased with Wanda's performance and had written a growth plan that Wanda felt was out of line and unfair. The coach listened as the expressions of frustrations and unfairness continued. After paraphrasing in a way to show that the coach was "witnessing Wanda's struggle," she made a statement like this: "Wanda, the language you are using, for example, 'I feel like my hands are tied; no one appreciates what I'm doing; I work hard and get nowhere because of what others think about me,' and so forth sounds like the language of a victim. How accurate is that?" Wanda became very quiet and said, "Oh my gosh! It does, and that is not the way I want to be. While I don't agree with what is happening, I do have control over how I move forward. I will no longer make excuses. I will move forward and change the way I am being viewed!" And Wanda did just that. She grew from that experience and kept her focus on who she was, even when moving through a hard time. She was a highly qualified educator who was open to ongoing opportunities to grow in her skills as a leader and is now flourishing in her district. Jim is no longer employed by the district.

Another resource that affirms the importance of listening is the late Laura Whitworth's (2011) book, *Co-Active Coaching: New Skills for Coaching People Toward Success in Work and Life*. In it, Whitworth and her colleagues offer three levels of listening.

- **Level I: Internal Listening**—This level is about listening to self and listening from the perspective of what something means to me. It's how I figure out things for myself—through reflection and creation of my own meaning. While a valuable form of listening, it is what a person being coached might be doing rather than the coach.
- **Level II: Focused Listening**—This level of listening is an intentional focus on the person speaking. One listens to both the energy and the information that comes from the speaker. Akin to *listening for* described above, it's like listening twice—once when it is initially spoken and again when you listen to the person's reaction to your response.
- **Level III: Global Listening**—This level of listening, sometimes called *environmental listening*, is when you and the other person are in your own world; you are at the center of the universe receiving information from everywhere at once. Everything you can observe with your senses such as what you see, hear, smell, and feel, including both tactile and emotional sensations, are involved. In addition, action, inaction, and the interaction are included. At this level, intuition is accessed.

ESSENTIAL SKILL #2: COMMITTED LISTENING AND PARAPHRASING

Described as the most underutilized skill, paraphrasing is often a skill we have learned that is at the bottom of our toolkit as communicators. When we ask you why paraphrasing is not used, here are some of the responses we hear:

- We learned parroting rather than eloquence in paraphrasing.
- We are afraid we will get it wrong.
- It sounds inauthentic, more like a pattern of speech we have learned.

Paraphrasing is a skill most of us learned prior to the more recent neuroscience regarding the S (Status) in SCARF, which is discussed in detail in Chapter 2. What we now understand about the importance of making our language about the other person reinforces the potential power of this skill. Learning to flip the language from "I" to "you" now makes sense when we consider it from the brain's perspective. The metaphor we use to illustrate this concept is a flashlight beam or spotlight. Our goal is to keep the beam of light on the other person. So instead of "what I hear you saying," which makes it about us, we change the language to "you want . . . your goal . . . your desire . . . or you're feeling . . . ," which makes it all about the other person, giving status and keeping the ray of light focused on him or her.

When done eloquently, paraphrasing holds the potential for a highly effective communication skill. It can even replace the need for a question. Paraphrasing is evidence of our committed listening. Without our full presence, we cannot paraphrase eloquently. So how is this done? By simply doing what was suggested above—*listening for* and *listening with*. Putting these two skills together as if they were bookends demonstrates our full presence for what is of value to the person. Rather than parroting back exactly what the person has said, we go deeper for the essence of what they want, the emotion they are feeling, or their vision of possibility.

Let's Practice

Listen for what these individuals want, the emotion or passion present, and the options or possibilities possible. There are many possibilities for responses. The only nonnegotiable is presumption of positive intent.

- "I'm working with Drew every day to improve his reading. His progress is so slow, and I'm getting frustrated."

_____

_____

- "Who has enough time to meet in PLCs? We have so many things to accomplish, and we aren't accomplishing anything."

_____

_____

Possible Responses

"I'm working with Drew every day to improve his reading. His progress is so slow, and I'm getting frustrated."

- "You want Drew to be a strong reader."
- "You're committed to Drew's success as a reader."
- "No matter what, you want Drew to be a good reader."
- "You want your hard work to have a purpose and be of support to Drew."

"Who has enough time to meet in PLCs? We have so many things to accomplish, and we aren't accomplishing anything".

- "It's important to you that your PLC is productive and addresses the work to be accomplished."
- "You want your PLC time to be of value to you and to your students."
- "You are dedicated to your work as a teacher, and you are striving to find value in the PLC time."
- "You like to get things done and you are looking for a way to guide your PLC into being focused toward accomplishing the team's goals."
- "You want your team to 'spin like a top,' doing great things for kids every time you meet."

Advanced Practice

Listen for what is wanted and flip these complaints into commitments.

- "I'm overwhelmed with all we are expected to do at the beginning of school: get our rooms ready, meet the parents, develop lesson plans, and so on."

_____

_____

- "I'm not sure how to teach this new science curriculum."

_____

_____

(Continued)

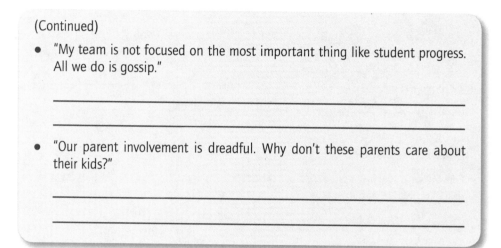

(Continued)

- "My team is not focused on the most important thing like student progress. All we do is gossip."

  _____

  _____

- "Our parent involvement is dreadful. Why don't these parents care about their kids?"

  _____

  _____

Worrying about getting the paraphrase wrong is not necessary. We say, "When you get it wrong, you get it right!" because you bring clarity to the conversation. An example that teaches this valuable lesson was a time when someone came to one of us visibly upset. The paraphrase was, "You are very angry about the way you were treated in this interaction." The person responded, "No, I am not angry. I am hurt and disappointed." _Now_ we knew what we were taking about. Hurt and disappointment are very different from anger. When you demonstrate a sincere attempt to _listen for_, the person will sense the intent, feel the safety, and will let you know when you have not hit the nail on the head. It may sound like, "Not exactly" or "Kind of, but what I really meant was . . . ." On the other hand, when you have hit the nail on the head, you may hear, "Exactly!" or "Yes! That's what I meant, and you said it better than I did."

Two additional lessons we have learned that add power potential to paraphrasing are the importance of silence and the notion of less is more. As educators, we are highly proficient with language. Often we use a lot of words in an attempt to ensure we are understood. We have learned that less is more with regard to a powerful paraphrase. When we listen for essence, passion, or possibility, we need fewer words than when we thought we had to repeat everything the person said in our paraphrase (parroting). When we flood the person with an abundance of language, it confuses the brain and invites fuzziness into the conversation. We listen for the heart of the spoken word and give it back in a brief, crisp paraphrase. Often, 15 words or less, or even three to five when applicable, will convey a much more powerful message than a paraphrase with an _and_ that extends the sentence and invites old patterns of speaking into the equation. In our seminars, when an _and_ creeps into our conversations, we playfully say, "Put a period at the end. KISS it—Keep it simple sweetie!"

In her book *Fierce Conversations*, Susan Scott (2002) writes, "Silence is sometimes the answer." In the context of paraphrasing, deliver the paraphrase followed by silence. Do not utter another sentence *and* most certainly not a question. Let silence do the heavy lifting. Silence is where thinking lives; it's where I can discover awareness, create my own answers, and consider my next steps. This is where we learn that paraphrasing followed by silence can replace many of our questions. Suzie McNeese, one of our elementary principals, discovered this for herself when she proclaimed, "Today, during a coaching session, I realized that when I wanted to ask clarifying questions, it was for me to try to solve the problem for the other person. Instead, by listening for and paraphrasing, I was allowing the person to solve the problem themselves."

One of the most frequent goals we hear as coach leaders move through our seminars is for increased automaticity with the skills. One participant, in particular, was totally committed to the integration of paraphrasing into her communication skill set. Debbie practiced with Karen for hours. She requested that Karen talk about something and then stop so she could paraphrase. Karen recalls, "I would offer feedback or ask for other possibilities." It was only when Karen pushed her to listen for what she really, really wanted (emotion) that Debbie was able to go deeper and move from the literalness of Karen's words to the heart of what she wanted. Instead of saying, "You love your grandgirls," which was true, she said, "You love your grandgirls so much you are willing to leave your home of 30 years to move to Florida because you want to be in their lives every day." "Yes!" That is what we call the "river that runs beneath." Listening for what a person is truly saying to you, listening for what they care deeply about is an eloquent paraphrase.

ESSENTIAL SKILL #3: PRESUMING POSITIVE INTENT AND POSITIVE PRESUPPOSITIONS

Chapters 1 and 2 establish the rationale for why positive language is so important in communication. Our words send messages to the brain that can be interpreted as safety or threat. In our first book, *RESULTS Coaching: The New Essential for School Leaders*, we describe in detail why language matters and how the presumption of positive intent holds the potential for influencing the conscious and subconscious mind, for creating safety for authentic sharing, and for opening the door for deep levels of trust and respect in a relationship. We also stressed this importance in Chapter 2 of this book as we talked about leading with the brain in mind.

A Matter of Distinction

Before we begin, a distinction is called for—the global perspective of pre-suming positive intent, which then spills out into the specific language of our statements and our questions, called *positive presuppositions*. The first is an adaptive change—a mindset—that we hold that presumes positive intent on the part of the other person. It's like an umbrella covering our way of thinking about how we work with others. Second, a demonstration of the mindset is the language of our statements or questions, which is called a *positive presupposition*. This is a technical change meaning the skill set of how we construct our statements or questions to presume positive intent. An example of the mindset is my overall belief in the other person to find his or her own solutions, thus eliminating the need for advice giving. The skill is the specific language of my statements or questions which demonstrates that belief such as, "When you spoke with the parents about their child, what was the response?"

Let's explore this more deeply. Here are some statements that demonstrate a mindset of positive intent.

- You believe all people want to be good at what they do.
- You believe people want to be valued and make a difference in this world.
- You believe that people show up to do the right thing and make good choices.
- You believe people care about those they teach or lead.
- You believe everyone is working hard and when things prevent their best it is due to life distractions.

We contend that if you invited us to your school for a professional learning experience that would dramatically impact the culture of your school, it would be teaching the concept of presuming positive intent. We would also state without reservation that this is the easiest concept to get cognitively *and* the most difficult to internalize in our language. Why? Because of brain hardwiring! We have practiced our language patterns for a long time, so the default is to continue that pattern especially when under stress. It takes intention, determination, and a strong commitment to create new wiring.

Creating the new wiring is truly an adaptive change: an inside-outside process. It requires that mind and body align with the language we speak—so easy to say and so hard to do. It takes us back to the concept of mindset that we discussed in the beginning of this chapter. The essential mindset of a coach leader is:

- **Belief in another's ability to grow and excel**—A growth mindset is mandatory. The minute I step off the belief that a person can grow is the minute I choose to diminish my own potential for impact with a person.

- **Recognition that "advice is toxic!"**—Now that we understand the importance of giving status to another, we get why advice does just the opposite. As mentioned in the section of this chapter on the Seduction of Advising or Telling, we recognize this feeds our status rather than the status of the other person.
- **Use of intentional language that aligns with our trust and belief in others**—This is the one that sounds really easy, and yet we know from our work with you that it's *really hard*. You report, "My head knows it, my mouth just says something different." Again, we realize it's about our years of practicing a language pattern. The hope is what we now know is possible—we can create new wiring.

Because of these nonnegotiables, it is important we show up for our conversations having considered how we want to "be" in the conversation. By bringing great intention to the conversation, we will enhance the relationship by:

- **Setting aside or suspending some behaviors**—For example, judgment will quickly shut down any chance of trust evolving in the relationship because it instantly feels like threat rather than safety.
- **Seeing the person as whole and capable**—Knowing the person is neither broken nor needs fixing keeps *belief* present as an accelerant for change. When we "hold able" that the person is capable and can do for themselves what is best for his or her own life, we will work from strengths seeing the possibility and potential of the person.
- **Being a model of committed listening and speaking**—We teach others through our own behavior. It is the best message of our beliefs and values. Walking the talk of a coach leader through the modeling of committed listening and speaking sends a clear signal of what is expected. From our learning about the brain, we understand the concept of mirror neurons—our behavior and language will be picked up by those with whom we interact. In turn, our greatest hope is that the mirror neurons of the teacher's behavior and language will be mimicked by the students. Now we are changing the culture of how we talk to one another in the school environment.

A Story From You: Coaching Begins With Me and My Mindset

One story that emerges from our work that illustrates both the essential mindset and how we show up for a conversation follows. Karen was working in the Houston area and was approached during a break for some coaching about a high school department head. The math coordinator described the department head as extremely negative, so much so, that her negativity was bleeding into the attitudes of the team members and affecting their productivity together. The coaching begins . . .

Coach:	It is the morning that you are going to work with this particular department head. As you get out of bed, what are you saying to yourself about the person and the work before you?
Math Coordinator:	Oh, I can hardly get up! Today will be excruciating, hard, and exhausting! All my energy will go toward trying to get this person to see my point of view about the work. There will be a vortex of negativity and little will be accomplished on behalf of the team or the students.
Coach:	(With humor.) Please stop! Thank goodness this day is over! It's a new day and you are getting out of bed to work with your *best* department head. What are you saying to yourself about the person and the work before you?
Math Coordinator:	Oh, I can't wait! Our work together is always invigorating and inspiring. Our ideas spiral up as we consider possibility after possibility. The team is on fire and future focused—what can they do next that will accelerate the learning of the team and their students?
Math Coordinator:	I get it! It's about me! What I put in my head is reality for how I will work with the department head. The work begins with me and what I say to myself.

BINGO! Through coaching, the math coordinator saw clearly what was the center of her struggle. The mirror changed from facing the department head to facing the math coordinator (or herself). She realized that the language or story she told herself would be actualized in how she showed up for her conversation with others.

Working on New Hardwiring

So how do we get this new pattern well established in our brains? Just as we said in our first book, we presume that others are doing each of the following:

- **Prior and current planning**—The person is already planning how they will address the topic or concern.

- **Prior and current thinking**—Clearly, he or she has been thinking about it because of wanting to speak to you for greater clarity.
- **Nobility of purpose**—Believing a person wants to do something even when they have not begun to do so is especially impactful to the brain. Because our brains are different, we each respond to change in different ways. My pace for change may be significantly different than your pace for change. Believing that I want to and just have not started yet sends a different message than language that carries judgment that I have not started yet. My brain may be planning for action, and when you approach me presuming positive intent, I am more likely to risk and take the next step. Approximation in the desired direction is progress!
- **Commitment to a standard or expectation**—Our brains hold so much information that we can forget a standard or expectation. Even those of us who are Type A go-getters can temporarily forget something we know for sure. When a coach leader uses his or her language to reconnect us to what we know, our status remains intact and we quickly plug back into an existing standard or expectation. One example is the leader who says, "When you checked our procedures for a responsive classroom, what options did you find?"
- **Positive intent for action or behavior**—Language that presumes positive intent almost always conveys an intention for follow-up action or behavior. For example, the question in the previous bullet presumes the person will check the procedures for a responsive classroom if they have not already done so. This is the language that "holds able"—presuming that the person will take action in the intended direction. Additional examples include: "Knowing the importance of being at your duty station first thing in the morning, what is your plan to make sure that begins to happen with regularity?" and "Knowing that budgets were due this morning, when is the earliest you can turn yours in to the office?"

A Story From You: My Map
for Change May Be Different From Yours

One principal experienced the value of presuming nobility of purpose firsthand. A standard or expectation for using cooperative learning as a strategy for high engagement had been established as a campus goal. Extensive professional learning had been provided over time. There had been many conversations, individually and collectively, about what the expectation would look and sound like in the classroom. Still, there was one teacher who was showing hesitation. As the principal conducted her walk-throughs, she went by one teacher's room to notice that while she had put the desks in groups, she was continuing to lecture as usual without any student interaction. The principal was upset as she entered the office area to find her assistant principal (AP). Presuming the worst, she spouted off her frustration to the AP. In response, the AP said, "Well, at least she has her desks ready for her cooperative groups." The principal stopped in her tracks realizing the AP was spot on. She had a new view or perspective that the teacher was moving in the intended direction. Quickly, her frustration turned into hope and she marched back down to the teacher's classroom and said, "How exciting! You've organized your room for cooperative learning groups. I can't wait to come back and see the level of engagement with your students."

Carol Dweck's (2006) notion of growth mindset vs. fixed mindset is fundamental and deeply embedded in the concept of presuming positive intent. When you presume I have, I am, or I intend to, you convey belief, value, and trust to my brain. You are also connecting to the significant work of David Rock's (2008) SCARF described in Chapter 2. At the heart of presuming positive intent is maintaining my status, which keeps me engaged with you rather than sensing you don't like me or thinking I may not be good enough and ultimately pulling away (taking flight) because I sense fear or threat.

What About . . . ?

One question we are frequently asked is, "How does one presume positive intent when we have a history with the person or we know for certain they have not done something?" One answer already described is nobility of purpose—believing I want to *and* that I have just not started yet. No one gets up with the goal of being the worst he or she can be. We all want to make a difference. So what can one lift up to presume positive intent? Here is a short list to which you may add:

- **Nobility of purpose** (see story above)
- **Effort**—I show effort in some way every day. What is it? Example: "You've worked really hard to ensure each student has access to the resources they need."
- **Knowledge and skills**—What are my strengths; what special gifts do I possess? Example: "Because you've been teaching for a number of years, you have a vast knowledge of classroom management strategies."
- **Integrity**—Defined as the quality of being honest and having strong moral principles can be a recognizable attribute. Example: "Your moral compass is a strong guide for what you see as right or wrong." Or "Knowing your word is like a promise, this goal will be accomplished in no time."
- **Caring**—How do I show kindness and care to others? Example: "Your sensitivity to the lives of each of your students is apparent in the kindness you show them every day."

- **Dedication**—Every person carries within them a set of beliefs and values aligned with what they hold dear to his or her heart. Sometimes in the midst of the busy work, we lose sight of that dedication. Comments from others offer opportunities for us to reconnect to that personal dedication. Example: "Even when the task at hand seems daunting, your dedication to your students always seems to carry you through the tough times and toward new successes."
- **Commitment**—In what ways do we stay engaged in areas where we have verbally or in writing expressed that we are all in? Example: "There is no doubt how committed you are to the mission and goals of our school. What are you envisioning as the most important next step in reaching parents that have yet to attend a parent conference?"
- **Perseverance**—What is that driving force that keeps us in the game when a part of us wants to give up or throw in the towel? Sometimes it's being reminded that we have the internal strength to carry on. Example: "As a person with a track record of not walking away from a challenge, what is giving you the strength now to persevere, even in the midst of numerous challenges?"
- **??**—What additional items would you add to this list of ways to show presumption of positive intent?

Having and showing a mindset of positive intent holds greater possibility for increasing productive responses from others. Your language and attitudes send a message of respect coupled with high expectations, which in turn increases the likelihood of inspiration and motivation for action. And when we presume a person has done something and they have not, typically they will do one of two things: (1) confess that they have not done what we presumed, which invites truth-telling in the conversation. My brain feels safe enough to be honest with you. Or (2) I will say to myself, "She thinks I have already done this. I better get busy and get it done." Either way, status is preserved. We want to influence, never manipulate. When a person has a pattern of behavior indicating standards are consistently unmet, we hold up the standard with a question indicating positive intent for action, such as, "Knowing the deadline for lesson plans is the end of the day Thursday, what is your plan for consistently getting your plans in on time?" or "Because one of our focus areas this year is increased parent involvement, how are you thinking you want to engage those parents you have not seen yet?"

Positive Presuppositions—The Questions We Ask

That brings us to positive presuppositions present in the questions we ask. As educators, we have perfected the art of asking questions.

Our point here is to offer a perspective about the questions we ask. First, we believe that in coaching there is a difference between questions that are for gaining information and questions that provoke thinking. While we want both, we want the majority of our questions to be those that promote thinking. Here are some insights about questions that make a difference:

- Most people have the answers to their own questions.
- Most people find the best answers for themselves, within themselves.

Seven Attributes of Questions That Make a Difference

Building on the insights, there are attributes of questions that make a difference. These six essentials include:

1. **Presume positive intent**—"Knowing that our focus is on science instruction this year, what goals are you focused on for the first 6 weeks?" This one question presumes positive intent, offers status, lifts up a standard, and holds able.

2. **Focus on solution**—"What options have you and your team determined as possibilities for your solution?" In this question, we see a standard and/or expectation for meeting with the team, talking about options, generating possibilities, and a focus on solutions over problems.

3. **Invite vision thinking**—"When June of 2018 arrives, what will you and your team be celebrating about literacy performance for your grade level?" This question begins with the end in mind. It suggests consideration of measures of success, that the team is talking about these important details, and that there will be a celebration.

4. **Focus on positive connections**—"As you plan for management of classroom behavior, what learning from your Love and Logic training will be most beneficial to your plan?" This question builds a bridge between what has been learned and the expected implementation. It models multiple standards—planning and strong classroom management—and it holds the teacher able to make it happen.

5. **Incorporate specific actions**—"As you implement your plan, what will be your first step or what do you want to do first?" which may be followed by, "What will you do next, and so on?" In a coaching conversation, this is an important question as the conversation nears the end. It consolidates all the thinking and possibilities generated in the conversation and narrows to the

intended action. Making it explicit rather than implied ensures the brain of the person speaking has crystallized his or her commitment to action.

6. **Consider resources**—"What resources are you thinking you want to consider or draw from as you move forward with your plan?" Checking in on resources provides an opportunity for another to think about a body of support that is available, from other people to well-respected best practices, research, and readings.

7. **Hold able**—"As we end, what are *you* thinking you want to do between now and the next time we talk?" This ensures the person is doing the heavy lifting instead of us. The language demonstrates my belief in you as a competent and capable person and gives you the autonomy to take action on your behalf. When we do for others what they can do for themselves, we sabotage ourselves because we send the subconscious message to status that you are *unable* to do this yourself.

Questions That Presume Positive Intent

For those of you who have been in our seminars, you have a strong visual image of the language that presumes positive intent when asking questions. In fact, many of you carry the picture on your phone as a reminder of how we actually "switch" language as if it were a light switch to ensure it sends a positive message. We ask that you draw a circle in the center of your paper with these words in the middle of the circle:

- Have you . . .?
- Did you . . .?
- Can you . . .?
- Could you . . .?
- Do you . . .?

Now, with a very bold marker, draw a diagonal line to signify this is the language that we do *not* want to use to begin our questions. Not only does the language presume negative intent, the questions are closed and are answered with a yes or no response. We want positive presuppositions that show clear declarations of belief in the other person. The replacement language that we write on the outside of the circle includes phrases such as

- What . . .?
- When . . .?
- How . . .?
- Which . . .?

with value adds such as

Based on . . .?

In what ways . . .?

Using data . . .?

Relying on . . .?

Having tried . . .?

Since . . .?

to beginning with a status statement such as

- Knowing your level of commitment . . .?
- As someone who . . .?
- Given you are a teacher who . . .?

This does not mean that we profess one should never use a closed question. Sometimes asking "Is this what you really want?" or "Would you like to stop and talk about this?" is very appropriate. We are saying there is an overabundance of closed questions, and in most cases, deep reflection comes from evocative and open-ended questions. This is also an opportunity to remind us that we refrain from asking questions that are leading others to respond in a way that has been determined by us to be the right answer. We do not ask leading questions, whether open or closed.

Another Perspective

Another frame that is sometimes helpful when designing questions is the power that comes from choosing the focus of our questions (Rock, 2006). Imagine a high-rise building that has five floors plus a basement. Each floor has the possibility of a different focus. The top floor is the penthouse where the focus is thinking: the what ifs, the possibilities, the potential. The fourth floor has a glass ceiling to the fifth floor because this floor is for visioning or seeing the future and wanting it. The third floor is where planning is the focus. It is for creating and designing, prioritizing and ordering, and determining our action steps. The focus of the second floor is to add supporting details. Without clear boundaries about how much detail is enough, we can experience the ancient wisdom of the "devil is in the details" and we can get lost in them. You are seeing that the power potential of our questions is diminishing as we continue down the floors. We are now on the first floor where the focus is on the problem. We know about this from earlier descriptions in this chapter. The problem is problematic in that it gets larger the more we focus on it. We've learned that flipping to solution recovers the energy, the passion, and the commitment to move forward. So what's in the basement? We're certain you know it because we've all experienced it—drama! Yikes! Let's stay out of the basement!

Figure 3.2   Designing Focused Questions

- Thinking (How long have you been thinking about this?)
- Vision (What is the vision you want to achieve?)
- Planning (What is the blueprint you are designing?)
- Details (What specific things are going on?)
- Problem (What kind of barriers are you encountering?)
- Drama (What if this doesn't happen?)

© edelZ / iStock

So why is this important to consider? Eighty-five percent of conversations typically take place on the third through the fifth floors, but the top two floors have the potential to move us to insight. Most of our conversations are about details, problems, and drama. As a coach, our goal is to be in the penthouse (thinking) and on the top floors (visioning and planning).

Let's Practice

Flip these questions from negative to positive presuppositions.

Figure 3.3   Turning the Negative Into a Positive

Negative Presupposition	Positive Presupposition
Did you check the student's scores before you made the plan?	
Can you answer a question for me and my team?	
Have you thought about using manipulatives to teach that concept?	
Do you know any good ideas for how to get high engagement?	
Do you meet with your PLCs every week?	
Have you done your homework?	
Did you know we are the lowest ranking school in science in the district?	
Did you call the parents of your students this year?	

Red Flags: Caution—Status at Risk

What have we learned about questions? Plenty! One that bears repeating here is that eloquent paraphrasing can eliminate the need for many of our questions. We've also learned that just because we have practiced questions as a major skillset of teaching, it does not transfer equally to coaching. Paraphrase first, question when needed. In addition, there are some roadblocks to consider with regard to questions. Here are a few:

- **Leading questions**—Questions, especially inquisitive ones, have the high potential to put us in the lead. When they include a conclusion or direction, we have clearly become the leader of the conversation. When we find ourselves wondering what we are going to ask or say next, it's a clue we've moved away from full presence. It's our signal to return to the default of listening and paraphrasing, which returns the person speaking to the lead.
- **Questions disguised as advice**—These questions are "a wolf in sheep's clothing" because they are advice. We can dress them up with our language, yet in the end, they are still advice. When we own the outcome of the conversation or the direction a person may take, we are in danger of being a wolf. Our goal as a coach is to explore in the direction of the outcomes a person has expressed.
- **Stacking questions**—Consider a coach asking you these questions in rapid-fire fashion: "So the work that we are doing, what would you like us to work on? What is our goal today? What would we like to focus on so that we can take another step forward in 30 minutes?" These are called stacking questions, asking multiple questions without pausing for a response. Karen's brother-in-law, David, broke this habit for her when he said, "Which one of those questions would you like me to answer?" The standard for coaching is that we ask open-ended questions, one at a time, at a pace that allows for thinking and reflection.
- **Why questions**—"Why" automatically moves the other person to a lower status. The amygdala releases cortisol, causing distractions that may take us to a defensive state. Blame often kicks in, and we move to preserve status rather than hearing what the other person is saying. Why questions impact status, and the brain uses all energy to recover. Instead, our intent is to ask about the person's way of thinking, his or her assumptions, beliefs, values, needs, and wants. Our questions are intended to explore beyond current thinking to new or expanded ways of thinking about self or the situation.

To conclude this section on the third essential skill, presuming positive intent and positive presuppositions, we offer a few examples of the thought-provoking questions we have heard you ask. These questions emanate from deep listening and full presence with another person. In addition, they expand the thinking in a way that invites the speaker to a new level of understanding about self and the topic being discussed.

- What is the most important thing you would like to communicate in this conversation with Jane?
- How will this message protect her?
- What will be most impactful for you in this plan?
- As you think about putting the pieces of your puzzle together, where do you want to begin?
- When the puzzle is complete, where will it lead you?
- How is the intervention plan supporting your own beliefs about serving students?
- Add your own . . .
- Add another . . .
- One more . . .

ESSENTIAL SKILL #4: REFLECTIVE FEEDBACK

Imagine teachers saying, "Give me more" . . . "Your feedback is critical to my ongoing growth as a professional." Well, that is a reality in more and more schools. Schools are making the shift to a coaching culture with a growth mindset that presumes positive intent. And they are using the evaluation process as the way to make it happen.

Take for example, Principal Keith McGee from the Little Rock School District, who after attending our Level II seminar committed to increasing his use of reflective feedback in the evaluation process. Specifically, he wanted to include more value and value potential statements in his conversations with teachers. When he said, "Your commitment to educate our students for the PARCC assessment is valued and is evidenced by students' engagement in your class as they prepare," the teacher expressed her appreciation for the feedback and requested *more* feedback. She asked the leadership team to give her more feedback because she viewed it as a way to improve as a teacher. In other words, she had a shift in her thinking and mindset about the value of evaluation for ongoing growth and development.

McGee's testimony is just one of many examples we hear from you about the impact of reflective feedback. According to emerging literature in the business world, the kind of feedback that promotes *growth + action* will be the required skillset for leaders who are exceptionally successful in the 21st century. Jenny Rogers (2012a) writes, "Giving feedback is a high-level art . . . more talked about than done." Additionally, while Rogers admits effective feedback is tough, she challenges us by saying, "You have to become an expert in the art of giving feedback."

Why Do We Want to Provide Reflective Feedback?

Why is a new kind of feedback required? Because we know better! The SCARF research from neuroscience coupled with over 3 decades of work from the Gallup group sends us a very clear answer. People do not grow from their weaknesses or deficits. They grow from their strengths and gifts. Status is a key factor! Knowing what I do well and seeing that you see it, too, acts as an accelerant for what I will do next. When feedback sends the message that "you see me!" my brain can calm down and hear what you have to say to me. That acknowledgment is an essential feature that has been missing from most feedback. When my brain feels threatened, I stop listening and move to defensiveness or some other coping mechanism.

Previously, Rock (2006) taught us that the best way to improve the performance of another is to improve his or her thinking. In a new article, Rock, Davis, and Jones (2013) note that when talent is seen as fixed, it becomes a limiting belief as discussed above. Most performance management systems built on indicators, scales, or checklists inadvertently encourage a way of thinking that limits the ability to grow talent. "A belief that talent can be developed, by contrast, will lead to more effective feedback, goal achievement, evaluation effectiveness, and a culture of collaboration and growth" (p. 16).

In the educational arena, John Hattie and Helen Timperly (2007) speak about the power of feedback to improve the process of teaching and learning. They say, "Feedback is one of the most powerful influences on learning and achievement, but this impact can be either positive or negative. The evidence shows that although feedback is among the major influences, the type of feedback and the way it is given can be differentially effective" (p. 81).

Most certainly! We return to the idea that effective reflective feedback requires an adaptive mindset—one focused on growth and skillfulness with the language and mindset of presuming positive intent. It does not mean that we sugar coat our language or show up as Susie Sunshine. Rather we use our words to say what needs to be said while maintaining the relationship. When reflective feedback is seen as a chance to learn and primes people for improvement, the environment becomes less reactive and shifts from a focus on a ranking to an opportunity for deeper processing through reflection and goal setting. Following is another story from you that describes the desired shift from a fixed to growth mindset.

A Story From You: How Reflective
Feedback Supports the Evaluation Process

School leaders across our country are working to integrate reflective feedback into their coaching conversations that support the observation and/or evaluation process. Principal Andy is working to show how evaluation and feedback are best accomplished through a coaching mindset. He, himself, had a mindset shift when he began to see the evaluation process as a tool for supporting his core value of growing teachers. As a result, he totally revamped his process for evaluation. Knowing the importance of certainty for the brain, he and his assistant principal, Sean, developed reflective questions that presumed positive intent, which they gave to their teachers prior to the observation (the "c" in SCARF). The questions became the focus of the growth conversation following each classroom visit. Teachers expressed value for this new process and feedback that was centered on their strengths and celebrations.

Andy, Sean, and others are finding their shift from a technical change challenge to an adaptive mindset change, has a huge ROI (return on investment). Being in classrooms and holding reflective coaching conversations is the essential work of school leaders so that a coaching culture emerges with a clear focus on the growth mindset for all.

Because effort is the pathway to mastery and success, feedback focused on effort rather than ability replaces threats and rewards with ideas and possibilities for new efforts. Shifting from a rating or numbers to recognition of effort and what a person is learning and how he or she is growing increases the odds for double and triple dividends.

Some of the most compelling reasons to practice reflective feedback come from the TNTP (2012) study called *The Irreplaceables* and focused on the real retention crisis: failure to retain the right teachers. While reinforced in Chapter 4, the study's conclusions demand our attention with regard to feedback. Defined, *the irreplaceables* are "teachers who are so successful they are nearly impossible to replace, but too often vanish from schools as the result of neglect and inattention." Here are the startling stats:

- "On average, each year they help students learn two to three additional months' worth of math and reading compared with the average teacher, and five to six months more compared to low-performing teachers" (p. 2).
- "When an Irreplaceable leaves a low-performing school, it can take 11 hires to find just one teacher of comparable quality" (p. 4).
- Lesson learned: "Good teachers don't leave demanding schools that hold them to high expectations; they leave schools that aren't serious about good teaching" (p. 28).
- Two-thirds of the leaving teachers reported that no one encouraged them to return for another year (p. 16).
- Of the eight simple, low-cost strategies identified to help boost teacher retention, giving feedback or public recognition (status) for a job well done was at the top of the list. (p. 16)

How Are We Perfecting Our Reflective Feedback?

With clear evidence from the section above addressing "why?" feedback is an essential skill for our success as leaders, let's focus on "how" to perfect this skill. A key understanding is that the information in this section builds on the knowledge about reflective feedback discussed in our first book, *RESULTS Coaching*. With that base, our focus is on new and deeper understandings of the essential skill of reflective feedback.

Three Options for Reflective Feedback

Based on the work of David Perkins (2003), the three options for reflective feedback are:

1. Clarifying questions for understanding
2. Value/value potential statements
3. Reflective questions for possibility

Several distinctions show up in our seminars. Questions in the first group are designed specifically to gain additional information before giving feedback while questions in the third group are present and future focused and designed to provoke new thinking. The feedback in number two is a statement rather than a question. A nonnegotiable for all feedback is that it presumes positive intent. It is often helpful to consider the attributes for each of the three options for feedback.

Clarifying Questions for Understanding

Characteristics of this option for feedback are:

- Presumes positive intent
- Open ended—cannot be answered yes or no
- Purpose is to gain more information and clarity
- Can be answered quickly
- Just the facts, ma'am!—just like Sergeant Friday in *Dragnet*, the question asks for the bottom line rather than all the details of the event.

Sample language:

- How many children are in the class?
- Of your 20 students, how many were off task?
- What time of the day does this behavior show up?
- What does the code of conduct say about this situation?
- When is your collaborative planning time?

- When does your team meet when they are doing their best work?
- Your turn _____
- Your turn _____

Value / Value Potential Statements

This option for feedback is recognizable because, in essence, it is an eloquent paraphrase. One distinction we make is the difference between value and value potential. Value is what I see in the present, right before me. *Value potential* refers to the impact that will be realized in the future as the result of my intention in the present. An example used is what we might say after visiting a first-grade classroom where the teacher is using small reading groups as a way to teach and monitor progress in reading. A sample value statement would be, "Your commitment to building strong readers is evident in the way you work with them in small groups." A value potential statement takes it into the future where we cannot see what might happen, yet we can predict it. "Your commitment to building strong readers in first grade will create successful students throughout their career as learners." Attributes of this option are:

- Presumes positive intent
- Purpose is to recognize and reinforce what is seen in the present or future
- Replaces vague statements such as "I like . . .," "Wow!," and "Good job!"
- Specific and measurable
- Sincere and genuine

A value or value potential statement is the antidote to the startling statistics in *The Irreplaceables* report mentioned earlier in this section. This is the way we ensure teachers know the value and contribution they make on a regular basis. We promote generosity with this option of feedback. It breaks our hearts when we hear stories from the field where highly competent and caring teachers are leaving our profession because no one is giving them feedback on their hard work.

Sample language:

- Your high standards invite students to be the best they can be academically.
- Because you want all your students to succeed, you regularly analyze benchmark data to monitor the progress of each one.
- Your attention to detail ensures your team does not miss a deadline.
- As a teacher who is passionate about literature, you want your students to share that love and recognize it is relevant in their lives.

- Your commitment to reaching each student is evident in your differentiation strategies to meet the needs of all.
- Your understanding of the new math standards is clearly impacting your team planning and influencing your colleagues' confidence.
- Your turn _____
- Your turn _____

Reflective Questions for Possibility

These are the questions that mediate and support our thinking for consideration of new ideas or possibilities yet explored. They are an invitation to excellence in our work and in our performance. Many a principal has recognized the value of these questions for all teachers and especially their talented, committed master teachers who are often overlooked. The attributes of these questions are:

- Presumes positive intent
- Open ended—cannot be answered yes or no
- Purpose is to provoke thinking for possibility, not leading
- Future focused
- Require time for thinking

Sample language:

- In what ways has your data informed the decision for next steps for your team?
- Because you are a teacher who considers each student individually, what are you thinking will get the best from Sam?
- How is your team addressing this discrepancy between where the kids are now and where we want them to be by December?
- Based on our desire to continue our improvement results in science, what plan is in place to ensure we show gains this year?
- Given your knowledge of math standards, what are you noticing about your student's ability to transfer from concrete to abstract?
- Knowing that parent communication is vital to healthy school cultures, what new ways are you thinking about for engaging parents in meaningful ways?
- Your turn _____
- Your turn _____

When Is Our Best Time to Provide Reflective Feedback?

As educators, our days are full of opportunities for giving reflective feedback. Typically, one of two situations appears as the time for giving feedback. One is the cycle of listen and give feedback; the other is observe and give feedback. Both are opportunities for growth.

Listen and Give Feedback

Let's take listen and give feedback as our first opportunity for growth. A teacher stops you in the hall and says, "Is this okay for my first parent newsletter?" Once we move from the distraction that the question can be answered yes or no along with the temptation to give the quick response, "Good job!" we hesitate because we are reminded that this kind of feedback is short lived. It lacks the specificity of what constitutes a good job. Not only does the teacher leave with the uncertainty of what was good, the likelihood of repeating or sustaining the behavior or action is diminished. So we might respond with a clarifying question such as, "Who collaborated with you on this grade level information?" This question accomplishes two goals. It gains clarity about potential partners and holds up the expectation that the grade level was included in the development of the content. A second option for our feedback may be a value or value potential statement coupled with a reflective question such as, "Knowing you want a consistent message to parents, what feedback did your teammates offer you regarding this plan?"

Now, it's your turn. You receive an e-mail from a fellow colleague asking for feedback on his or her plan for an upcoming professional learning day with staff that recommends everyone working with their department.

What clarifying question might you ask?

_____

What value or value potential statement would recognize the effort and/or core value of this person?

_____

What reflective question for possibility will "push" the colleague's thinking for additional considerations?

_____

Check Up—Ask someone to give you feedback on your language to ensure internalization of presumption of positive intent.

Observe and Give Feedback—The second situation where feedback can motivate and inspire growth is after a walk-through or a formal observation. This is where reflective feedback holds the potential to make the greatest difference. Many of you tell us about observation processes you are currently using in your schools. Often the conversation rolls around to the fact that the observation is well and good; yet there is uncertainty about the language to use in the conversation following the observation.

Because we know the potential for real learning *is* the conversation, reflective feedback becomes even more critical. We know language matters because it will keep us engaged and listening or it will push us away. Hmm! Here's the real dilemma! A threat state is an inherent part of feedback. So what can we do (say) that immediately moves the conversation to a safer state? One possibility is we can feed status with a value or value potential statement. Again, the brain calms down, and we are all breathing again! Here are other possibilities adapted from the work of Jenny Rogers (2012b) in her *Manager as Coach* book.

- **Ask for permission, when appropriate**—"Knowing you are working to incorporate language that presumes positive intent, would you like data on the questions you asked?" (p. 129) or "Because we are all working to include literacy strategies in our classroom, would you like feedback on your word wall activities?" (p. 129)
- **Stick to the facts**—Use the specific data you have collected to offer feedback. Separate fact from opinion. "Of the ten questions you asked, half presumed positive intent. How might you flip the remaining five?" (p. 129) or "Of the ten questions you asked in this lesson, two were asked of girls with the remainder going to the boys. What system will ensure equitable opportunity to respond for your class?" (p. 129)
- **Avoid assumptions**—We know about assuming! It can really get us in trouble. Making up our own stories about what is really going on or interpreting through our lens can be dangerous to hearing the real message. As a result, our feedback can be off-base and not heard because it may come across as advice.
- **Offer as "the truth" vs. "THE TRUTH"**—When feedback is offered as "the truth," it comes across tentatively as possibility rather than the certainty of something being in fact "THE TRUTH" with ALL CAPS. Even a paraphrase, "You're angry," stated as if it were fact can affect me differently than you saying, "You seem to have strong feelings about this," or even, "You seem angry about this." It's left to me to confirm or not; it's a possibility rather than a given. Another example might be when you are talking with another person and you sense there are two conversations going on at the same time. For the sake of clarity, you know you want to raise the intuition. It might sound like this, "It seems we might be talking about two things in this conversation. Let me just put them on the table and see if there is any truth to that possibility."

Again, it's your turn. Your campus has a peer review process for visiting classrooms to observe for specific areas of focus. High engagement for all students is the goal everyone is working on. On today's walk-through visit, data were collected to show that three students were off-task without redirection for the duration of the visit.

What clarifying question might you ask?

_____

What value or value potential statement would you say to this teacher?

_____

What reflective question will hold up the data for the teacher in a question that presumes he or she wants to take action?

_____

Check Up—Ask someone to give you feedback on your language to ensure internalization of presumption of positive intent.

SUMMARY

Before we engage the skills of a coach leader, it is imperative we check our mindset. Successful coach leaders have transformed their mindset from coaching being something they *do* to someone they *are*. They have made an adaptive change so that coaching has become the core of their being.

After a decade of work in the field, the essential bundle that positions us to be coach leaders has remained the same. While there are layers of other skills and competencies the ESSENTIALS are:

- Committed listening
- Paraphrasing
- Questions that presume positive intent
- Reflective feedback

The intent of this book is to offer new understandings about the essential skills. It is a companion to the first and in no way is intended to replace what is taught there with regard to the skills.

Evidence continues to amass regarding the importance of listening in the communication process. Without it, all other skills are in jeopardy. The concept of *listening for*—first and second dimensions—is transforming the listening of many coach leaders.

Language matters. Three of the essential skills are about skillfulness in speaking. Paraphrasing, presuming positive intent along with positive presupposition questions, and reflective feedback can all send messages to the brain that can be interpreted as safety or threat. Using our language to ensure a safety state holds the potential for influencing the conscious and subconscious mind, for creating safety for authentic sharing, and for opening the door for deep levels of trust and respect in a relationship—all required elements for our work as successful educators.

REFERENCES

Auerback, J. E. (2006). Cognitive coaching. In D. R. Stober & A. M. Grant (Eds.), *Evidence based coaching handbook* (pp. 103–128). Hoboken, NJ: Wiley.

Campone, F. MCC—Results Coaching Global Master Mentor.

Covey, S. (2006). *The SPEED of trust: The one thing that changes everything*. London, UK: Simon & Shuster.

Dweck, C. (2006). *Mindset: The new psychology of success*. New York, NY: Random House.

Fredrickson, B. L. (2013, July 15). Updated thinking on positivity ratios. *American Psychologist*, Advance online publication. doi:10.1037/a0033584

Gladwell, M. (2007). *Blink: The power of thinking without thinking* (Kindle locations 499–501) [Kindle edition]. New York, NY: Little, Brown.

Goulston, M. (2010). *Just listen*. New York, NY: AMACOM.

Haden Elgin, S. (2000). *The gentle art of verbal self-defense at work*. New York, NY: Prentice Hall.

Hattie, J., & Timperly, H. (2007). *The power of feedback*. University of Auckland, New Zealand: Review of Educational Research.

Heifetz, R. A. (1998). *Leadership without easy answers*. Cambridge, MA: Harvard University Press.

Kee, K., Anderson, K., Dearing, V., Harris, E., & Schuster, F. (2010). *Results coaching: The new essential for school leaders*. Thousand Oaks, CA: Corwin.

Kegan, R., & Lahey, L. (2002). *How the way we talk can change the way we work*. San Francisco, CA: Jossey-Bass.

Kegan, R., & Lahey, L. (2009). *Immunity to change*. Boston, MA: Harvard Business Review Press.

Orem, S., Binkert, J., & Clancy, A. (2007). *Appreciative coaching: A positive process for change*. San Francisco, CA: Jossey-Bass.

Perkins, D. (2003). *King Arthur's round table: How collaborative conversations create smart organizations*. Hoboken, NJ: John Wiley & Sons.

Rock, D. (2006). *Quiet leadership*. New York, NY: HarperCollins.

Rock, D. (2008). *SCARF: A brain-based model for collaborating with and influencing others*. Retrieved from www.neuroleadership.org

Rock, D. (2009). *Your brain at work: Strategies for overcoming distraction, regaining focus and working smarter all day long*. New York, NY: Harper Business.

Rock, D., Davis, J., & Jones, E. (2013). One simple idea that can transform performance management. *People & Strategy, 36*(2), 16–19.

Rogers, J. (2012a). *Coaching skills: A handbook*. New York, NY: McGraw-Hill.

Rogers, J. (2012b) *Manager as coach: The new way to get results*. New York, NY: McGraw-Hill.

Scott, S. (2002). *Fierce conversations: Achieving success at work and in life—one conversation at a time.* New York, NY: Berkley.

TNTP. (2012). *The irreplaceables: Understanding the real retention crisis in America's schools.* Retrieved from http://tntp.org/assets/documents/TNTP_Irreplaceables_2012.pdf

Whitworth, L., Kimsey-House, K., Kimsey-House, H., & Sandahl, P. (2011). *Co-active coaching: New skills for coaching people toward success in work and life.* Boston, MA: Nicholas Brealey.

4

Supervision vs. Coaching

It's Time for Change

Memo to Leaders: "Your central function is to engineer intelligent, spirited conversations that provide the basis for high levels of alignment, collaboration, and partnership at all levels throughout your organization and the healthier outcomes that go with them."

Susan Scott, *Fierce Conversations*

People don't need to be managed, they need to be unleashed.

Richard Florida

SUPERVISION IS COACHING

Wherever we go and share the power of coaching, it's inevitable that the topic of supervision and appraisal or evaluation enter the conversation. There is a deep abiding belief among many that coaching is indeed necessary for a few but definitely not all teachers. Based on our combined 180 years of experience in education, it is evident this mindset originates from experiences and role models that ingrained the message, "I have too many other demands and am constantly fighting fires, so I can invest significant time in only the weakest teachers." This is the hard-wired, default response. It's time to build new wires in our brains, to realize and implement strategies to provide supervision and learning for all. Together, let's learn a different response to the question of the value and importance of coaching in the role of supervision.

FROM TRADITIONAL SUPERVISION TO 21ST CENTURY SUPERVISION

Every person who has ever been supervised has stories to tell about their experiences. At times the stories are filled with wonderful memories and important examples that have impacted their own leadership skills when it became his or her time to lead. In other instances, the stories show how much we have grown from the old ways of supervising to the current views of supervision that focus on leading over managing. Here is Kathy's story.

Kathy Kee's first encounter with supervision was in 1970, when she began teaching in Baton Rouge, Louisiana, and her first supervisor would drop by. The supervisor came and inspected what was being done in the classroom, and without exception, identified the things that needed to be improved, and usually added with what seemed like a little pat on her head, a "good job." Kathy never was certain what had been good considering all the things that her supervisor said still needed improvement. As a new teacher she just kept trudging along, hoping she was getting it right. In 1976, while teaching in Missouri, another supervisor repeated the behaviors of her first supervisor. By this time there had been several supervisors—their behaviors were all the same. They were hard wired to emphasize what she was doing wrong.

As a teacher certified through the federal Teacher Corps program (one of the first alternative teacher training programs), Kathy thought she was well trained. Students wanted her as their teacher, her discipline issues were minimal, if at all, and she used strategies she had learned to engage students. Her students appeared to learn and have fun at the same time.

By the time Kathy got to Norman, Oklahoma, she thought her experience would be more of the same with regard to supervision. And then a different kind of supervisor entered her life and changed everything! Her principal, Lee Ann Kennedy, talked to Kathy as though she were the expert, as though Kathy knew what she was doing. Lee Ann would drop by Kathy's class and cite specific things she was doing that would really impact the success of her remedial reading students. Kathy discovered an amazing thing. She found herself working harder to implement more innovative strategies with her students. She wanted her principal to think she was as knowledgeable about teaching reading as her principal thought she was. When her team leader echoed similar feedback and invited more collaboration with the department to share ideas and talk about students needing some unique strategies, Kathy jumped at the opportunity. Her team at the Norman school represented colleagues who were committed to having the best department—not just because the teachers were collegial—but because the team successfully got kids back on their instructional reading levels. Outside the department, other teachers envied their enthusiasm. It was special all right, but the enthusiasm was because of the principal.

Those 2 years in Norman set the standard for what Kathy knew she wanted in a supervisor. She had learned a career lesson that was profound: *Supervisors have the power to influence how people feel about their work, their energy, their passion, their commitment, their very drive for personal mastery.*

From 1978 forward, the imprint was made. Kathy had officially learned that the single most important job of supervisors, principals, and leaders is to build capacity and inspire teachers to be their best professional selves.

In the mid-1980s, while studying the new concept of Cognitive Coaching, Kathy had the pleasure to hear Carl Glickman present with Bob Garmston and Art Costa. Glickman added the dimension to coaching that was the dilemma in her district. Everyone wanted to learn about coaching and let the teachers enjoy the skills and tools for coaching each other, but few supervisors believed that coaching was their role. Glickman offered the connection.

Glickman's (1990) Developmental Model was the link for direct assistance and support to teachers. Among the methods of support Glickman recommended were professional learning, group learning, curriculum development, and action research. By this time, new appraisal and evaluation models had spread to districts across the country; they were called *professional development appraisal models* or systems. The models meant supervisors had to be knowledgeable about developmental supervision and how employees grow and develop throughout their careers, including areas of pedagogy, the science and art of teaching and learning, effective school characteristics, adult development, interpersonal skills, and the technical skills of effective teaching. This new developmental supervision model required ongoing personal contact with individual teachers and groups of teachers. It required thoughtful planning and reflection, clear expectations, clear goals, understanding of the standards for the disciplines, and knowledge of the research-based high-impact strategies to engage students. This was a big paradigm shift in supervision.

Glickman (Pajak, 1993) offered five principles of supervision, which we believe align closely with what we are learning about leading with the brain in mind. The five principles are as follows:

Principle 1—Supervision should encourage teachers to invest in a cause beyond themselves.

Principle 2—Supervision should enhance teachers' feelings of efficacy in influencing student outcomes via classroom management and effective instruction.

Principle 3—Supervision should encourage teachers to share ideas and materials and support each other's efforts in improving common instructional goals.

Principle 4—Supervision should stimulate teacher involvement in professional learning and curriculum and instructional action research to strengthen collective action.

Principle 5—Supervision should challenge teachers to think more abstractly about their practice of teaching. This is accomplished by giving feedback, questioning, and creating safe environments for teachers to self-appraise, reflect, self-modify, and adapt their practices to the ever-changing needs of students.

Given that society was and is still hardwired to have traditional, top-down, directive supervision models and styles, Glickman's vision of a developmental supervision model hit the ball out of the park, transporting 20th century supervision into the 21st century. His model holds answers for today's coach leader. The vision he gave us connects to the growth mindset research today. His thinking was to teach the supervisor how to support the continuous learning of teachers throughout their careers.

Reflecting on the principles above, the vision of building capacity in others and inspiring others to accomplish great things for kids is clear. It focuses on the teacher/employee, who is committed to the work and who desires to get smarter right along with his or her students.

What is so interesting about our work world is that when a profession grows unhappy with the current results, the go-to thinking seems to look to redesigning or constructing a new appraisal, evaluation, or performance management system. Think about the lowest level of intention when the primary vehicle for professional growth is the belief that by assigning numbers, ratings, and words such as "below expectations," people will be better. What possible chance could there be for real change? It's as if we simply identify, again, what standards must occur in the workplace or classroom and by scoring and labeling employees, the behaviors and outcomes desired will just magically appear or happen. As you will see below, there is absolutely no evidence that this approach makes teachers better. It may coerce temporary compliance accompanied by resentment, but not much authentic change.

PERFORMANCE RESEARCH

In 2014, Human Capital Institute (HCI) published research on performance appraisals. HCI reported that while the objective of performance evaluations is ultimately to enhance organizational functioning, they often lead to poor quality performance, lower job satisfaction, and lower organizational commitment and higher turnovers. Supervisors expressed contempt for appraisals; next to firing employees, appraisals were the most disliked task. The struggle is the same in education. Appraisals are time-consuming endeavors, and leaders struggle to effectively balance their daily responsibilities with monitoring their staff. Additionally, 55% of the supervisors in the study believed they weren't even accurate, and only 39% of professionals agreed that their appraisals would improve performance. Performance appraisals are still an important function of leadership and talent management. When done in an effective way, evaluations can still fulfill their ultimate purpose of improving performance and developing employees. David Rock (2006) offered what we believe to be the new mindset: "If you want to improve performance, you must improve thinking about performance."

A research study in *Strategy + Business* (Rock, Davis, & Jones, 2014) showed that the ability to grow talent is ranked 67th out of 67 competencies for supervisors, despite 30-plus years of investment in training. The study reported that *supervisors (managers) are the weakest at developing their employees than anything else they do.* We must find ways to assess people that will reverse the destructive effects of traditional evaluation. We must use current knowledge about the human brain, have a growth mindset, and see employees eager to grow and learn under the right context and conditions.

What might happen if we view our employees as we do students: always growing and getting better? What might happen if we ditched the ratings and rankings that trigger the fight-or-flight response? A study at Kansas State University found that "the mere act of receiving a numerical rating can be perceived as negative feedback, and even people with a growth mindset don't react well to negative feedback" (Rock et al., 2014).

What is happening that triggers the fight-or-flight response? As explained in Chapter 2, David Rock's (2006) SCARF Model postulates that five organizational factors have an immense, but often unnoticed effect: They produce negative emotional reactions and responses. As previously addressed, the factors are:

1. **Status** (the perception of being considered better or worse than others);

2. **Certainty** (the predictability of future events);

3. **Autonomy** (the level of control people feel over their lives);

4. **Relatedness** (the experience of sharing goals with others); and

5. **Fairness** (the sense of being respected and treated equitably).

When an organization's perceived level of any of the SCARF factors is low, people feel threatened and perturbed. Even if they don't express it, the feeling is there and it often impairs their productivity and willingness to show commitment.

Let's connect all this to labeling and ranking in schools. While this has been done throughout history, it does not erase the demoralizing impact it can have. Imagine ranking family members by who is the most talented and what type of impact that could have; imagine the impact on kids throughout their lives when they are publicly ranked on learning; and here we go again ranking our teachers—real or perceived. We can predict the impact.

Carol Dweck—*Mindset*

All over this country schools, districts, and businesses are reading Carol Dweck's (2006) *Mindset*. From her research, she finds that people have two mindsets: a fixed mindset or a growth mindset. Her research suggests that people's beliefs about whether intelligence and talent are innate or can be developed dramatically impact the success or failure of a whole performance management system. The other surprise is that people fall fairly evenly into both beliefs. Sadly, the tools that most organizations use today are unintentionally sending people down the wrong belief path—that talent is fixed. Research consistently shows that our belief about our capabilities impacts our success. In addition, our belief about whether or not we have control over oneself impacts our success, our ethics, and how we collaborate with others.

David Perkins—Feedback

David Perkins (2003) of Harvard University confirms that feedback is essential for people and organizations to grow, develop, and continually improve. Feedback fails because it motivates either by approval or disapproval. Approval takes the emphasis away from intrinsic motivation to gain mastery; disapproval spirals most people down to either eating up themselves from the inside or fueling a negative attitude toward the organization. Feedback in any form, evaluations or appraisals, must have one goal, and that is to ignite a deep fire within someone to grow, to be great at something, to love what they do and continually strive for personal mastery. See our book *Results Coaching: The New Essential for School Leaders* (2010) to learn how we have used Perkins's ideas to develop more effective reflective feedback approaches.

Daniel Pink—*Drive*

Daniel Pink (2009) makes the strongest case for motivation in his best seller, *Drive: The Surprising Truth About What Motivates Us*. To make his case he draws on multiple studies and real examples. He includes a powerful quote from Meddius CEO Jeff Gunter: "Management isn't about walking around and seeing if people are doing their work; it's about creating conditions for people to do their best work" (p. 86). Pink shares a personal story of his dad who appeared to view people as human resources just like two by fours needed to build a home. For Pink, leadership "is a partnership between the employees and me." He offers three motivation drivers: autonomy, mastery, and purpose.

> We forget that "management" does not emanate from nature. It's not like a tree or a river. It is something that humans invented and hasn't changed much in a hundred years. Its central ethic remains control; its chief tools remain extrinsic motivators. It presumes that to take action or move forward, we need a prod. Being passive and inert is not our "default setting." (Pink, 2009, p. 88)

Autonomy

When we enter the world we are wired to be active and engaged. Research is screaming that we reawaken our deep-seated sense of autonomy. This innate capacity for self-direction is at the heart of Pink's Motivation 3.0 (presumes people want to be accountable) and Type I behavior (driven by an intrinsic, self-directed, curious nature). Autonomy means acting with choice. A sense of autonomy has a powerful effect on individual performance and attitude. Numerous studies show autonomy promotes greater conceptual understanding, better grades, enhanced persistence, high productivity, less burnout, and greater levels of psychological well-being. Studies indicate that there are four essential features of autonomy—what people do, when they do it, how they do it, and with whom they do it—which correlates to the four Ts: Task, Time, Technique, and Team. Autonomy leads to engagement. The opposite of autonomy is control, which leads to compliance. What do you want—compliance or engagement?

Mastery

The best predictor of success is perseverance and passion for long-term goals. Mastery is the desire to do something because you find it deeply satisfying and personally challenging. Only engagement can produce mastery—becoming better at something that matters. It is a constant pursuit. It takes grit. The joy of mastery is in its pursuit. What environments are we creating that ignite mastery?

Purpose

The most productive and satisfied human beings, by their nature, seek purpose—a cause greater and more enduring than themselves. Glickman reminds us that "supervision should encourage teachers to invest in a cause larger than themselves" (Pajak, 1993, p. 237). How do you inspire and maintain the focus on our greater purpose?

Pink (2009) humorously observes that our way of structuring work is a "slightly more civilized form of control." The ways we are supervising in schools today run counter to the times and the nature of humans doing their best work. He sums it up in these words:

> Perhaps it's time to toss the very word "management" onto the linguistic trash heap alongside "icebox" and "horseless carriage." This era doesn't call for better management. It calls for a renaissance of self-direction. (p. 92)

Robert Marzano, the most prolific educational researcher of this century, continues to pass along the same "change" message about teaching. If we indeed want teachers or employees to be motivated by purpose and mastery, traditional supervision behaviors and language must change.

Carl Glickman—Model of Supervision

After studying Glickman's model during her own leadership training, Kathy Kee had a wonderful opportunity to collaborate for over 3 decades with her colleague, Dr. John Crain, around their passion for a new kind of supervision that builds capacity and inspires greatness. Crain was a professor at both University of Dallas and University of North Texas. He served as assistant superintendent in Dallas ISD and Highland Park ISD and continues to be the go-to expert on curriculum and instruction. He is coauthor with Dr. Frank Kemerer (2013) of the best-selling *Documentation Handbook for Appraisal, Nonrenewal, and Termination*. While based on Glickman's initial research model, Crain has continued to enrich Glickman's model with his own experience, state and national data, and direct application of the model. Because the *Documentation* book is a guidebook for supervisors with staff who are the least effective, both Kee and Crain have found that *for all practical purposes documentation means "writing someone up" and is often the first and generally the least appropriate option for change rather than the last*. For this reason Crain has collaborated on this section of the chapter in an effort to share his giant knowledge base and enhancements to Glickman's model. This practical and experiential knowledge offers to the reader leadership and supervisory strategies for powerful change by focusing on 95% who are meeting the standards, rather than the 5% who are not.

David Rock (2006) has made it clear: "If you want to improve performance, you must improve thinking about the performance" (p. xxiii). Rock has also offered the metaphor of the iceberg about how important and how difficult this can be.

Figure 4.1   Results—Performance Behaviors

Outcomes/performance

Thinking and emotion

© jgroup / iStock

If the work of the supervisor is to impact results and performance, how do the supervisor's behaviors and actions impact those results?

Glickman says in Principal 5: *Supervision should challenge teachers to think more abstractly about their practice of teaching. This is accomplished by giving feedback, questioning, and confronting teachers to self-appraise, reflect, self-modify and adapt their practices to the ever-changing needs of students* (Pajak, 1993, p. 238).

> Clearly, teaching is a skill, and like any skill, it must be practiced. . . .
> Teachers must . . . examine their practices, set goals, and use focused practice and feedback to achieve those goals. These reflective practices are essential to the development of expertise in teaching.
>
> Robert Marzano, 2009

The gift of Glickman's model is that it begins with the supervisor reflecting on his or her own staff. This offers the supervisor the opportunity to consider specifics about each teacher: experiences, special interests, special talents, level of commitment, thinking processes, approaches to identifying and solving problems, and so on. The criteria are different, but similar to how a teacher plans for differentiation among students. The supervisor thoughtfully reflects on the staff and considers the best approach to influence capacity and inspire individual teachers. According to Carl Glickman, *two factors lie at the heart of performance.* One factor concerns a teacher's (or employee's) *level of abstraction*—the ability to identify problems and generate solutions. The other factor is related to a teacher's *level of commitment*—the willingness to accept responsibility for the work (student learning) and to place students (not adults) first in the adult decision-making process.

Let's consider how these important factors, *commitment* and *abstraction*, hold the potential to influence the supervisor's language and behaviors and impact positive change in an employee.

(Note: While the model is Dr. Glickman's, the interpretation and application are those of the authors.)

Level of Commitment

Think about your own level of commitment. How do you measure your commitment to your work, to your family, to your health? What do you see yourself doing to demonstrate that commitment? In schools we want to believe people are committed to the work of designing engaging, deep, complex, and connected learning for students. We believe that 95% of the time we will see varying levels of commitment described in the following ways:

Teachers or employees

- want to learn; are eager to engage in professional learning opportunities.
- come early or stay late to make sure plans and materials are ready for students or whatever a situation demands.
- know the importance of working collaboratively to accomplish common goals; they realize one person can't do it alone.

Figure 4.2   Factors of Performance

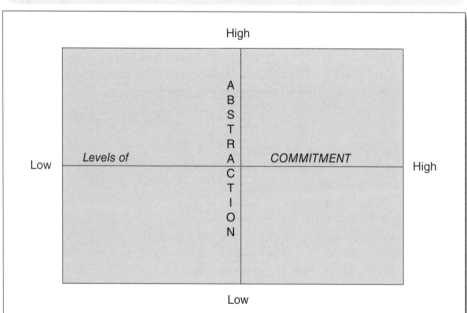

- desire feedback, and when they receive it, they ask questions to clarify and act on that feedback; they understand or talk about what they want to do to improve performance.
- try a wide variety of strategies to accomplish a task, whether it is finding a strategy to engage a student, reading more about something to influence success, doing action research to test ideas, or stepping right out of their comfort zone to get better at a skill they want.
- take on leadership roles, by their own initiative or when asked, with enthusiasm and zeal.
- see themselves as part of a bigger mission and goal; they view their work as a calling rather than a job.
- believe that what they are doing and trying will make a difference.
- ask courageous questions in the spirit of inquiry to understand.
- pick up on the urgency or the seriousness of a situation and step up to do what is needed or required to support the mission or goals of the work.
- demonstrate positive intent with others; they mentally consider the possibility that is within the situation or what the learning might be.
- motivate and inspire others when the going gets tough; they are intentional in building and maintaining trust with all (team, parents, students, colleagues, and administrators).
- strive to reach every student, meet each student's needs; they persevere—they don't give up on kids.

You are probably seeing faces in your mind now as you read these commitment descriptors. You are thinking about situations where you witness commitment in your own work. Commitment is that DRIVE—Pink (2009) speaks to and gives tools to influence it.

Low levels of commitment may look like the following:

- A deliberate "why bother" attitude
- A belief that there is no need to change; everything is just fine
- Occasionally may commit to something but fails to follow through
- An attitude of "What's in it for me? Will I get a raise, advancement, a new position?"
- Being overwhelmed, asking "Why do I care," or "What is the system doing for me?"
- Thinking "The students don't care and don't want to do anything and their parents provide no support—why should I work so hard?"

In an *Atlantic* magazine article, "The Ongoing Struggle of Teacher Retention," author Paul Barnwell (2015) reports that some of the schools with the lowest performance rankings have the highest percentage of teachers with 4 years' experience or less; and similarly, schools with the highest percentage of students on free or reduced-price lunch have the highest percentage of inexperienced teachers. This formula of least experienced and knowledgeable paired with the greatest pressures and demands to succeed continue to quickly drive away those who come to the profession. While a few new educators jump into the demands of teaching early on, for most it takes years, even decades, to become truly effective in the craft of teaching. We also know from the Harvard research study that high-poverty public schools lose on average a fifth of the faculty annually, a fact that is hugely expensive to our kids and our society.

Susan Moore-Johnson (2004), who directs the Project on the Next Generation of Teachers at Harvard, found that several factors strongly influence teacher satisfaction with the work, including

- a provision for ample time for teacher collaboration during the school day (shared commitment to get the work done);
- strong and supportive principals (commitment to believe in and support staff); and
- a shared and common vision, shared and executed by teachers and staff (commitment to the work).

In other words, retention results from work conditions that support success in teaching. From brain research we know that *commitment* to the work is the engine that drives success. It can be reignited, rekindled, and reenergized. There are many reasons people lose their commitment—for example, feeling devalued, not receiving recognition, feeling unfairly treated, or feeling invisible and overlooked. The list goes on and on.

Conversations about our own value and importance to the organization and the work offer the opportunity to reignite our commitment. We all were originally hired because someone saw something in us that was needed in the organization. What was it? How do we want to reengage that special something to the purpose? Highly committed individuals also tend to be very resilient. If they try something and it fails, they are willing to jump in and try again . . . and again . . . and again.

Now let's consider Glickman's second factor at the heart of performance, the level of abstraction.

Level of Abstraction

It may be helpful here to differentiate between abstract learning and a person's level of abstraction. Abstract learning typically is driven by academic concepts that are completely new to and out of the schema (prior knowledge and experiences) of the student. Conceptual learning generally moves from the abstract to the concrete through one or more personal experiences or connections, through interaction with other people and/or technology, and/or through pictures and mental images. Marzano, Pickering, and Pollock (2001) posit that this is often done by using or creating "non-linguistic representations of the learning" (p. 73).

Level of abstraction, on the other hand, is an entirely different issue. Abstraction, in this sense, is closely related to an individual's ability to quickly identify problems, generate and act on solutions, and monitor and adjust to the ever-changing classroom environment. Teachers who have higher levels of abstraction might be described as situationally aware or "with-it"; they may be perceived as thinkers or problem-solvers or as having a large and diverse toolkit of teaching and learning strategies.

We know from brain research discussed in Chapter 2 that when the brain senses threat, fear, or criticism, bad things happen in the brain (e.g., blood leaves the brain, the chemicals needed to make connections decrease or stop). Even if people have developed to a point at which their level of abstraction is high, they cannot always access that power if their brains sense threat, fear, or criticism. If we want employees to fully engage in building their skills, take risks, and be NASA-level problem solvers, supervisors must take care with their own behavior and language to continuously send the message of trust and respect.

Teachers with high levels of abstraction demonstrate thinking in some of these ways:

- They recognize when students have gotten off task and are no longer engaged and have multiple tools in their toolkit to stop or redirect the behavior.
- They recognize when it is time to shift an activity to less or more activity and appear to do so seamlessly.
- They realize that when they say or do something, it has an impact on the environment and on students and choose language and behaviors that are aligned to positive outcomes.
- They recognize when parents should be brought into the loop on a situation, and they have the communication strategies and language tools to effect a positive outcome for everyone.
- They recognize when the principal should be informed regarding certain situations because they can predict outcomes and communicate with the principal in a positive and professional manner.
- They understand that changing their mindset about something holds the potential to change their attitude, behavior, and language.
- They recognize when a situation or behavior requires new thinking and responses and seek out information from research and other professionals.
- They recognize the importance of collecting data, doing research, or investigating a situation before responding and base their behavior and language on the insights from what they find.
- They exhibit high levels of emotional intelligence by being aware of internal triggers, by being sensitive to others around them, and by reading a situation for the most effective or appropriate response and consistently choosing responses tailored to the situation.
- They know that thoughtful reflection and planning impact results.

The higher the person's level of abstraction, the more the person can and will respond to problems, situations, and dilemmas with speed, decisiveness, appropriateness, and confidence.

With commitment and abstraction—two powerful developmental factors—in mind, supervisors have the tools to influence their own behavior and language as they plan for supervisory conversations.

Figure 4.3 illustrates the model and its four quadrants. Think of each quadrant as graph paper; individuals can be at a variety of places within one quadrant. Remember the quadrant is just a guide that offers the supervisor insight into the teacher's developmental level:

- Who am I dealing with?
- What is the person's level of commitment?
- What is the person's level of abstraction?
- How will these understandings help me customize my language and strategies to effectively help the teacher grow?

The supervisor must initially determine which quadrant characteristics the person exhibits and where the employee is within the quadrant. The supervisor can be intentional in deciding what strategies and language might be most effective in helping the employee grow and improve. Commitment can be fragile and is contingent on an employee's perceptions. The strategies and language selected for any employee have the

Figure 4.3   Where Is the Employee and What Language and Strategies Will Have the Greatest Potential for Impact?

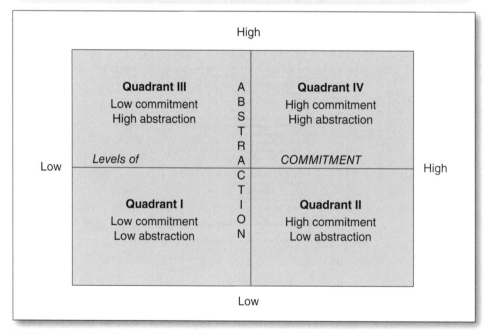

SOURCE: Adapted from Kemerer & Crain, 2013.

potential to create an environment of safety and trust, reduce stress, and provide for reflection and deep thought—always fundamental goals in any supervisory conversation or conference. The NeuroLeadership research in *SCARF: A Brain-Based Model for Collaborating With and Influencing Others* (Rock, 2008) can *inform* the supervisor's planning for the conversation. Abstraction comes from opportunities to think, to reflect and consider options, and to evaluate the impact, consequences, and results of a decision. A skillful supervisor creates a safe place to think.

Thoughtful assessment guides the supervisor in choosing one or more of the following approaches.

Once the supervisor has reflected on the employee's levels of commitment and abstraction, it is time to consider the *issues* involved in the supervisory conversation.

The Issues Involved in Supervision

In instructional supervision, there are at least three issues that will form the essential elements for a productive and focused conference or conversation with the teacher: diagnosis, prescription, and timelines.

Figure 4.4   Quadrant Reflections

Q III	Q IV
• Abstraction is high. There is knowledge and skill. How does the supervisor want to acknowledge and give status to it? • Commitment is low. How does the supervisor desire to rekindle energy or mission to the work?	• Abstraction is high. How does the supervisor want to recognize and give status to the person's abilities to problem solve, innovate, and create? • Commitment is high. How does the supervisor keep it so? What are the specific actions and behaviors that are producing results?
Q I	Q II
• Abstraction is low. Knowledge and skills are deficient. What are the possibilities of this person successfully increasing the size of his or her skills and level of thinking? How long will this take? What might be impacted by the wait? What's at stake? Can you afford to wait? • Commitment is low. There is evidence over time that the person is unwilling to consider changes. How might the supervisor ignite or reignite commitment to the work? How willing are you to commit the time and effort?	• Abstraction is low. What standards and expectations are offered to collaborate on strategies? How will choice and belief encourage energy and risk taking? • Commitment is high. How will the supervisor recognize the effort and energy given to the work? How will the supervisor create focus for the work and build capacity as he or she increases levels of abstraction?

SOURCE: Adapted from Kemerer & Crain, 2013

Diagnosis

The diagnosis responds to the questions "What is effective and what is ineffective. What is working and what is not working?" The diagnosis may address issues related to the level of student participation and success, depth and complexity of the learning, connectivity of the learning to other disciplines and the world beyond the classroom, or the degree to which the classroom environment was supportive of student learning. The diagnosis may address issues related to standards and expectations: for progress monitoring, scope and sequence of the curriculum, engagement in the classroom, behavior in the classroom, and other factors. What nonjudgmental, relevant data support results or lack of results for this diagnosis?

Prescription

Depending on the diagnosis, the prescription sets a direction for improving or maintaining teaching behavior and best practices. The prescription responds to the question "What must (or could) change?" Teachers with high levels of abstraction and commitment may generate their own prescription, but teachers with low abstraction and/or low commitment will need help in identifying areas for change and the direction in which changes must take place.

The examples in Figure 4.5 illustrate the language and the relationship between the diagnosis and the prescription.

Timelines

Timelines establish checkpoints at which teaching behaviors will change and what professional learning activities, book studies, coaching, mentoring, and so on would provide support to the teacher. When considering improvements in instructional behaviors, a common question is "How much time is reasonable for change/improvement to occur?" The answer may be somewhat ambiguous because the length of time that is reasonable

Figure 4.5   Examples of Thinking

DIAGNOSIS	PRESCRIPTION
Students appear disengaged or disinterested.	Goal: that the teacher plan and implement instruction in such a way that all or almost all students are engaged with the learning; adjusting instruction and activities to maintain student engagement.
Enforcement of behaviors that comply with the campus rules and procedures resulting in behaviors impeding learning in the classroom.	Goal: that the teacher reviews and/or reteaches the campus and classroom behavior code of conduct. Monitors, intervenes, or redirects behavior that is inappropriate or disruptive in such a way that appropriate behavior is evidenced and positively reinforced.

Figure 4.6   Factors Affecting Timelines for Improvement

Longer Time to Improve		Shorter Time to Improve
● Term or continuing contract	vs.	● Probationary contract
● Multiple years of experience	vs.	● New to teaching
● History of good evaluations	vs.	● No evaluations or consistently weak evaluations
● Minor/remediable problem	vs.	● Serious/irremediable problem
● Complex changes in teacher behavior	vs.	● Simple changes in teacher behavior
● Employee politically connected/ popular	vs.	● Employee not politically connected/ popular

SOURCE: Kemerer, F., & Cain, J. (2013). *Documentation handbook for appraisal, nonrenewal, and termination.* Fort Worth, TX: Park Place Books.

depends on a number of variables, including the teacher's contract, length of service, previous evaluations, seriousness of the behavior, and the complexity of the needed changes in the teacher's behavior. Figure 4.6 shows Kemerer and Crain's recommendations when setting timelines.

When the desired changes in behavior are complex (e.g., designing student-centered, inductive or inquiry lessons instead of teacher-centered, deductive lessons), it is reasonable to expect an extended period of time for those changes to occur. However, if the desired changes in behavior are rather simple (e.g., post rules for student behavior in the classroom), it is reasonable to expect changes within a much shorter time frame.

There may be some behaviors that are not remediable and will require no time for improvement. Using physical force with a student would most likely be considered irremediable behavior.

MATCHING SUPERVISORY STYLE WITH TEACHER LEVEL OF DEVELOPMENT

Who Controls These Three Issues?

The three supervision styles or approaches are based on the following questions:

1. Who will control and/or make the decisions about the diagnosis?

2. Who will control and/or make the decisions about the prescription?

3. Who will control and/or make the decisions about the timeline?

Figure 4.7   Supervision Approach

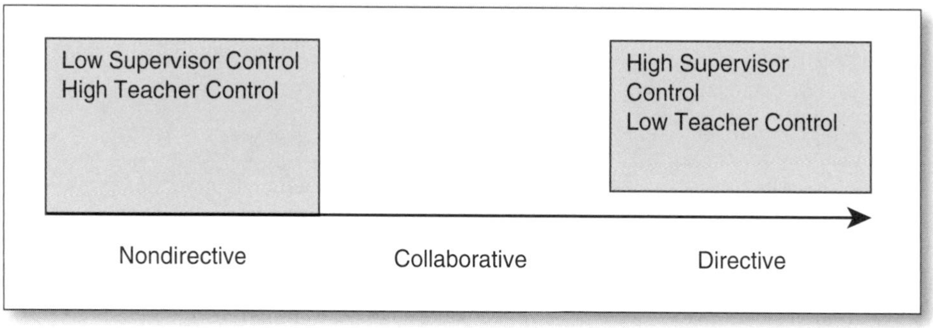

Low Supervisor Control
High Teacher Control

High Supervisor
Control
Low Teacher Control

Nondirective   Collaborative   Directive

SOURCE: Kemerer & Crain, 2013.

Each of these styles or approaches requires a different level of supervisory control of the three decisions. When the collaborative approach is employed, the supervisor and teacher share control of diagnosis, prescription, and timelines. A nondirective approach places the teacher in control of these three issues. And a supervisor implementing the directive supervisory style and/or approach retains control over all three supervisory issues. Each of these supervisory styles or approaches supports improved instructional practice when properly implemented and appropriately applied (Kemerer & Crain, 2013).

As the supervisor, you have now reflected on the following:

- The employee's level of commitment and level of abstraction
- The *issues* involved in the supervisory conversation, including diagnosis, prescription, and timelines
- Objective, credible standards of instruction and behavior that will guide the conversation without imposing one's personal judgments and without criticism of the teacher—essential decisions for a thinking, reflective conversation

Here are a few examples of how decisions might play out:

- If classroom management is the area of discussion, what principles, found in the campus or district guidelines, will be helpful to review with the employee?
- If communication with parents is the area of discussion, what expectations are found in the handbook or website that guide the level of relationship and communication?
- If high levels of student engagement is the area of discussion (and knowing teacher engagement impacts student engagement), what curricular and instructional expectations are found in the curriculum, appraisal system, or campus initiatives that may be reviewed? What is the teacher's level of engagement with the area of discussion?

- If collaboration with team members is the area of discussion, what professional learning community (PLC) principles, guidelines, or training materials describe and/or address the expectations?
- If having strong content knowledge is the area of discussion, what appraisal instrument and what content standards will support the expectation?

You are now ready to match your style or approach with the teacher-employee level of development. Figure 4.8 can help you determine who is in control or takes the lead on the issues.

Quadrant IV

Characteristics: High Commitment and Abstraction

Preferred Supervision Style/Approach: Nondirective/Coaching

We have chosen to begin with a discussion of Quadrant IV teachers because they are typically the masters of their craft. They are quite talented and committed to the best interests of their students.

In July of 2012, the New Teacher Project (TNTP) published an article: *The Irreplaceables: Understanding the Real Retention Crisis in America's Urban Schools.* The *irreplaceables* were defined as the top 20% of teachers, based on district student data. The impact of an irreplaceable teacher on students was 5 to 6 more months of student learning each year than the average

Figure 4.8   Supervision Approach

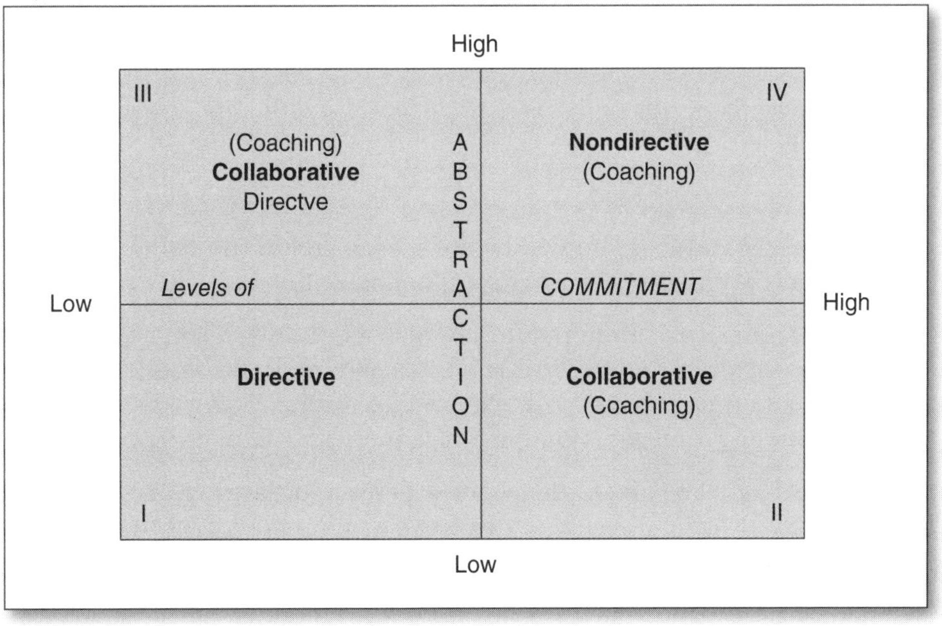

performer. Sadly, the study concludes that there are two major reasons that the irreplaceable teachers leave.

1. **Principals made too little effort to retain irreplaceables or remove low-performing teachers.**

2. **Where principals created cultures of respect and trust, high percentages of irreplaceables were found. Good teachers don't leave demanding schools that hold them to high expectations; they leave schools that aren't serious about good teaching.** (TNTP, 2012)

The following might be the most surprising information:

- Only 47% of high performers had been informed that they were high performing.
- Only 26% had received opportunities or paths for teacher leadership roles.
- Only 37% were encouraged to keep teaching at their school for another year. (TNTP, 2012, p. 5)

Irreplaceable teachers felt they received little positive feedback or public recognition for a job well done. *The report offered five ways principals can keep these indispensable, irreplaceable teachers:*

1. **Start the school year with great expectations.** The best teachers want clarity and certainty of standards and expectations. Use meeting or orientation time at the start of the year to rally teachers around a clear and specific definition of excellent teaching and a set of goals for making the school a better place for learning. Limit best practices to prevent a feeling of being overwhelmed. *Choose 2–3 "high leverage" issues to achieve focus. Ask yourself, "If I could get or sustain focus around 2–3 issues that would significantly impact the quality of teacher/learning in all classrooms, what would they be?"* (see tntp .org/irreplaceables). Then, with the teacher, set individual goals aligned to that vision. Tell teachers that you will observe them frequently and that you will be honest when they are falling short. Be clear that ineffective teaching is not an option.

2. **Recognize excellence publicly and frequently.** Don't let success be a secret. Set aside 5 to 10 minutes in regular meetings to publicly celebrate teachers who have done exceptional work in the classroom or achieved a notable milestone with their students.

3. **Treat your irreplaceable teachers as though they are irreplaceable.** Make it difficult for them to leave your school. List the teachers who are most critical to your school's academic success and spend time with them. For a while, consider ignoring the nay-sayers and holdouts.

4. Start having "stay conversations" by Thanksgiving.

5. **Hold the line on good teaching.** Administrators who refuse to tolerate poor teaching keep more of their top teachers. Keep the focus on reading, learning, and conversations focused around your 2–3 high leverage issues. (TNTP, 2012)

Why is attention to Quadrant IV teachers/employees so important?

The conversation a leader or supervisor has with Quadrant IV teachers and employees is critically important. They get results. They drive the mission of the work and they ultimately will be the next generation of leaders of our schools.

With the Quadrant IV teacher, the goal is to coach and expand this professional's thinking. Quadrant IVs are committed and are great thinkers. Conversations with these teachers provide the opportunity to give lots of specific positive feedback on the value of what they are doing and offer powerful and provocative reflective questions about why and how they are getting results—to push higher order levels of thought for creativity, innovation, and/or design.

Coaching is the essential skill and tool for working with Quadrant IV employees. A supervisor who applies the language and skills of coaching provides the environment for safety and deep thought. The supervisor listens deeply like a coach to really hear a point of view or perspective. The supervisor listens for the emotion, the energy, and the desire for possibilities within the teacher. The supervisor—the coach leader—is truly a thinking partner with this teacher to design and create student lessons and classroom environments that produce the highest levels of learning.

A conversation might sound like this:

"Jim, I know you have been reviewing the data on our math scores and are crazy upset about this. Given that you are always five steps ahead of the rest of us, what are you uncovering within the data that is directing your plan?"

Or

"Shauna, your continued use of the data and then varying the approach when needed for your students continues to accelerate their success. Just look at what Joshua, Mary, and Kanya did on the last benchmark. Look at this. Your actions demonstrate your commitment to our kids every day. Your detective approach is going to skyrocket your results. So what are you noticing, right now, as you monitor and contemplate the approaching state assessments?"

Quadrant III

Characteristics: High Abstraction and Low Commitment

Preferred Supervision Style/Approach: Collaborative/Coaching

The Quadrant III teacher can be complex and challenging. With a high level of abstraction, the teacher is knowledgeable and skilled, competent to share in the control of the issues in the conversation (diagnosis, prescription, and timeline). The issue of low commitment may make this person more difficult because it makes visible his or her unwillingness to step up to the expectations and accept responsibility for results. The Quadrant III teacher may have an attitude of "been there, done that" or "retired on the job" or "why bother—this too shall pass."

The supervisor must maintain an ever-present belief in possibility. This teacher was once, possibly, a very good teacher who may have lost trust, hope, or purpose along the way. With *SCARF* as the blueprint and by identifying a list of strengths, contributions, and qualities that make this person special, the supervisor has the potential to reawaken commitment. Remember, as Oprah Winfrey has commented, every person on this planet wants the same thing: "Do you see me? Do I matter?"

The supervisor—the coach leader—engages the teacher in a safe conversation and while doing so

- values the history and/or results of the teacher;
- authentically holds up the data and expectations for the campus or for this class;
- invites the teacher to look at the diagnosis;
- collaboratively considers and determines what changes the teacher might choose; and
- agrees on the plan or actions needed to get the required results within an expected time frame.

The caveat here is to remember that while this teacher's abstraction level is high, the commitment level is low. While you should attempt to approach all three supervision issues (diagnosis, prescription, timelines) collaboratively, that may not always produce the results you want. Depending on the teacher's level of commitment, you may end up having to use a directive approach on some issues. For example, the teacher may blame the students for poor performance saying things like, "They don't care; they won't try; they're lazy." Collaboratively use your coaching strategies to influence the teacher to reconsider and accept the responsibility for poor student performance. If the collaborative route is not successful, you may have to shift your approach and become directive on the diagnosis: "When students are not achieving, we know for sure that there are problems with the instructional design and delivery or the classroom learning environment. That diagnosis is really not negotiable."

Having taken control of the diagnosis (directive), attempt to shift back into a collaborative mode for the prescription: "You are a very experienced teacher with a big toolkit for teaching. As you think about your successful experience, what kinds of learning activities hold the greatest potential for engaging and motivating your students?"

As we discussed earlier, David Rock (2006) uses the acronym TARP to communicate the requirements for real change:

Time

Attention

Repetition

Positive feedback

It is up to the supervisor to provide a structure for TARP and adhere to the committed timelines and check-ins.

Educators land in Quadrant III for a variety of reasons: burn out, frustration with kids, demographics, how things used to be, personal pressures, and so on. When the supervisor isn't ready to give up on a Quadrant III, still sees them with possibility, and has some belief in the efforts to reconnect them to their passion, conversations may sound like this:

"Helen, for years you have been a leader on our staff, a fierce advocate for struggling kids. As you have reviewed and reflected on the math data that we just received on the percentage of students not mastering the target objectives, what powerful tools are you getting out to turn your kids around? (Teacher shares concerns but quickly identifies some strategies she is already putting in place.) "Hey, it is clear you are on top of this, so let's get together next Tuesday to examine some specifics of impact that you are seeing with your kids" (reignite passion/bring focus).

Or

"Jim, you are clearly frustrated because all the things you've done in years past just aren't getting the results you must get today. Change is hard, especially when it feels like we have to start all over learning to do things in a different way. As your supervisor, it is clear to see the possibilities for meeting the different needs of your students today, just as you must have when you first started teaching. You care deeply about the content and talk about it with the love and zeal of a college professor. Since you recognize the requirements placed on us to take our kids to extraordinary heights in learning, I'm thinking you just want a reset button or a little turbo charge to rekindle the teacher in Jim who loves challenges and obstacles. Let's have some spirited conversations over the coming weeks and find that sweet spot in you. How about every Tuesday and Thursday the first 30 minutes of your planning time? Sound like a plan that might support the results you want?"

Even with the best follow-up, sometimes a Quadrant III teacher remains unwilling to change. The supervisor has laid out the expectations for what needs to change with specific clarity (diagnosis), possibilities for how it might change (prescription), and the timeline to make it happen. Should the teacher make the decision that he or she is unwilling, the principal must move forward in response to the teacher's decision or unwillingness to make a decision. There do not have to be angry words, loud voices, or threats. It's simply a decision the teacher makes: that he or she does not want to do what is required—an example of low commitment. So without emotion, the supervisor might offer that since a decision appears to have been made, maybe this position is not the right placement or maybe the teacher is considering other options outside this district or even education.

The conversation might sound like this:

"Ms. Jones, there was a time when you eagerly accepted the responsibility and demands of teaching; it sounds like something has changed. In our conversations you have reviewed the data and committed to turning around student engagement, and with it, student results in your class. From your actions and the progress in your class, it appears you have decided this is not what you want to do. What options are you considering for yourself? What possibilities are you considering that will provide the satisfaction and enjoyment you desire for meaningful work?"

Should the teacher report too much is required and they will probably be looking for something different, the supervisor may offer:

"Well, you are a professional, and given that we still have 12 weeks to instruct and support your students, I believe in your professionalism to finish strong in this position. I will drop by each week to see how things are going and support your strong finish."

Quadrant II

Characteristics: Low Abstraction and High Commitment

Preferred Supervision Style: Collaborative/Coaching

It is always exciting to have eager and committed teachers. They will most frequently fall into Quadrant II. You will find beginning teachers, those returning to the profession or changing positions, as well as those new to an assignment and eager to perform well. Because the situation is new, Quadrant II teachers or employees don't always know what to do or how to do something as required or expected in the new position. But Quadrant II teachers want to do the job well! The response of the supervisor is extremely important to maintain and support their energy and commitment as they learn the new expectations and nuances of the position. Because there are gaps or lack of knowledge or expertise, the supervisor will intentionally scaffold success for these worker bees by clearly articulating

- the expectations of the position, via job description or appraisal matrix;
- the conditions of the work environment;
- how data will be used to measure success and results; and
- the core values and norms in existence as to how people work together.

When new employees for any position know coming in what is expected specifically and how they will be assessed on their work, their potential for success is increased tenfold. The influence of the supervisor, the coach leader, is critical. How the coach leader will influence, support, retain, grow, or move an employee into a profession that is more aligned with the employee's commitment, interests, and talents will dramatically influence satisfaction and joy for the work.

The effective supervisor will have articulated these things previously to the whole staff and periodically throughout a work year. The supervisor who is clear in the focus of the work based on targeted data will support each employee and teacher to set clear, meaningful, and measurable goals that support the focus. Even with the best of communication, things are often fuzzy, and supervision conversations support the teacher or employee to understand the concrete and to move to the abstract in using content, tools, and strategy.

For example, after being in a classroom, the principal shares with a teacher some of the data she gathered while in the classroom. The principal, with great intention and knowing the fragile nature of new teachers and feedback, considers *SCARF* as feedback is given. Beginning with value statements, the principal identifies what things were going well in the class—the creative environment, evidence of clear procedures and rules, positive interaction with students, and eager engagement from the students. The principal then reminds the teacher of the month-long focus on corrective feedback to students and asks, "What are you noticing in your practice, and what results are you seeing in students?" The teacher shows in her facial expression that she might not have been thinking about that and just says, "I think, okay."

The principal states that part of her responsibility is to share observed data gathered during the observation and asks the teacher if it might be helpful to hear some of the data on feedback that she gathered. Being a highly committed Quadrant II, the teacher responds with an eager "Yes!"

The principal then shares the observation data in an intentionally objective manner: "You called on Mimi, and she was successful. You immediately called on Kiante, and he was successful." (For this approach, use as many examples as needed to make the point.)

The principal then invites the teacher to reflect on the information she shared: "As you are reflecting on this information, what are you seeing or thinking?"

The teacher is surprised. "I really thought I was using positive reinforcement with the kids. I really like them, and I want them to feel good." The principal responds, "Of course you do. You know that when students receive specific, positive reinforcement, the learning is reinforced and the confidence level of the students goes up. It also sends them the message that is so important to you: I care about you."

The teacher then admits that she is not very good at giving corrective feedback and prompting: "I am afraid that if I prompt or give corrective feedback, I might embarrass them or make them feel dumb. Can you help me with this?" The principal offers options: "Well, there are some things other teachers do and that I have learned about in my own professional development. Here are three that come to mind.

1. Let students talk first with a partner and wait for partner hands.

2. Direct students to facets of the content. Does it meet the definition, the required conditions, the criterion, and so on.

3. Direct attention to anchor charts, teaching guides, posters."

The principal then asks, "What has come to mind for you?" If the teacher responds that she can't think of anything, the principal continues. "Which one sounds like something that would work best for you and your students or one that you want to learn more about?"

The teacher is intrigued by #1: "I never heard of 'Letting students talk first with a partner and waiting for partner hands.' That sounds really interesting."

The principal then suggests opportunities for learning and professional development: "Here are some possible ideas for learning opportunities. You could observe in another class. Mr. Redmond is a real expert in giving positive, supportive reflective feedback. And we could both look for a workshop on instructional strategies to get lots of ideas.

What might hold the best possibility for providing you with the skills and confidence to give reflective feedback in ways that do not demean or embarrass your students?"

The teacher leaps at the opportunities offered: "I'd really like to do both. Maybe get some training first and then observe Mr. Redmond to see how he does it."

The principal agrees that both are appropriate options: "If we can locate some training available this month, how quickly after that would you like to observe Mr. Redmond's classroom?"

The teacher shares in the decision on timeline: "I'd like a couple of weeks to practice what I learn in the training and then go observe Mr. Redmond."

The principal invites the teacher to share a second timeline decision: "When do you think might be a good time for me to come back and observe all the new strategies you are going to be learning?"

The teacher and principal agree on a date for 1 week after the teacher observes in Mr. Redmond's class, and the principal acknowledges and affirms the teacher's commitment: "You are so committed to your students and to growing your skills. I am so eager to get back to your classroom and see the great results you are having."

When the brain feels safe, one is free to be authentic and open about things that seem scary or difficult. With a principal knowing what this Quadrant II teacher needs, he or she is able to support, provide positive feedback, and just watch this teacher soar. Quadrant IIs are aware of some issues and not of others. Often they don't know what they don't know or how to solve problems. This is typically indicative of a lower level of abstraction. Because the principal's goal is to build capacity and grow the talent of the teacher, the principal shares control of the diagnosis and prescription. The principal presents objective data from an observation and offers or elicits a range of options or possibilities from which the teacher may choose. In the situation just described the teacher has a high level of commitment and really wants to get better and learn more strategies. The low level of abstraction is seen in not knowing how to identify or even identifying the problem. Both the principal and the teacher may share control of the timeline, because the teacher has high commitment and may be inclined to overcommit to both the complexity and speed of change. Quadrant II teachers hold great potential to become outstanding teachers, with time, practice, reflective feedback, and thoughtful reflection for our profession. Glickman's Principle 5, *"Supervision should challenge teachers to think more abstractly about their practice of teaching,"* begins here and takes a teacher or any employee to their personal best simply because they are nurtured to be thinkers and reflective practitioners. Tomorrow's leaders start here in Quadrant II!

Quadrant I

Characteristics: Low Abstraction and Low Commitment

Preferred Supervision Style: Directive or Collaborative

When, for whatever reason, we have a teacher or employee with low commitment and low abstraction, there is much reason for concern. They were either hired inappropriately or have lacked supervision resulting in this situation. A Quadrant I teacher can range from solid Quadrant I to being on the edge of Quadrants III or II. People vary in their attitudes for a variety of reasons. It may seem a bit confusing to note that the preferred supervision style for Quadrant I teachers or employees is directive/collaborative. That does *not* mean that there is a fourth, hybrid style. It means that in choosing among supervision styles, you must consider each of the three conversation or conference issues separately. Remember, the three issues in the supervision conference: diagnosis, prescription, and timelines. The reality is that for the issue of diagnosis you will probably have to be directive. You may simply tell the teacher what is acceptable practice and what is not—no collaboration, no arguing. You may then shift to a collaborative style for the prescription and invite the teacher to discuss solutions to the problem. (In later research, Glickman offered two different types of directive. Directive Informational where the supervisor provides options for possible changes the teacher need to choose from and then plans with the teacher the specific details. The second is Directive Control, where the supervisor tells the teacher what she must do. They are both directive but the first involves choices and the second does not.) If the teacher is willing to authentically participate, you can continue to collaborate on both the prescription and the timelines, if you as the supervisor agree. If the teacher is unable or unwilling to authentically participate, you remain in a directive mode and take control of all three decisions.

Low commitment often manifests in ways such as doing as little as possible, viewing the job as a nuisance or bother, failure to follow instructions, failure to meet standards and expectations, failure to move in any forward direction for results, negative attitude, and blaming results or lack of on everyone other than self. Low abstraction only adds to the problem because the person doesn't demonstrate the mental capacity to recognize problems or make connections for cause and effect. The combination of low commitment or low abstraction requires the supervisor to take control of all the issues in the conference: the diagnosis, the prescription, and the timelines. This conference is not a true conversation, but a monologue or perhaps I talk and you talk. Being directive means that you are in control of all the decisions. There is no arguing, no negotiating, and no opportunities for the teacher to make choices. At the end of your three-part monologue, you may ask the teacher what questions he or she has about the directives and timelines, but you have determined the action plan and it is nonnegotiable. Consider the following data:

In a classroom observation you observed four students passing notes with no action by the teacher. In the 45 minutes you were in the class, 3 of 28 students participated in the lesson; other students were passive listeners and taking notes.

The principal begins the conference by inviting the teacher to listen to some data that were collected during the observation. When the principal shares about the note passing, the teacher responds, "Which students?

When were they passing notes?" When the principal shares data about 3 of 28 engaged students, the teacher asks, "Is that a problem?" When asked what changes the teacher would make if he were to teach the same lesson again tomorrow, the teacher replies, "I'd probably do pretty much the same thing. These remedial-level kids aren't going to do anything, no matter what I do." Later in the conversation the teacher comments that the students are the problem and nothing he can do will change them. The principal asks the teacher to return to his office after school for more conversation because the teacher must return to class.

When the teacher returns, the conversation is dramatically different.

The principal begins with, "Mr. Green, you have been a teacher in this district for several years, and I am sure you want to be a good teacher for our students. Unfortunately, the evidence and data are confirming that kids are not mastering the objectives of the curriculum. Our teacher contracts require that teachers teach the curriculum and assume some responsibility for student results. The records show you asked for this remedial class, so my hunch is you wanted to make a difference with kids who were challenging. Given the district expectations and campus expectations for high levels of learning, I have identified the highlighted areas of the curriculum for your focus over the next 3 weeks, and I have compiled four instructional strategies you are to use with your students. I'll drop by a couple of times a week to support your progress and will expect to see the following:

1. All students engaged with the learning objective. Although they may be doing a variety of tasks, they must be engaged with the learning.

2. Small and whole group instruction to support engagement as well as use of the collaborative strategies shared in our last professional learning session.

3. You will be teaching or monitoring small groups and your whole group with multiple strategies for checking student understanding.

4. Your positive actions and behavior will match your initial desire to teach and challenge the best in these students.

We will meet again at the end of the third week and look at the impact on your students' learning."

The teacher is invited to speak and begins to offer an excuse about why the plan will not work. The principal listens, then interrupts the excuses and responds, "Mr. Green, it is important for you to understand that students not learning is not acceptable and violates the job description and appraisal expectations. You have accepted a professional role, and you are qualified to meet the expectations of the role. My hope is that you will. As a parent, you would want only a teacher who believed in your child's ability to succeed. If you determine that you are unwilling to meet the expectations of the professional teacher role, then I am happy to meet with you to talk about some of your employment options. I look forward to being in your class next week."

In a directive conference, the supervisor is in control—he or she is the decision maker. There is no negotiating, arguing, convincing, or reaching any consensus. There is a professional demeanor of calm, confidence, and courage that holds up the standards and expectations of the position and accepts nothing less than effort and results for students.

In the resource section you will find several conversations that offer examples and practice activities of how Glickman's model may be utilized.

In a 2011 TEDx Orange Coast presentation, Carl St. Clair (2008) talks about musical innovation. The conductor demonstrates how by whispering honest feedback and direction, he encourages musicians to create exceptional music that mirrors their souls and delivers a level of performance that is exceptional and awe-inspiring. To the musician, ears are the mirror to the soul. By respecting the professional and what they do, with quiet encouragement a transformed orchestra is developed. Why not classrooms? The space in the middle of our work is the child who must learn successfully for their best life. May we, as supervisors, be the soft, gentle, every present voice that whispers reminders to teachers of our great purpose and why we hold the power to change the world—one child at a time.

SUMMARY

- Most people want to do good work.
- It is critical that the supervisor examine his or her own beliefs and mindset about people and why they do or do not change their behavior.
- To do great work, developmental supervision and coaching offers a safe environment to learn and grow in the ability to think abstractly about the work we do.
- When the brain feels safe, feels status from the coach leader, the ingredients are present to develop talent.
- 21st century applications of Carl Glickman's Developmental Supervision Model hold great alignment to current brain research and great potential to create real change for results in schools.
- Leaders must be intentional in choosing the supervision style that will best assist the teacher.
- Leaders have the opportunity to influence the level of commitment and abstraction of those they lead. When leaders hold reflective conversations that express value for specific actions conducted by a teacher or employee, they offer the possibility to increase the impetus and desire within the employee to repeat such actions. When leaders ask reflective questions of the teacher or employee in

a manner that demonstrates a belief that he or she can, it increases the likelihood that the employee level of thinking will expand as he or she responds to the questions. This is how supervisors—coach leaders—grow talent!

- When leaders observe and collect data that demonstrate a low level of commitment and/or abstraction on the part of the teacher or employee, they hold thoughtful and specific conversations with the employee based on three critical factors: diagnosis, prescription, and timeline.
- The chief goal of leaders is to improve thinking, performance, and results by

  o helping people think about things that are worth thinking about such as student success and active participation in learning;
  o believing if people begin to think differently, they will, over time, choose different behaviors; and
  o realizing authentic change takes time, attention, repetition, and positive feedback!

- Glickman suggests that most teachers are unlikely to initiate or pursue change independently, due to the unchanging and controlling work environment of schools that constantly reinforce conformity and unimaginative thinking. Supervisors have an obligation to challenge the ineffectiveness of the traditional role of supervisor to a professional level that facilitates deep thinking and problem solving, reflection and insights that will produce new ideas, solutions, actions, and continuously improved results.
- The greatest leadership challenge of our century is changing the mindset about how real change occurs in others. Traditional supervisory practices are hardwired into our culture, environment, habits, and behaviors. To lead for real change and growth will take deep commitment, courage, and a deeply held belief that the payoff in supporting others achieve more will be the reward.
- Let's be the change we want to see. It begins with us.

"Supervision needs to be clearly focused on the real nature of practical coaching and mentoring. Reflectiveness results in mindful work where we constantly consider what to do, why we do it and examine it to see how we can do it better. Supervision is a forum for reflecting on work in the presence of another or others who facilitate that process."

Dr. Mike Carroll

"The key to successful leadership today is influence, not authority."

Kenneth Blanchard, University of
Massachusetts, Schatz, Mana

"A good leader inspires confidence in the leader, a great leader inspires people's confidence in themselves."

Unknown

"The goal of many leaders is to get people to think more highly of the leader. The goal of a great leader is to help people to think more highly of themselves."

J. Carla Nortcut

"A successful school is foremost an organization that defines good education for itself, through its goals and desired practices, and then engages in the 'moral equivalent of war' in achieving that vision."

Carl Glickman

REFERENCES

Barnwell, P. (2015, May) The ongoing struggle of teacher retention. *Atlantic Monthly*. Retrieved from http://www.theatlantic.com/education/archive/2015/05/the-ongoing-struggle-of-teacher-retention/394211/

Dweck, C. S. (2006). *Mindset: The new psychology of success*. New York, NY: Random House.

Glickman, C. D. (1990). *Supervision of instruction: A developmental approach* (2nd edition). Newton, MA: Allyn and Bacon.

HCI: Human Capital Institute. (2014). Talent Pulse Research, A quarterly research ebook on management and leadership. Retrieved from http://www.hci.org/files/field_content_file/Talent%20Pulse_Dynamic%20Appraisal_8-14-15.pdf (membership required)

Kemerer, F., & Crain, J. (2013). *Documentation handbook for appraisal, nonrenewal, and termination*. Fort Worth, TX: Park Place Books.

Marzano, R. J. (2009). *Becoming a reflective teacher*. Bloomington, IN: Marzano Research.

Marzano, R. J., Pickering, D. J., & Pollock, J. E. (2001). *Classroom instruction that works*. Alexandria, VA: Association for Supervision and Curriculum Development.

Moore-Johnson, S. (2004). *Finders and keepers: Helping new teachers survive and thrive in our schools* (with the Project on the Next Generation of Teachers). New York, NY: Jossey-Bass.

Pajak, E. (1993). *Approaches to clinical supervision: Alternatives for improving instruction*. Norwood, MA: Christopher-Gordon.

Perkins, D. (2003). *King Arthur's round table: How collaborative conversations create smart organizations*. Hoboken, NJ: John Wiley & Sons.

Pink, D. (2009). *Drive: The surprising truth about what motivates us*. New York, NY: Riverhead Books.

Rock, D. (2006). *Quiet leadership*. New York, NY: HarperCollins.

Rock, D. (2008). SCARF: A brain-based model for collaborating with and influencing others. *NeuroLeadership Journal, 1.*

Rock, D. (2009). *Your brain at work.* New York, NY: Harper Business.

Rock, D., Davis, J., & Jones, B. (2014). Kill your performance ratings. *Strategy + Business, 76.*

St. Clair, C. (2008, June 8). Carl St. Clair – Innovation whispers [Video]. Retrieved from http://www.tedxorangecoast.com/videopick/carl-st-clair-innovation-whispers/

TNTP. (2012). *The irreplaceables: Understanding the real retention crisis in America's schools.* Retrieved from http://www.tntp.org

5

The Power of the Conversation

I need to have a conversation, but for some reason I'm holding off, or I'm not sure of the best approach to take.

A typical statement heard by the authors of this book

In this chapter we provide clarity on reasons why holding conversations are both expected of leaders and at times challenging for leaders. We propose a proven process for holding thoughtful conversations that reflect coach-like behaviors for the leader while also addressing the most important points related to the conversation topic and outcome. You will be introduced to the Results Coaching Global (RCG) Coaching Conversation Frame that can be used when holding any conversation where you want to increase clarity and strengthen both relations and intentions for forward-moving thinking and action. We provide sample conversation scenarios as well as ways to use the Conversation Frame when holding conversations often described as *difficult*. When you put learning from this chapter into practice, people will thank you for both the time-efficient processes that you use and the way in which they feel as a result of being in conversation with you.

During a recent Internet search for books on having conversations, 48,225 were listed as possible options. Clearly, there is no shortage of books about a variety of processes and practices with regard to conversations, yet leaders continue to seek best approaches to use when holding conversations with others.

The intent within any conversation, whether personal or professional is for human beings to interact through the use of words and feelings to communicate thoughts and ideas, make connections, understand from different perspectives, gain clarity, and consider possible actions as a result of the conversation. When asking people to describe conversations, one might hear *warm, energizing, productive, valuable, fun, needed, thought-producing, relationship-building, respectful, humbling, joyful, appreciative,* or *growth-producing.* Or, depending on the situation and experience, one might also hear conversations described as dreaded, harmful, devaluing, emotionally charged, time-consuming, boring, empty, aggravating, draining, complicated, energy-depleting, unclear, heavy, or disrespectful.

Typically, we don't tend to dread or put off conversations that offer productivity, unless time, energy, and/or location are barriers. As leaders, it's the tough or difficult conversations that cause many of us to pull back and think very carefully before moving forward with a conversation that could be described as walking barefoot through a field covered with grass burrs. In this situation, we tread very carefully and watch each step we take, to pass through the area as pain-free as possible, with few or no repercussions.

What if you didn't have to walk through grass-burred fields or paths that seem overwhelming in size and scope? What if you could hold conversations that actually enrich relationships and impact positive change? What if you felt the consistent and productive power within conversations regardless of the topic or situation you are dealing with? We propose this is possible and offer concrete ways to achieve this big goal. And you don't have to read 48,225 books to get there. It all begins with you, your self-awareness, and how other people respond to you.

As was emphasized in Chapter 2, whenever people come together for a conversation, they are scanning for safety or threat. Our words matter and have an impact on others. And because we stand in the role of leader, it's as if our words and behaviors multiply in size and strength. After all, as Heatherton (2011) tells us, "Humans have a fundamental need to belong, are incredibly sensitive to social context, and are strongly motivated to remain in good standing with their social group and avoid social exclusions" (p. 1). If people feel safe and respected, they will more likely open up. If, however, feelings of threat overtake safety, it's a different story. Social threats inhibit perceptions, cognition, critical thinking, creativity, and collaboration (Rock, 2015).

Leaders have a huge responsibility to hold conversations where the people involved feel free to speak openly without reprimand while also being willing to listen to understand from multiple perspectives. As Susan Scott (2009) wisely directed leaders, "Your central function is to engineer intelligent, spirited conversations that provide the basis for high levels of alignment, collaboration, and partnership at all levels throughout your organization and the healthier outcomes that go with them" (p. 5).

The intent of this chapter is to awaken within each of us the importance of and commitment for designing and holding conversations, whether easy or difficult, that offer clarity, demonstrate respect for differing ideas and viewpoints, and ignite an impetus for change, while also holding clear opportunities to positively impact people's status, certainty, autonomy, relatedness, and fairness, or SCARF as described in Chapter 2. Because, as Susan Scott (2009) so profoundly says, "the conversation is the relationship" (p. 15). While conversations do take time, anything else, especially when dealing with the aftermath of not holding the conversation, or holding one that is not carefully engineered or orchestrated, is most likely to take even more time. Let's live toward the positive end of the message so beautifully articulated by Scott (2009), "Our careers, our companies, our personal relationships, and our very lives succeed or fail, gradually then suddenly—one conversation at a time" (p. 15).

Let's also agree that not every conversation is a coaching conversation. We have many conversations, at home and at work, which are more social and personal in nature that offer opportunities for people to enjoy each other's company. We contend that within any conversation, when we show up with a commitment to listen to understand, use the gift of silence, offer paraphrasing, ask thoughtful questions, and share personal thoughts in ways that demonstrate attitudes of respect for those engaged in the conversation, we can strengthen opportunities to enrich relationships and ultimate results. Regardless of the conversation, when we show up coach-like in our skills and attitudes, we have a greater opportunity to have a positive impact on others, be it family, friend, colleague, parent, child, or stranger. We earnestly believe that the majority of the conversations held in the workplace hold the potential to be coaching conversations. When we show up coach-like, we are there to support the other person's or group's thinking, reflections, and decisions for actions. When we are coach-like, we understand that the spotlight, described in Chapter 3, is shining on him or her much more than on us.

Recently, during one of our seminars on Leadership Coaching for High Performance, a principal said early in the training, "I want to learn how to have more productive conversations upfront so that I don't have to have as many difficult conversations on the backend. I want to help teachers improve before they get to the place where they are in danger of not staying with us." Yes! We want that, too!

Often, leaders come to our seminars wanting to know how to have difficult conversations. We contend that once leaders learn and consistently incorporate the essential skills of committed listening, powerful paraphrasing, asking questions that presume positive intent, and offering reflective feedback in a consistent manner, they will decrease the number of difficult conversations they are called to have. We also believe that when leaders use the RCG Conversation Frame as a guide to holding conversations, they will experience an efficient and effective way to navigate through most conversations regardless of the multitude of topics or the scope of emotions. Let's explore this conversation frame.

First, the concept of a frame is offered as a way of holding in place a view or visual of what happens within any coaching conversation.

Figure 5.1   RCG Coaching Conversation Frame

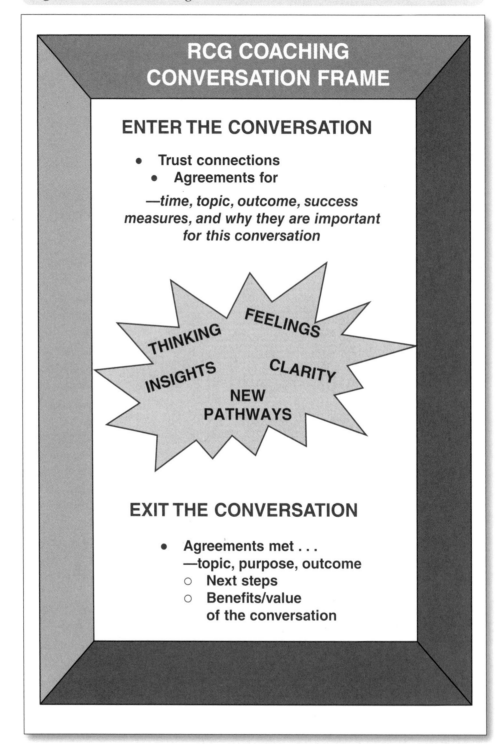

COACHING FRAME

Sample Language for
ENTERING THE CONVERSATION

- Given we have about 10 minutes, what would you like for us to focus on?
- At the end of our 15 minutes, what would you like to take away?
- What are you wanting to accomplish by the end of our 20-minute conversation?
- I'm here to be your thinking partner for the next 15 minutes. What would you like to focus on? What are you thinking would be the best use of our time?

Sample Language for
EXITING THE CONVERSATION

- What has been the most helpful in our conversation today?
- When we started our conversation you wanted_____; how did we do?
- Of all the things we have talked about, what has been of greatest value?
- What is clearer for you now that was not as clear when we began our conversation?

NEXT STEPS:

- When we began our conversation, your goal was to_____. How are you feeling about your great thinking? What will be your first steps?
- What actions are you ready to begin based on the plan you have designed?
- When we talk again where are you thinking you would like to begin?

(Continued)

(Continued)

COACHING FRAME

Sample Language for the RCG – GPS

SOLUTION FOCUSED:

- If ideal, how would the situation be?
- When you have encountered this situation before what did you do that resolved it successfully?
- What three things are you thinking would have the greatest impact on achieving your solution?
- Would it be helpful to generate numerous options to consider?
- How will you know (what data will you use) to evaluate your success with this situation?

GOAL FOCUSED:

- When this goal is achieved what will the impact be?
- What people or resources are you thinking will be the greatest support in achieving your goal?
- What strategies [specific #] are you assessing will have the most influence on achieving this goal?
- What will be your first steps? What data will inform you of your achievement?

PLANNING FOCUSED:

- What do you want?
- What will it look like, sound like, be like when accomplished?
- What strategies are you thinking will get you there?
- How are you wanting to assess your success?
- As you consider your timeline, what are your first three steps?

REFLECTION FOCUSED:

- As you have reflected on this, what was the greatest insight (learning) for you?
- What did you do specifically that influenced the outcome?
- To what did you pay attention, to ensure your goals were accomplished?
- As you take this learning forward, what will you keep with you; what will you refine; what will you leave behind?

SOURCE: Influenced by the International Coach Federation Coaching Competencies

THE CONVERSATION FRAME

Entering the Conversation

Trust Connections

It is worth our thoughts to consider how we want to begin the conversation for people to feel they are entering into a safe and respected place. As leaders, we know the importance of offering personal regard as we begin the conversation. This doesn't have to take long. It's offered through our tone of voice, our body language, and the words we use.

- **Example**: "Hello, Jane. Thanks for coming by. You are always on time for any meeting you attend, and I'm looking forward to spending this time with you. Let's sit over here where we can be comfortable. How are you today, Jane?"
- **Example**: "Hello, Mr. and Mrs. Smith. Thanks for taking time out of your busy schedules to come and talk with us about your son, Johnny. First we want you to know that we think that Johnny is a super young man! Come, let's sit here and talk together."
- **Example**: "Hi, Jim. I was glad to see that you had asked for a time for us to talk today. I always enjoy our visits. Please, come in and let's sit over here."

Trust continues to grow throughout the conversation as you intentionally use the skills of committed listening, paraphrasing, and presuming positive intent. And we all know that having a good beginning to a conversation is extremely important. When we start well, we increase the likelihood of ending well.

Agreements

This is such an important part of a well-orchestrated conversation. Agreements are strongly connected to the C in SCARF. Agreements offer certainty about what we are going to talk about and how we will move through a conversation. When people feel that they are part of the decisions made around agreements, they are more likely to feel safe and respected (status) and thus engage in the conversation at a much deeper level. And as we move through the agreements you will also see how the A (autonomy) in SCARF shows up when people are asked questions to contribute to the process and focus of the conversation. You will also make connections with the R (relatedness) and F (fairness). In other words, the whole of SCARF encompasses the entire RCG Conversation Frame and the interchange within it.

We offer the following agreements. It's important to remember that these are only examples and yet without agreements you may be traveling down different paths to outcomes that are misaligned from what is expected by each person.

Time

Let's be clear about the time all have dedicated to the meeting. Typically, when scheduling a meeting we offer a time frame for the meeting. (That means that we do not send out a message that says, "See me." That is too vague and also holds potential for the receiver to think something is wrong.) Once a time agreement has been established, we do our very best to meet the agreement. And, yes, we can set new agreements as needed and schedules allow.

- **Example:** "Jane, with your agreement, let's dedicate about 20 minutes to this conversation. And if we decide we need more time, then we can either go longer or reschedule, based on our calendars and needs. How does that sound to you?"
- **Example:** "Mr. and Mrs. Smith, we have set about 30 minutes for this conversation. How does that sound to you?"
- **Example:** "Jim, I have about 20 minutes for our conversation. How does that meet with your needs?"

Topic

This is the main focus for the conversation. Since we can only tend to one theme, issue, concern, challenge, puzzlement, or topic at a time, it's critical to get clear on the "one thing" that we agree to as the subject or main topic of the conversation and the importance of this one topic. Sometimes you bring the topic, but if it is truly a coaching conversation, the other person brings the topic.

- **Example: When you ask for the meeting.** "Jane, today, I'd like for us to talk about you and your development as a grade-level leader. You have strong leadership potential and yet you seem to hold back on taking on more leadership responsibilities. I'd like for us to talk about this to better understand your desires and thoughts around leading your peers. How does this sound to you?" If Jane does not feel comfortable talking about this topic yet, then together you and Jane will adjust the agreement. Even when you bring the topic, you want Jane to agree to the topic or both agree to a revision to the topic. Think of the trust this builds as Jane thinks and feels that she has a part in determining the topic of the conversation. Also, consider how this approach speaks to the F in SCARF (fairness) and the R (relatedness).

- **Example: When you call for the meeting**. "Mr. and Mrs. Smith, the purpose of this conversation is to talk about Johnny [the topic] and to celebrate his accomplishments, share his current status with his school work, and consider ways we can together continue to support and challenge him as he moves through this school year [importance of the topic]. How does that sound to you? What else would you like to include in this conversation?" (If the parents say they want to talk about a specific incident that happened with another student or a teacher, then together you will renegotiate the agreement. Maybe something has happened that takes priority over the topic you were bringing and you are flexible to adjust the topic within the time frame to which you both agreed.)
- **Example: When they ask for the meeting**. "Jim, you have something on your mind. What is it that you would like to talk about today in our 20 minutes together?"

Getting clear on the topic is critical to the conversation and may take some exploration to reach clarity. Many times someone brings a topic that they think they want to discuss and then discovers through the conversation that there is even a more important topic coming to the forefront. If someone brings what appears to be multiple topics, then together you will determine which topic to deal with first, or how all the topics possibly fit into a broader topic, like how best to deal with highly demanding parents, or ways to better balance work and home schedules. This is such an important point. It often takes a little time to get clear on what is the most important topic to talk about in the time you have together. That is why in a coaching conversation we might explore the topic some before we settle on the actual topic for the conversation.

Outcomes and Measures of Success

Many times we move into a conversation and never clearly articulate the desired outcome for the conversation. We just keep talking until time is up. Typically, before getting to an agreed-upon outcome, there is a time for exploration around the topic to be clear on what is really desired as a result of the conversation. Exploration is a critical component of a coaching conversation.

- **Example:** "Jane, while I asked for this meeting, what do you think will be the most productive outcome for our conversation today?"
- **Example:** "Mr. and Mrs. Smith, as we all understand the intent of this meeting, and we've had an opportunity to share some opening thoughts regarding Johnny, let's determine together what will be the most important outcome or outcomes for us today. I have some options to offer, and I'm also interested to hear what you would like to have as a result of this meeting."

- **Example:** "Jim, you said that you wanted to talk about a situation that has arisen between you and a fellow teacher. Please share what is most critical about this situation for you so that I quickly understand the real concern here and understand why it is the most important topic for us to focus on today." (Jim begins to talk. You listen and use your other valuable coaching skills. Then, you ask for the conversation outcome.) "Jim, to best support you as we continue to talk, what would you like to have by the time we end this conversation?" (Jim might say that he wants clarity on how to move forward. We then ask for a measure of success.) "Jim, how will we both know that you have more clarity by the time we end this conversation?" Jim will offer his own measurement of success (it might be a couple of ideas about next steps; it could be a way to begin a conversation with a coworker). When Jim brings the topic, Jim also determines what he wants for an outcome and a measure of success. We might offer other possibilities, but Jim makes the final decision.

Coaching for Desired Results

You see this portion of the conversation represented with the symbol of sparks and insight which can happen anytime during the conversation. We sometimes call this *deep dancing*. It's in deep dancing that we use coaching processes and competencies to expand thinking, create new insights, and ignite energy for actions, while always staying focused on the desired conversation outcome and measure of success for that outcome. We also check at varying points during the conversation to make sure we are moving in the right direction or the best way to accomplish the conversation outcome. And, yes, at times there may very well be a change in outcome based on new agreements for both the outcome and the measure of success.

Exiting the Conversation

Agreements

As the agreed-upon time begins to come to a close, we should return to the outcome agreements and measures of success and check in on how we did.

- **Example:** "Jane, how did we do on reaching the outcome that you desired for this meeting?"
- **Example:** "Mr. and Mrs. Smith, when we began we agreed to discuss both Johnny's celebrations and to determine ways in which we will work together to continue to motivate and inspire him to reach new challenges. How do you think we did on reaching that outcome?" (Parents talk, and we may add comments as well.)

- **Example:** "Jim, when we began, you said that you wanted to have greater clarity on how best to move forward. What is clearer for you now?" (Jim shares.) "How did we do on reaching your measure of success?" (Jim shares.)

Next Steps

This is the portion of the conversation where we agree on actions to be taken as a result of the conversation. In an authentic coaching conversation, the person being coached determines the next steps they want to take, including any support or resources they desire.

- **Example:** "Jane, as a result of this meeting, what are you already considering to be your next steps related to possible actions you would like to take?" And "When shall we meet again to continue our dialogue about this important topic?"
- **Example:** "Mr. and Mrs. Smith, what follow-up actions would you like to offer on your behalf? We offer these follow-up steps on our part." Also, "How would you suggest we stay connected in support of Johnny?" (We give the parent an opportunity to offer suggestions, and we also offer a few follow-up suggestions.)
- **Example:** "Jim, what do you think you want to do next as a result of this conversation?" (Jim will respond.) An additional question might be, "What, if anything, do you think you may need to move forward in the way you intend?" And because we know that follow-up is critical, we might say, "When we next talk, I'll look forward to hearing how you are moving toward what you really want in this situation."

We believe that the more leaders practice using the components of the RCG Coaching Conversation Frame, the greater the capacity for results and deeper relationships. We also believe that this format works well with most any conversation, whether colleague to colleague, supervisor to employee, teacher to student, parent to child, or educator to parent.

As educators who have spent many years in leadership roles, we do know that the time comes when leaders are called to hold a difficult conversation. And because we have committed to deep lasting change, we desire to give time, attention, repetition, and positive feedback in our conversations throughout the year. We have learned that by regularly holding productive conversations, we are much more equipped to navigate a tough conversation when the time comes.

After much thought and consideration, we have created an RCG Difficult Conversation Frame to support leaders during those difficult conversations. It is no coincidence that this frame follows the same format as our first Conversation Frame and includes the majority of components. Let's take a closer look.

DIFFICULT CONVERSATION FRAME

Figure 5.2   RCG Difficult Conversation Frame

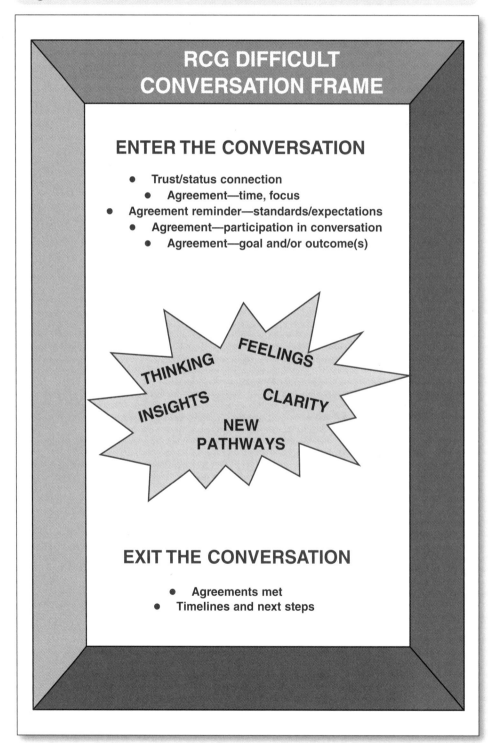

COACHING FRAME

THINKING · FEELINGS · INSIGHTS · CLARITY · NEW PATHWAYS

SAMPLE LANGUAGE

QUADRANT I—DIRECTIVE

- You came into this profession to make a difference. You were hired because of your knowledge, skills, and/or tools—which are . . .
- The expectations of the position have been articulated to be . . .
- The urgency of your actions is . . .
- It is immediately critical to see the following . . .
- Some evidence of it would look like . . .
- Your timeline for it is . . .
- On a scale of 1–10, what is your commitment to this goal/action/timeline?
- I look forward to your success and reviewing your evidence on . . .

QUADRANT II—COLLABORATIVE/COACHING

- Your energy and commitment to your work are evident.
- This conversation is just to review and revisit the standards/ expectations that will be so important to your success in the position.
- How are you assessing your success? What evidence are you noticing?
- What do you want to be celebrating about this in a couple of weeks?

QUADRANT III—COACHING w/specific follow-up timelines

- You came into this profession to make a difference and have been doing that for many years. Your years of service are . . . Your knowledge, skills, or gifts are . . .
- You are very aware of the huge accountability changes in our profession and the expectations that we face today; you are very aware of the standards we are held to; you have been at this long enough that you know . . .
- As you think about this requirement, what comes to mind as your best strategies or moves? How are you hoping to put this into action?
- With your knowledge and expertise, what will guide your self-assessment of your progress?
- Let's talk again in 10 days so you can share what you are seeing and how it has impacted your results.
- So your understanding of your focus and work is . . .?

QUADRANT IV—SELF DIRECTED—COACHING

An important theme throughout this book has been that relationships matter, and as leaders we deepen relationships as we intentionally give our time and ourselves to conversations with those we lead. At the heart of work-related conversations is a desire to grow forward together in accomplishing the goals with which we have been charged to undertake. We have all signed a contract, which represents our written commitment, to fulfill the specific expectations related to our jobs. As leaders, we have a responsibility to support purposefully ways for the entire team to never lose sight of who we are, individually and as a team, and what we are charged to do. We are best able to achieve this goal when we move together toward, rather than away from, our desired results.

With this in mind, leaders commit to having ongoing conversations with staff members, both in a team setting and as individuals. It's not enough to meet with multiple people at a time. While this is one important way to build relationships and increase clarity around specific expectations and initiatives, nothing takes the place of private meetings with the leader.

When we consistently hold conversations with our staff members, be it a quick 5-minute conversation as we walk together or one that takes much more time, and are intentional about providing ongoing and specific communications and feedback, we lessen the number of those difficult conversations we are called to have. After all, we don't want our first conversation to be a difficult one.

Let's say that you have held numerous conversations with a teacher, and yet you have a growing concern as you observe her teaching or interacting with others. Because you are a dedicated and committed leader, you have data that inform you and support your decision to have a more direct conversation to discuss areas that are in need of improvement.

Many times, this is where a coach leader may very well have a coaching conversation with his or her own coach prior to holding the conversation with the teacher. One sign of a high-performing leader is that he or she is very thoughtful about how they best want to plan for and conduct a difficult conversation, and how they want to *be* (meaning specific attitudes and behaviors) as they move through the conversation. For example, "I want to stay calm and listen with an open mind, using language that is respectful to the person/s and specific to the situation." In fact, this may be the best time to remind us of one critical way that leaders succeed or fail in their jobs. It has to do with their interpersonal skills or emotional intelligence and the way they work with others—or perhaps in some cases, the way they do not work with others. As Goleman tells us in Scott's book (2009), "As a leader moves up in an organization, up to 90 percent of their success lies in emotional intelligence." Scott goes on to say, "Nine out of ten executives who derail do so because they lack emotional competencies! The three primary causes of derailment are difficulty handling change, not being able to work well in a team, and poor interpersonal relations" (p. 77).

Personally speaking, through our work as school leaders and as professional certified coaches through the International Coach Federation, we know the value of thinking first before holding a difficult conversation. We offer five guiding questions for leaders to consider as thinking prompts in preparation for these meetings.

FIVE KEY QUESTIONS TO CONSIDER BEFORE HOLDING A DIFFICULT CONVERSATION

1. What is the key focus or concern to be discussed during the conversation?
2. How have standards and expectations connected to this concern been previously articulated to the person?
3. What is the desired outcome for the conversation?
4. How involved would you like the other person to be in thinking through solutions to the concern? (Remembering that coaching and collaboration work best with Glickman's Quadrants II-III-IV staff.)
5. Knowing that you are committed to your role as a coach leader, what will you intentionally do and how will you *be* during this conversation?

Because you have spent dedicated time using the RCG Coaching Conversation Frame, the questions above make much more sense to you and you understand the value of getting clear about the key focus or concern to be discussed during the conversation. It can take patience and time to get to the heart of the concern.

Here is an example of one such concern that comes from our experience coaching a principal whom we will call Tim. It took at least 15 minutes of conversation with a coach for Tim to get to the heart of his concern and how he wanted to best move forward with his conversation with Jane.

Example

Jane is a middle school social studies teacher with 16 years of experience. She uses a traditional teaching approach, lecturing to students sitting in straight rows, taking notes, and responding to questions posed by her. Student results on the first benchmark testing indicate that 75% of her students demonstrate a basic understanding of the concepts measured, and yet the principal, Tim, believes with increased levels of active student engagement, stronger results are obtainable. Tim believes Jane has the ability to make the needed instructional adjustments and feels it's time to openly face the current situation in an honest and collaborative dialogue, while using the skills and mindset of a coach leader.

Tim's biggest concern is how to begin the conversation so that Jane does not feel attacked or reprimanded. He does not want Jane to shut down or become guarded in expressing her true thoughts and feelings. Tim wants to provide a space where Jane will openly share what's keeping her from aligning her teaching methods with those specifically listed in the state and district teaching standards and expressed in staff meetings as an expectation by Tim. He also wants the two of them to think together about ways for Jane to begin the process of moving toward alignment with the student engagement standards and expectations. This is Tim's first year as principal at the school, and it is now the 7th week of school.

Tim works with a RCG leadership coach and has created a plan for how best to move through the conversation he will have with Jane. Tim thinks that Jane most likely is a Quadrant III teacher based on the Glickman Supervision Model. He believes that Jane knows how to make the required instructional changes and yet is holding on to the more traditional approaches for reasons he doesn't understand.

Tim:　"Hello Jane. Thank you for coming. Let's sit over here where we can both be comfortable. We have about 20 minutes today of uninterrupted time, and I'm looking forward to spending this time with you." **(Trust connection, time agreement)**

Jane:　"Thanks, Tim." **(Jane is scanning for safety.)**

Tim:　"Jane, as I mentioned when we talked briefly yesterday, the focus of our conversation today is for you to share how you are feeling about the new instructional requirements that have begun this year, specifically as it relates to active student engagement. Something is holding you back from beginning to make some of the changes, and I want to understand what that might be so that together we can figure out how to move forward in the best way possible. It's a given that you are a dedicated teacher who cares strongly for your students and this school. I sincerely thank you for that. It's also a given that the expectations for student engagement have shifted from a heavier emphasis on a teacher lecture mode to one where students are expected to be more actively engaged in the learning to learn, retain, and apply the learning in other situations." **(Conversation focus, why important)**

"While I'm bringing the topic for our conversation, I want this to be a time when we can have a thoughtful conversation where we both agree to speak what is on our minds and listen with the intent to understand. How does that sound to you?" **(Asking for agreement about the conversation focus)**

Jane:　"Ok. And thanks for taking the time for us to talk in private. I do appreciate that fact that you are giving me an opportunity to share where I'm coming from about moving away from a method of teaching that has served me well for over 15 years." **(Agreement)**

Tim: "Great! I'm interested to hear. I'd also like to go ahead and identify the outcome for this meeting. How does that sound to you?" **(Agreement on outcome)**

Jane: "Sure. What will that be?"

Tim: "One outcome is for us to come to an agreement on the first two or three steps that you want to take to move toward more student involvement in the learning. How does that sound?" **(Agreement on measures of success)**

Jane: "Ok. I agree."

Tim: "What else would you like for an outcome of this meeting?"

Jane: "I'm good with this. I have a few things that are bothering me about this new requirement. If I can get that off my mind then I think I can be open to some ways to move forward."

Tim: "Knowing that we have about 15 minutes left, Jane, where would you like to start?"

Jane: "Well, why don't I just share what's on my mind as it relates to some of these new requirements." **(Agreement. Even in this situation, Tim is giving Jane autonomy on how she wants to start.)**

Tim: "Great. I'm ready to listen."

Jane talks for about 7 minutes while Tim listens, paraphrases, and asks a few questions. The essence of what Jane says is that she is really struggling to make the instructional changes. She has taught the content for over 10 years and knows it by heart. She has an ill husband at home and knows that to make some of the changes expected, it will take more time for planning, and she's not sure that she has the extra time to give.

Tim listens, expresses empathy for Jane's situation.

Tim: "This is a hard time for you, Jane. You have lots of expectations on your time both at home and at school. It feels a little like you are being pulled at both ends." Jane agrees. **(Tim offers empathy for Jane's situation.)**

Tim: "Jane, it also sounds like you are very open to moving forward with the expected instructional changes and are looking for the best way to handle the planning portion of your teaching so that you don't have to spend untold hours on it." **(Tim stays focused on what is expected for Jane as she moves forward. He does this in a nonthreatening, yet forward-moving way.)**

Jane: "Yes. I know I have to make some changes, and I don't want to quit my job. I love this school and the work. I just have to figure out a way to balance my responsibilities at home and at work so I have more time to spend on planning."

Tim: "Absolutely. What are you already thinking about some of the easiest ways to begin the process of moving forward?" (**Solution focused**)

As the conversation progresses, Jane decides that she would like to begin by having a conversation with her team. She knows that they have moved away from straight rows, and she wants to understand what strategies they use for student grouping that engages the students in the learning and not just in idle chit-chatting. Jane says she will talk with her team later that day. The next thing that Jane decides she wants to do is to take a current lesson and create a section of the lesson where students, working in partners, create a current connection to the historical concept. She says she'll think through the details tonight at home and have it ready to share with the class tomorrow. It is evident that Jane had turned a corner and is thinking on her own about new ways to actively engage the students. (**Jane is creating actions around what is expected and is given autonomy in the choices she decides. If Tim were not in agreement with the actions, he would ask for greater specificity.**)

Tim: "Jane, thank you for your willingness to talk about this and for the energy that is sparking from your own creativity. As you plan, you'll remember that we have other resources to help you with this, including our own instructional guides that provide suggestions for student engagement. It will be interesting to see how you find these resources helpful and what new ideas you come up with on your own. I'd like to drop by next week to see your efforts in action. I can come by any day next week. Which day and which class would you prefer I visit?" (**Next steps**)

Jane: "Let's make it on Wednesday. That will give us time to get some of the routines down. And come by any time. Thanks, Tim. I've been dragging my feet, and this has given me the energy to move forward."

Tim: "Thank you, Jane, for your honesty and your commitment to your work. I'm looking forward to our next conversation when we are celebrating your success with the new teaching methods. As we begin to end our conversation for today, how do you think we did on reaching our outcomes?" (**Outcome agreement**)

Jane: "I think we did great. I'm walking away with four new steps: (1) Talk with my team about collaborative grouping strategies that are working for them, (2) reorganize my classroom so that the students are working in groups and not sitting in straight rows, (3) create a partner activity for students that connects history with current happenings, and (4) I'm going to take a look at the online curriculum resource guide to see what activities they have for student engagement." **(Measure of success)**

Tim: "I look forward to visiting your class next Wednesday. Your willingness to make these changes in your instructional methods has the potential to excel the learning of your students and speaks volumes about your dedication to your job. Thanks for your time today, Jane."

Most likely, Jane came into the meeting having slipped into a Quadrant III teacher profile (see Chapter 4) and will hopefully now begin to move back over into the Quadrant IV teacher that she really is. And we all understand that this conversation is not the only conversation the two will have. Remember, they agreed to meet again for Jane to share her progress. This is important for us to remember. Follow-up is critical. When there is a concern and decisions are made about next steps, it is up to the leader to meet his or her commitments just as it is expected that the teacher meet his or her commitments.

What if Tim had not handled this conversation in the thoughtful way that he did? In what ways might this conversation have had an entirely different feel and result if Tim had come down hard like a hammer? It's possible that he might have lost a beautiful and powerful nail that holds an entire portion of the building together.

Meeting With a Teacher
Where There Is a Critical Concern

Here is another example of a difficult conversation where the stakes are even higher. There is a critical concern, and this principal has very thoughtfully prepared to address the major issues in a respectful and direct manner. In this conversation the principal will do more talking and offer fewer options to the teacher. However, we will see clearly how the principal shows up with a professional attitude of respect, using coach-like behaviors as much as possible. Clearly this is a Quadrant I teacher who is in need of immediate improvements. This example, as with the first one, is based on an actual event.

In developing this format, we called on key components from the RCG Conversation Frame, our experience as coaches and school leaders, thoughts from organizational psychologist Dr. David G. Javitch (2009), as well as what we have learned from Susan Scott (2009) in *Fierce Conversations*.

CONVERSATIONS WHEN THERE IS A CRITICAL CONCERN

Example

Enter the conversation.	"Thank you for coming in today, Barbara. Let's sit here at the table where we can both take some notes as we talk." **(Trust connection)**
	"It's evident that you came into this position to make a difference and you were selected because of your skills, prior knowledge, and your expressed commitment to serve the students of this school and our district. How accurate is my description?" **(Listens as the teacher responds. Is prepared to interrupt if the teacher gets off topic or talks too long.)**
	"We are now at a place where there are some specific concerns about your job performance here at our school. What is clear to you about your current status with your job performance?" **(The principal listens and offers a paraphrase that shows he understands both the teacher's perspective and her feelings. Again, this is done in a timely manner.)**
State the purpose of the meeting.	"The purpose of our meeting today is for me to share with you concerns that I have regarding your job performance and for us to determine a plan of action for moving forward to ensure increased results in your performance and in student results. We will know that we have succeeded when we have a written plan that we both agree to." **(Meeting outcome with success measure)** Teacher nods in agreement and says she understands.
	"We have scheduled 45 minutes for this meeting and that will give us ample time to reach our outcome. If we both decide that we need to take more time, I'm prepared to stay a bit longer and I would ask the same of you." The teacher agrees to the time frame. **(Time agreement)**
State the concern in a concise manner. Base what you say on data and be specific. State it as what *is* rather than what it *should be*.	"First of all, Barbara, it is important for you to know that I believe that you have the ability to rectify the concerns, if you are willing to put forth the time and effort required. "The major concern is about the level of performance of the students in your classroom. The overall benchmark scores of fifth-grade science students that you teach are running 20% below those of students taught by the other science teachers in our school." (The school has three science teachers in fifth grade, and all groups are of even distribution of abilities.)

	"While your lesson plans represent engaging lessons that address the science objectives for your grade level, your students are not retaining the content as indicated on results from the benchmark assessments. "Data seem to reveal that this discrepancy has to do with the way in which you personally interact with your students. As I have observed, in and out of the classroom, you are often curt with the students; you use an argumentative tone, and you appear to have little personal connection with them. Your language indicates a low level of belief in your students' ability to learn at high levels. "For example, last week as I walked past your classroom, I heard you call out in a loud tone, 'Marcus! You will never learn this! Sit down and stop talking!' "And, as you know, we have met before about five separate complaints I have received from parents who voiced concerns about the demeaning way in which you talk to their children." If the teacher begins to interrupt, the principal is prepared to stop the interruption. It could sound like this: "Barbara, please stop and listen carefully to what I'm saying. You will have an opportunity to talk in a few moments, and I will listen to you. Right now is your time to listen."
State what is at risk if nothing changes.	"If nothing changes, and we continue to see both a gap in your student benchmark results as measured against results of other fifth-grade science classes at our school and if there is no improved evidence that you interact with your students in a respectful and caring way, your continued work at our school and within our district is at risk. "Your lack of response will be conveying that you do not share the beliefs and goals of our school. It will also indicate that you are thinking this is not where you want to work and you are ready to consider possible options in and outside our district."
State what is expected to change and by when.	"Here is what I expect to see changed beginning now and until spring break, understanding big changes happen over time. 1. Continued lesson plans that demonstrate your compliance with the written lesson plan expectations for our school. This is an area that you already do at a high level.

(Continued)

(Continued)

	2. Specific ways in which you are working to build personal relationships with the students and their parents that represent high levels of professionalism, as described in the district handbook, and personal regard for each student in your classroom. 3. Comments from parents and students that indicate students are enjoying learning in your classroom. 4. Increased benchmark scores on future benchmark assessments that indicate student growth at a rate similar to other classes."
Ask the employee how they would best like to resolve the concern.	"You do have input into the best way for us to resolve this concern. How are you thinking you want to work to resolve these expectations?" Teacher voices language that she wants to get results and also offers excuses and barriers that prevent her from possibly doing the things expected. Principal responds: "When you began your work here you agreed to the goals and beliefs of our school and were willing to grow and learn to have great results and strong relationships. Nothing has changed, and you have the ability to make it happen."

Develop the improvement plan.	"Now, let's develop your improvement plan together. I have some points that will be included in the plan, and you are invited to put what you want included in the plan.
	
	Here are my key points:
	
	1. You will create specific strategies for providing personal regard to your students and share those strategies with me in scheduled meetings held twice a month.
	
	    a. Personal regard strategy/focus
	    b. Impact on student learning and behaviors
	    c. Data to support growth in this area
	
	2. You will read the RCG article on trust, "Building Trusting Relationships in School," and share key insights with me in our twice-monthly meetings.
	3. You will develop a method for communicating with parents to share both student success and challenges."
	
	The teacher agrees and also lists key points she would like included in the improvement plan.

	"Key points you would like to include: 1. You will visit two other classrooms that will be determined jointly by the two of us to observe ways in which other teachers present content and learning experiences in such a way that students are actively engaged and demonstrate enjoyment in the learning. 2. You will meet with the school counselor to gain knowledge on ways to meet the emotional needs of fifth-grade students and identify specific strategies you will implement from your learning."
Ask the employee to state back the determined steps of action with due dates.	"We have created a plan with five steps. To ensure clarity, please review and state your understanding of what is expected of you and by what dates." **(Outcome agreements and success measures)**
Schedule next meeting where employee brings proof of accomplishments.	"Let's schedule our next meeting where you will have the opportunity to outline your successes and how you are fulfilling the requirements of this plan. "Let's schedule for 2 weeks from today. In the meantime, feel free to provide ongoing updates via email or notes." **(Next steps)**

SUMMARY

From reading this book so far, it should be evident that leadership for this century requires the confidence, competence, and courage to continually lead through conversations. Conversations about the daily focus of the work and conversations about the challenges of the work influence positively the best in results for all—students, teachers, staff, and leaders at all levels of the organization.

Recently in a webinar by the NeuroLeadership Institute, David Rock (2016) said that the focus of leadership development is to transform the quality of conversations. Wow, that takes us right back to another favorite *Fierce Leadership* quote by Susan Scott. Memo to leaders: "Your central function is to engineer intelligent, spirited conversations that provide the basis for high levels of alignment, collaboration, and partnership at all levels throughout your organization and the healthier outcomes that go with them" (p. 5).

When our view of leadership is focused on our ability to influence and inspire the best from others, to grow others' talents and abilities to be the best they can be, we believe educational organizations can be transformed. It begins with the confidence and skill to have conversations to that end.

The vast majority of people who enter the profession of education are committed to a deep purpose of educating and supporting kids to grow and become tomorrow's productive citizens. How leaders talk and engage in everyday conversations, full of belief in others, holds the potential to keep teachers in the field and grow the next level of leaders. It's all about the conversation! *And it's important to remember, not every conversation is a coaching conversation. But every conversation offers the opportunity to use the powerful skills of coaching.*

REFERENCES

Heatherton, T. F. (2011). Neuroscience of self and self-regulation. *Annual Review of Psychology, 62*, 363–390 (p. 1).

Javitch, D. G. (2009, May). Five steps to deal with difficult employees. *Entrepreneur.* Retrieved from http://www.entrepreneur.com/article/201950#ixzz2rpF71Efx

Rock, D. (2011, May). The conversation is over. Long live the conversation. *Harvard Business Review.* Retrieved from https://hbr.org/2011/05/the-conversation-is-over-long

Rock, D. (2015, May). How neuroscience can aid collaborative leadership. *Ideas for Leaders, 473.* Retrieved from https://www.ideasforleaders.com/ideas/how-neuroscience-can-aid-collaborative-leadership

Rock, D. (2016, January). Rethink your leadership development strategy. Retrieved from https://neuroleadership.com/rethink-ld/

Scott, S. (2009). *Fierce leadership: A bold alternative to the worst "best" practices of business today.* New York, NY: Broadway Business Press.

6

Creating a Coaching Culture

School culture is an incredibly powerful but often invisible force that shapes a school community's work. It is more powerful than new ideas and innovative practices.

Dennis Sparks (2015)

This chapter answers three questions. WHY is a coaching culture of critical importance in this century? WHAT exactly is a coaching culture? And HOW does one make it a reality? We believe coaching is the leverage for transformation of the culture of a school or district, and we hold significant evidence of the *power of one* as the impetus for beginning that change.

WHY is a coaching culture of critical importance in this century?

We are increasingly aware that telling others what to do, how to do it, who to do it with, and when it must be done has never worked especially well. This top-down model omits the motivating force of autonomy and the individual efficacy of thinking people. We see example after example in the literature and research of many of the very brightest and best leaving the education profession because their ideas are not heard and valued (see Chapter 1, pp. 20–21, on teacher engagement).

WHAT exactly is a coaching culture?

A coaching culture is one that is based on the growth mindset. Rather than focusing on the past and a blaming culture, the focus is on the present and future. No excuses. Learn from the past, take forward the strengths and successes, and continue moving forward. Leaders provide a model of accountability while holding others able to perform their various and individual job responsibilities. Taking risks and being vulnerable are valued, while perfectionism and shame are pushed aside to make room for flexible thinking and experimentation. When this support is provided, individuals develop confidence and the willingness to push past restraints that block their willingness to be bold.

HOW does one make it a reality?

We believe coaching is the leverage for transformation of the culture of a school or district and we hold significant evidence of the power of one as the impetus for beginning that change. Margaret Mead famously said, "Never ever depend on governments or institutions to solve any major problems. All social change comes from the passion of individuals" (www .interculturalstudies.org). And "never believe that a few caring people can't change the world. For, indeed, that's all who ever have." Cultural shift begins with one, then a small group, which ultimately reaches a tipping point for the larger group culture to change.

WHY IS A COACHING CULTURE OF CRITICAL IMPORTANCE?

In his blog called School Culture Matters, Dennis Sparks (2015) writes about the critical importance of attending to school culture when he states, "School culture is an incredibly powerful but often invisible force that shapes a school community's work. It is more powerful than new ideas and innovative practices. Administrators and teacher leaders who ignore school culture or underestimate its influence will almost certainly fail in improving teaching and learning for all students."

Benefits of a Coaching Culture

There are many benefits of developing and sustaining a coaching culture in schools as described by school leaders and our experience in the field. Employee engagement, high levels of performance, continuous growth and development, collaboration, resilience in the face of change, and the ability to lead through difficult situations are some of the benefits that are evident in coaching cultures.

New ways of leading are called for in our ever increasingly complex world. To move away from debating who or what is right or wrong, we are asked to think together. In *Collaborative Intelligence: Thinking With People Who Think Differently*, Markova and McArthur (2015) bring forth the idea of mind sharing, which essentially means that if you have an idea and I have an idea and we exchange them, we then each have two good ideas. In other words, the more we share, the more we have. Our capacity to generate, share, and enact ideas becomes most valuable. In this way, we learn to use influence with others rather than power over them. Mind sharing requires developing the capacity within ourselves to be influenced by others. This idea of being open to being influenced by others relates directly to the notion of the transformative mind being at the most complex level of human thinking (see Chapter 1, Socialized Mind, Self-Authoring Mind, and Transformative Mind). Mind sharing asks what is possible. Leadership becomes a verb—*to host*—rather than a noun—*the hero* (Markova & McArthur, 2015, p. 11).

In an earlier work, *Community: The Structure of Belonging*, Peter Block (2009) defines *leadership* as convening. He states, "In communal transformation, leadership is about intention, convening, valuing relatedness, and presenting choices. It is not a personality characteristic or a matter of style, and therefore it requires nothing more than what all of us already have" (p. 85). Leader is a capacity that can be learned by all of us. Leadership begins with an understanding that every gathering is an opportunity to deepen accountability and commitment through engagement. Each gathering serves two functions: to address its (the purpose of the gathering/meeting) stated purpose and to be an occasion for each person to decide to become engaged as its owner. The leader's task is to structure the place and experience of these occasions to move the culture toward shared ownership. "Engagement is the means through which there can be a shift in caring for the well-being of the whole, and the task of leader as convener is to produce that engagement" (p. 87).

Markova and McArthur (2015) and Block (2009) speak of the power of engagement through listening and sharing. When people's ideas are invited and valued, when others ask and care what we think, when the expectation is that each of us will contribute and will continue to grow our own knowledge and skills, and improve our thinking, the culture begins to shift. Accountability becomes an internal force for excellence rather than an external monitor that carries a punitive connotation.

Therefore, the answer to the question, "Is school and district culture really that important?" is a resounding "Yes . . . absolutely . . . without a doubt!" Many a school improvement goal has been focused on the improvement of the culture of a school. Whether you define *culture* as the learning environment, the morale of the school, or the symbols, rituals, and traditions of the school, its health and vibrancy have a direct impact on student performance.

Deal and Peterson (2009) say it this way, "A school culture influences the ways people think, feel, and act" (p. 7). Additionally, they say,

"Being able to understand and shape the culture is key to a school's success in promoting staff and student learning" (2002, p. 10).

One School's Story

Following is an illustration of how one middle school applied Kent's statement by deciding to intentionally reshape the culture of their school. While their mission and vision statements were written over 13 years ago, their school was growing and evolving in new and different ways. Their student population was changing. Tweaking the current statements was an option; however, they preferred to begin anew. As they engaged in a collaborative process, their hopes and dreams spilled out, filling the room with the hope and promise for a brighter future for themselves and their students. Their high standards for excellence were evident in their thinking and the language that aligned with it. The words, "WE WILL . . ." demonstrated their intention to hold themselves accountable to the ideas and concepts of the mission.

As the work evolved into action thinking, new ideas emerged for how they would move the new mission and vision out of the room into the lives of their colleagues, their parents, and most important, their students.

Through focused conversation with intentional listening, the leadership team created a strong root system addressing the reason this school exists in the first place. By practicing new ways of thinking and talking with one another, the invisible force of culture became explicit, exposing their underlying assumptions and beliefs. And through honest and open dialogue, the process moved from completion of a task to "heart work" where passion and inspiration could emerge.

Because the group had created a safe and secure place to be honest and authentic, several people shared that they began the day thinking the work was going to be too difficult because of the diversity and strong opinions held by the group. Instead, they found commonality by surfacing what they cared deeply about—a river of passion and shared commitment to their students' success.

With their core values explicit in the new mission and vision, their work is now about creating the conditions to ensure their success. No doubt it is happening!

Witness the emergence of a coaching culture from this one event. With norms or working agreements in place about how this group wanted to work with one another, they chose full presence for all points of view, a focus on students, presumption of positive intent, suspension of judgment, and a commitment to live in options and possibilities for the future. Admittedly, they acknowledged the power of the work, the connectedness they felt as well as the energy they generated for the actions they designed.

In Chapter 1, we spoke about the concept of "what got us here won't get us there." Today the standards and expectations for how we work are different. We work with other adults to achieve the performance outcomes we have for our students. As stated in Chapter 1, a different set of skills or competencies are required for our work with adults. Where did we learn these skills? For most of us, the answer is "never" or "not at all," unless we have had the good fortune to attend a seminar on developing our interpersonal skill set. You tell us regularly that you wish you had learned about the mindset and skills of coaching earlier in your journey as an educator.

As we coach teams, it is evident within the first few minutes what is important in their culture. It is clear if they have been exposed to and practice the skills of coaching, including committed listening, paraphrasing to understand, and a mindset of positive intent. Their questions to one another demonstrate high emotional intelligence, and they offer feedback that shows value or value potential and questions that provoke thinking and support future action. More important, the focus of their work is student centered and what they can do to ensure student success.

WHAT ARE THE CHARACTERISTICS OF A COACHING CULTURE?

A coaching culture exists in organizational settings in which formal and informal coaching occurs. The standard is that most or at least a large segment of individuals in the organization practice coaching behaviors as a means of relating to, supporting, and influencing each other. Coaching cultures exhibit all or most of the following characteristics:

- Internal coaching
- External coaching
- Expectations for consistent presence of coach leader mindset and behaviors
- Relating, supporting, and influencing each other
- Employee engagement and retention

The International Coach Federation (ICF) in partnership with Human Capital Institutes: The Global Association for Strategic Talent Management (HCI) conducted research studies in 2014 and 2015 on the topic of developing a coaching culture (Filipkowski, 2014, 2015).

HCI found more and more organizations have recognized the value in building a culture of coaching that offers employees at all levels—not just executives and managers—the opportunity to grow their skills, enhance their value, and reach their professional goals. Additionally, it was found that not all coaching is equal: Variation in styles and approaches to coaching impact its effectiveness and results. To ensure successful results that go beyond skills training and truly enable the company to increase employee engagement and retention, the organization must develop a comprehensive and cohesive coaching plan that addresses both current and future needs. The challenge arises not only in determining the types of coaching that will be most impactful, but also in attaining the internal buy-in and support for the mindset and skills to be promoted by the organization.

Organizations continue to seek coaches who exude necessary qualities, such as listening actively, establishing trust, and maintaining high professional standards. Additionally, organizations must ensure that internal and external coaches, as well as leaders using coaching skills, have received the appropriate amount of training and are integrating skills in their leadership activities. The company must also actively evaluate the coaching initiative to determine its return on effectiveness (ROE) and return on investment (ROI) to maintain continued support and funding.

Our work in schools affirms the presence of a coaching mindset, which holds that individuals have their own answers within. Additionally, there is a recognition that offering advice sends a message that they don't know what to do and must be directed. People are at various levels of knowledge and experience and have differing needs (see Chapter 4). In professional education settings, around 95% of people need and prefer coaching as a way of interacting with peers and leaders. Coaching, first of all, requires committed listening. Listening is confirmed through powerful paraphrasing. Clarifying and reflective questions based on what is heard continue to sharpen thinking. Feedback is essential to growth and change and must be offered with the intent to foster growth and received without threat. These essential skills of coaching, whether practiced with individuals, teams, groups, or entire faculties support the development of a coaching culture. When people know that they will be heard, understood, supported, and challenged, they are free to collaborate and initiate without competition or fear.

As we compare our work in schools to the studies cited above, our experiences and stories that follow corroborate the elements found in the research studies conducted by the ICF and HCI. Coaching is offered at many levels, not just the top leadership. Not all coaching is equal. Results of coaching initiatives are impacted by variations in approaches. Because coaching is relatively unregulated as of now, anyone may call himself or herself a coach and may engage in activities not supported by the same definition or concept of the word "coaching." Many coaches in education are experts in a teaching field, content, or in pedagogy or curriculum and wear the label "coach" without having any training or expertise in the mindset and skill of coaching. Because of differing definitions, coaches, coaching, and the impact of coaching may be inconsistent from school to school.

HOW DOES ONE CREATE A COACHING CULTURE?

The understanding of why a coaching culture is desirable and what defines or describes a coaching culture leads to the next step. How are coaching cultures intentionally created? We combine the work of Scott Peck's (2003) stages of community, Bryk and Schneider's (2002) research on trust in schools, and our work in developing coach leadership to provide a potential framework for developing true communities. We also offer real-world examples of how individual coach leaders have created coaching cultures in their schools, districts, and departments.

Understanding how groups evolve and grow supports our efforts to create a culture for coaching. Creating healthy subsets such as grade levels or departments in schools holds the potential for health in the larger context. While there are a number of models that describe group dynamics as they work to achieve higher levels of performance, our work has been influenced by the descriptions from Scott Peck's book (2003), *The Road Less Traveled*. He offers, without judgment, these stages of group development or stages of community.

Pseudo

When asked, seminar learners offer synonyms such as *false*, *fake*, or *surface* for this stage of community. True, and we also acknowledge it as a necessary first step for knowing one another, which is an invitation for trust to enter the relationship. It's difficult for me to trust you when I do not know you. This shows up in our work with large schools when we discover that people in one hall acknowledge they do not know teachers in another hall. Hard to trust. And we know how important trust is to our best performance. Findings from Bryk and Schneider's (2002) *Trust in Schools* taught us that schools with high levels of trust have high levels of performance and schools with low levels of trust have low levels of performance. Trust matters!

So knowing *you*, the human *you*, is a way to ensure trust is high so that our relationship can survive any withdrawals of trust when we have competing points of view. This stage is also referred to as the *cocktail effect*, similar to the way we might converse at a cocktail party. "Hi, how are you? How is your family?"

In schools, this stage is especially evident when there has been a break. For example, when teachers return from the summer break, you hear things such as, "How was your summer?" "Where did you go for vacation?" "What great books did you read?" Again, this necessary stage says, "I see you; I care about you."

All it takes to move to the next stage of community is an innocent question from a new staff member such as, "Now, why do we do it this way?"

You can feel the slight push, which begins to rock the boat. Most of us would not even react to this question—we would see it as a quest to know more. However, those who are deeply invested in "why we do it this way" may take exception, puff up their chest a bit, and reply, "Well, let me tell you why we do it this way."

Remember conflict, in and of itself, is not a bad thing. The inability to resolve conflict is the bad thing. And this is what we have learned: Most teams are not equipped to navigate the conflict that naturally bubbles up in our work. The question is not, "Is conflict going to show up?"; it's "When is conflict going to show up?"

Chaos

Some of you say, "This is not a stage I want to experience." Yes, it is. When we reframe this as a team looking to make changes, to move, to get out of the box, the stage takes on a different look—a desirable one. Let's resume our metaphor of a rocking boat. When we ask you what people want to do when a boat starts rocking, here are your responses.

- Jump off the boat—While this response may not be a literal description of what happens, it does describe metaphorically what team members may do. They may check out: i.e., body is present; mind is not. When a staff member is not fully present for the team's process of thinking and decision making, the full potential of the team is compromised.
- Rock the boat even more—For some, this is an exciting move because staff members may sense the team is trying to move, to go where they have never gone before. Without skillful intention on the part of the team to stay the course, excitement can easily be replaced with frustration and withdrawal (jumping off the boat).
- Stabilize the boat—Stabilizing quiets the rough waters by returning the group to pseudo or "nicey nice." We get back to a safe place; however, the price we pay is extremely dangerous because it only temporarily brings a state of calmness. It is a given our boat will start rocking again. When this happens, an insidious cycle can occur: pseudo—chaos—pseudo—chaos, which equals *burnout* because we are unable to push through to the next level of community.

A team in the chaos cycle may benefit from outside support from someone who teaches or equips the team with knowledge, skills, tools, and strategies for advancing to the next stage. Peck (2003) reminds us that we cannot force a team from one stage to another; we can only invite. Further, he says a team entrenched in the cycle or pattern of back and forth, back and forth, may not hear the first invitation. Patience is a virtue!

A coach leader possesses knowledge and skills learned in our seminars that may provide the leverage for assisting a team's advancement. Certainly, SCARF and TARP are at the top of the list. Knowing how to apply the principles learned from neuroscience can enable coach leaders to normalize that chaos is a desired stage of transition from where a team is currently compared to where they want to be. Committed listening and paraphrasing are essential skills for how a team demonstrates full presence to one another. The mindset of presuming positive intent holds the potential for greatly influencing the way a team works together. In the words of Kegan and Lahey (2009), "how we talk can change the way we work." And when we use that mindset to formulate our questions, we model for our colleagues that we believe in them to do their best. Finally, working agreements or norms are the hallmark of high-performing teams. High-performing teams not only have working agreements or norms, but they also hold themselves accountable for following them.

Emptying and Listening

The characteristics of this stage of community include full presence, full engagement, and an appreciation for differing points of view. We value collaboration and are attentive to feeding the health of our team. We check in personally before we begin our work. Our norms or working agreements are clear, including how we will handle conflict when it arises. We hold ourselves accountable to the norms, and we keep our promises to one another. We use protocols to ensure each person is heard. When searching for solutions, we often share without crosstalk so that each voice can be heard. At this stage, another characteristic is truth telling. We allow ourselves to be vulnerable to address the elephant in the room, saying what needs to be said knowing it is a safe place for the deeper conversation. In a grade-level or department meeting it might mean the vulnerability of a teacher, possibly a new one saying, "I'm not sure what that strategy looks like. Watching you would be helpful."

If you were the proverbial fly on the wall observing us work at this stage, you would see each person having the space to offer options or possibilities for the topic being addressed. It would appear as if there were a basket in the center of the table for collecting our ideas. After all have shared, you would observe us committing to one of the ideas as a focus for our upcoming action. When we resume, you would note how we share our results—one at a time—so that our next step can become clear. Once a team is here, it's very likely they will organically transition into a true community.

True Community

At this stage, we live and die together. We celebrate the highest highs and lowest lows. No one slips through the cracks—students or adults. We are intentional about ensuring the health of our team by practicing a check-in that is about us personally before we begin our work. In our sessions, when we ask you if you stay in this stage once you've arrived, you emphatically say, "No." You know it's like a good marriage requiring one's attention and daily deposit of personal regard. Those of us who have experienced the synergy and productivity of true community search for it in each and every team we join after that. The energy and motivation are undeniable, levels of trust are exceedingly high, and the work is fun and surpasses all expectations.

HOW INDIVIDUALS ARE CREATING COACHING CULTURES

The Power of One

Once upon a time there was a principal named Shannon who was introduced to coaching by her district. She immediately recognized its value and declared she would bring it to her elementary campus—first at a school in the Allen Independent School District (ISD) in the North Texas area and second at a school in East Central ISD near San Antonio, Texas. For her first step, she introduced coaching to her leadership team, which included herself, her assistant principal, two coaches, and a librarian. While the team had had some learning and exposure to coaching concepts and ideas, they self-reported that they still did not know *how* to coach. Shannon recognized there was a missing link because she had been coached for a number of years beyond her initial learning.

Year 1

Partnering with Results Coaching Global (RCG) over a year's time, the leadership team at Highland Forest Elementary continued their growth and development as coaches. Team commitment to the study and focus of the specifics of coaching language were evident as team members began the process of embedding the language in their daily work. Coincidentally, Shannon invited central office administrators to attend the sessions, which evolved into a district focus as well.

Year 2

In August of Year 1, the leadership team made a presentation to the faculty specifically to address these questions: "What is coaching? What does a coach do or not do? What does coaching look and sound like?" With that understanding in place, the leadership team felt comfortable beginning to coach individuals and teams of teachers on a regular basis. The leadership team continued their learning and internalization of coaching along with another elementary school. This school, Harmony Elementary School, also included their leadership team with the same composition as Shannon's school. The focus of study was deeper internalization of the art and science of coaching through coaching labs designed for observation and feedback to each coach on her coaching. Simultaneously, the district began to schedule regular opportunities for RCG to work with administrators in the district including coaches, principals, assistant principals, and central office personnel.

With a solid base of the competencies of coaching present in the behaviors of the campus leaders, Year 3 moved to full implementation of coaching conversations throughout the two campuses. Influenced by *Leverage Leadership* (Bambrick-Santoyo, 2012), the idea of weekly conversations with teachers other than the ones an administrator supervises was included in the process. This strategy supported the mindset that coaching is for everyone and was in opposition to the mindset that coaching is a deficit or fix-it mindset for those with a "problem, issue, or concern." It sent the message that coaching is for all who wish to improve and be the best they can be.

In addition, the leadership teams worked with grade levels on a regular basis. The role of the RCG coach morphed into a *meta coach* (external coach) who observed the team at work and offered feedback to them regarding their coaching in the moment.

In one school, the focus was grade-level planning. Each grade level rotated into the planning room to discuss each of the upcoming target objectives for every curricular area. Norms and working agreements, previously created by each grade level, were posted around the room. A process for establishing roles in the meeting (record keeper, facilitator, time keeper) was determined before the work began. At the end of the hour, another grade level entered the room to repeat the focus on the standards and expectations for teaching and learning for their grade level. Feedback was offered in two areas: on the process and on the coaching of teams.

In the second school, the focus was on individual teacher Response to Intervention (RTI) strategies. While each grade level had a specified time, teachers rotated into the planning room one at a time. Having used baseline data to identify the lowest 15% of students in the class, the focus of the coaching conversation was how teachers were advancing the progress of the identified students. Evidence of growth was presented, and plans for continued action were considered. Coaches paraphrased to demonstrate committed listening and asked questions that presumed positive intent while provoking thinking for future possibilities. The process continued teacher-by-teacher until all had shared his or her plan for supporting growth for high-needs students.

Year 3

The focus of the third year was continued growth through observation and feedback—one day at each school and a third day with both leadership teams together. In addition to continuation of the work with these two schools, the district secured 9 days for district work with coaching. Four of the days were devoted to ongoing work with administrators in the system, 2 days were specifically for campus-based coaches, and 3 days were for campus-based conversations with the leadership teams of *six new schools* that requested the option.

These two schools, Harmony and Highland Forest Elementary, showed improvement in reading and math, which surpassed both state requirements in all areas from 2014 to 2015. According to Shannon, "Coaching provided us the tools and language to be thinking partners with teachers and hold them able to do their best work with students."

Clearly, the vision of "one" has power potential for transforming a system. By working her sphere of influence, sharing her vision with others through invitation, and maintaining the focus over time, Shannon slowly, but surely, influenced the culture of her school and district. Now that she has moved from principal to curriculum director for the district, just imagine what is happening!

Figure 6.1 Third Grade Reading and Math Comparison Data (State Assessment in Texas)

			2014		2015	
			Percentage Met	Percentage Advanced	Percentage Met	Percentage Advanced
3rd Grade	Harmony	Reading	65	11	77	15
	Harmony	Reading Spanish	33	0	37	3
	Highland Forest	Reading	62	7	74	14
	Highland Forest	Reading Spanish	77	27	81	25
3rd Grade	Harmony	Math	63	11	78	14
	Harmony	Math Spanish	33	0	57	0
	Highland Forest	Math	45	4	72	6
	Highland Forest	Math Spanish	63	11	91	15

Used with permission of Shannon Fuller and Debbie Grams. Table created by Shannon Fuller and Debbie Grams using public domain data from the Texas Educations Agency STAAR Data (2015).

An Award-Winning Coaching Culture

The Lewisville Independent School District (LISD) was awarded the coveted PRISM award by the North Texas Chapter of the International Coach Federation in 2011. The PRISM distinction is granted to organizations that exhibit a strong coaching culture throughout the organization with data pointing to its success. This award is not specific to schools. Other nonprofit organizations vying for the PRISM award in 2011 included United Way of Dallas and Southwestern Medical School. LISD's recognition for this award was based on the areas of impact below that continue today.

Coaching and coach leaders are making an impact in these areas:

- Development of leadership capability
- Enhanced performance
- Confidence in ability to manage change
- Higher morale
- Focused solution-finding capability
- Increased satisfaction in personal lives
- Greater confidence in working and personal relationships
- Maximized effectiveness while meeting individual needs
- Increased retention with attrition attributed to advancement, retirement, or relocation

The work has surfaced implicit and explicit beliefs and assumptions:

- The "experts are among us"
- All stakeholders benefit from the enhanced communication prevalent in coach-like interactions
- Coaching supports results for students
- High-impact instruction provided by outstanding teachers is fostered through coaching
- Coaching aligns with the district's commitment to sustaining a learning organization
- Coaching supports innovation

LISD has been intentionally creating a coaching culture in the district since 2008. Through the vision and leadership of Dr. Beth Brockman, Assistant Superintendent of Strategic Initiatives and Community Engagement, the concept of coach leader continues to infiltrate LISD. (Dr. Brockman has received three promotions since 2008.) Superintendent Dr. Kevin Rogers supports the coaching culture from his leadership post and was promoted to superintendent from within LISD in May of 2015. LISD is implementing coaching at numerous levels across the organization—from superintendent, executive leadership team, central office administration, campus administration, teacher leaders, classroom teachers, instructional support coaches, data coaches, and instructional technology specialists at all levels. Since invitational training sessions are a part of the initiative, personnel from functions such as purchasing, technology, and parapro-fessionals are choosing to join the learning to further the coaching culture.

The mindset and skills of coach leader permeate all levels of the orga-nization as the communication and collaboration are transforming rela-tionships one person at a time, impacting small collaborative groups, such as professional learning communities (PLCs), system-wide departments, leadership teams, and so on.

What brings about this intentional creation of a coaching culture? For LISD, it is a focus on invitational learning experiences encompassing beginning, intermediate, and advanced levels. The expectations are that skills are applied at all levels and that leaders exhibit coach leader mindset and communication. A condition of promotion within or hiring from out-side the district is that leaders embody the coach leader identity.

LISD is on the cutting edge of a trend described by Jack Welch, former CEO of GE, who has reportedly said, "In the future, people who are not coaches will not be promoted. Managers who are coaches will be the norm" (see http://thinkingintegral.com/2014/06/28/weekend-thought-63/).

In LISD, promotion, retention, and hiring decisions are based on the experienced or emerging leader exhibiting the attitudes, characteristics, and skills of growing others. The district adheres to a standard of all principals, zone leaders and others in support positions receiving extensive leadership training (a minimum of 8 full days) involving the mindset and skills exhib-ited in the coach leader identity. The authors are privileged to be able to share this leadership journey through our partnership with LISD.

Lewisville uses a combination of external and internal coaches. External coaches provide coaching to principals in their first 3 years of principal leadership. Principals and assistant principals coach staff members of all levels, and coaching trickles down as leaders at all levels model the coach leader mindset and skills in formal and informal interactions. As adult leaders practice these behaviors, the bottom-line impact is that students see the benefit of effective communication modeled daily in their classrooms.

With LISD's commitment to a coaching culture, they are well posi-tioned for the advent of the new principal appraisal system to be imple-mented in Texas in 2016–2017. Included is a component for assessing the principal's coaching effectiveness. The district is currently in the process of developing an in-house teacher appraisal system that will be built around the coach leader identity/coaching model.

From Executive Coaching to Coaching for All

Little Rock School District (LRSD) in Arkansas began partnering with Results Coaching in 2009, based on the vision and research of Dr. Lloyd Sain. (You read about Dr. Sain's personal transformation from a judgment-criticism focused leader to a coach leader in Chapter 1.)

Figure 6.2   Leadership Behaviors

Executive Coaching	Directive Coaching or Controlling/Telling
Partnering (co-thinking) with leaders in a thought-provoking and creative process that inspires them to maximize their personal and professional potential, which is particularly important in today's uncertain and complex environment. (Definition adapted from the ICF definition of *coaching*.)	A stance that similarly matches the role of a supervisor or mentor in which the leader is told, controlled, or led by the supervisor's primary thinking and experiences.

Dr. Sain found a need to identify additional options beyond the traditional means of support for school leaders with these outcomes in mind:

- to improve student achievement and
- to increase confidence, skills, and competency with instructional leadership. (personal interview, October 4, 2015)

He and other leaders in LRSD identified executive coaching as the option to pursue to achieve these outcomes. The vision began with this unique distinction.

The following characteristics were identified in the selection of the first external executive coaches for LRSD:

- Possesses a natural *coaching identity* to work with a school leader through being trustworthy, nonjudgmental, results focused, intentional, and a committed listener;
- Has the ability to assess the needs of the individuals they are coaching within the context of the leader's school setting, to mediate resources, and to identify multiple options;
- Exhibits a high level of integrity and ethics to ensure a trusting relationship with the school leader so that sensitive and confidential matters are respected;
- Demonstrates knowledge, competency, and skills to challenge and support the leader in achieving high levels of performance in various areas of leadership;
- Models the specialized training in leadership coaching from an accredited ICF training program (RCG); and
- Possesses experience as an educator in a K–12 or higher education setting.

Implementation of Executive Coaching in LRSD

Implementation began with the writing of an extensive proposal outlining the scope and goals of the program for district consideration and approval for a 3-year implementation. Once the proposal was approved by the district, 15 current and retired school leaders were invited to participate in a 4-day Leadership Coaching for High Performance seminar, provided by RCG. Of those who completed the training, seven who possessed the potential coach leader mindset were selected to serve as executive coaches in the first year of implementation (2009–2010). Principals who would receive this gift of an external executive coach were identified and notified. These principals were selected if they were a first-year principal, new to the district, or leading a school with a school improvement designation.

Supervisors and selected principals were asked to meet to identify and discuss performance goals or areas of potential focus for work with the executive coach. Executive coaches met with district leaders to become familiar with the district's expectations, key initiatives, district and school data on performance, and performance standards and indicators. This information was intended to set a context for district standards and expectations. Executive coaches were not expected to be the expert or holder of the data and performance indicators. An orientation session was held to outline the purpose of the program, describe how the principals participating were identified, define the program format, and introduce principals and executive coaches to each other. Figure 6.3 shows the growth of the executive coaching initiative.

Executive coaches are provided annual training and support, including seminars of Powerful Coaching and Advanced Coaching, customized follow-up, book studies, webinars, coaching circles, and the opportunity to continue additional coaching study of their choice.

LRSD and RCG continue to partner in learning and development and research and evaluation to grow the coaching culture in LRSD. The combination of external coaching and internal coaching through the coach leader identity continues to provide school leaders a forum for professional conversations that ultimately lead to the constant thinking and examination

Figure 6.3   Growth of Executive Coaching in Little Rock School District, 2009–2016

Year	Number of Leaders Receiving External Executive Coaching
2009–2010	11
2010–2011	13
2011–2012	17
2012–2013	20
2013–2014	21 (including 6 assistant principals)
2014–2015	17
2015–2016	19

necessary for the improvement of student achievement and to maintain employee engagement and retention.

A number of evaluation studies have been conducted to measure the ROE of the coaching initiatives in LRSD. The nature of leadership and coaching make it difficult, if not impossible, to find a direct correlation to such endpoints as student achievement. The studies are based on interviews of participants. Responses are coded and entered into a qualitative software program, NVivo.

KEY FINDINGS FROM THE 2013 STUDY

- These participants corroborated earlier findings that coaching promotes self-confidence in school leaders.
- Several coach leader techniques that were modeled by coaches were embraced by the participants as new leadership behaviors for themselves.
- While participants might have been vague or negative prior to the coaching experience, once they were coached, they felt it was an asset.
- Most felt they would like to continue coaching as their leadership development for another year.
- Coaching has had an impact on the beliefs of the leaders on the success for their school.
- Coaching has had a positive impact on participants' own leadership role.

KEY FINDINGS FOR THE 2014 STUDY

- Coaching has impacted the leadership of the respondents in seven major ways:

  1. Improved communication
  2. Improved decision-making
  3. Greater collaboration
  4. Building the capacity in others to solve their own problems
  5. Enhanced reflective and critical thinking skills
  6. Enhanced skills to diffuse situations with parents
  7. Leveraging resources

Unintended positive impacts began to show up throughout the district. Those who had not originally been assigned an executive coach began to request the services of a coach. Those whose coaching was coming to an end began to request to keep their coach for an additional year and through this request were able to keep their coach for a second year. Principals and other school leaders began to request the same training that the executive coaches received because they were personal recipients of the growth-producing impact of the coach leader mindset and skills. The district offered additional training to those 75 school principals, central office administrators, and assistant principals who voluntarily selected to attend Level I and/or Level II. By the 2012–2013 school year, instructional coaches received the entry level of coaching per their request for professional development, totaling 200 trained coach leaders through the district. Because of the impact of coaching, all personnel in instructional support roles, especially those called coaches, are now expected to meet the established standard of at least 4 days of coach training with RCG.

From Executive Coach to University Coach

One of the executive coaches serving the LRSD is Dr. Peggy Doss, Dean of Education at the University of Arkansas, Monticello (UAM). Her leadership of her department is an outgrowth of her training as an executive coach and her experience beginning with LRSD beginning in 2008.

Dr. Doss's colleagues began noticing "something different" in the way she communicated and responded in conversations (personal communication, December 8, 2015). That difference was that the language and mindset of coaching had become a part of everyday conversations with faculty and staff, which opened doors for more authentic and meaningful conversations. Because her colleagues began asking, Leadership Coaching for High Performance was offered for each UAM faculty and staff member who desired to participate. Leadership Coaching was also offered to partner school district leaders through UAM. Follow-up and ongoing learning is available through coaching circles, book studies, and continuing practice on a daily basis in every conversation.

THE IMPACT OF LEADERSHIP COACHING AT UAM AND PARTNER SCHOOLS

- Coaching conversations have become the norm for discussions regarding problems to be solved or plans to be made. Dr. Doss has replaced, "This is what I think," with "What are your thoughts and ideas?" This mindset and language shift have created a greater sense of community as well as bolstered the individual's sense of ownership in the organization. The result has been an increase in faculty offering solutions to problems rather than merely submitting the problem to the dean for her resolution.

- Faculty members model the mindset and language of coaching with students. They ask open-ended questions, paraphrase student comments, provide reflective feedback to students, and use specific value statements to validate student thinking and to encourage participation. Faculty colleagues hold each other accountable for meeting the standard and expectation of employing coaching skills.
- Faculty members feel freedom to express opinions and ideas on critical topics. Conversations in small and large group meetings are much richer, and participants are much more likely to be engaged in and support what they have created. Conversations are more authentic and deep, whether in formal settings (meetings, e-mail) or informally, such as hallway, office, or lunch conversations.
- The faculty and staff have a greater awareness of how they frame conversations and the power of their words. This heightened sense of the importance of listening and giving feedback to each other and their students builds individual and unit capacity to continue to grow and develop.
- Faculty seek others to be thinking partners and use coaching skills to brainstorm ideas, solve problems, or remove barriers.
- The coaching culture is contagious. As faculty (and family) experienced the benefits and outcomes of a conversation with someone who received the coach training, they began to model some of the same strategies and to say, "Who *are* you? What have you learned that has made such a dramatic change in your behaviors and interactions with others? We want to also learn the secrets you have learned."

According to her faculty, Dr. Doss's leadership has evolved dramatically since 2008, when she began her transformation into the coach leader identity. Evaluation sessions have evolved from directive to more reflective. Instead of directing commands, such as, "Let me tell you what you do well and what you need to improve. You need to do it this way and by this time," her language has progressed to more reflective questions, such as, "What do you believe you currently do well? What are your thoughts about the future? Where do you want to grow? How will you look different as a teacher next year, the next 3 years, and so on? How will you accomplish your goals? How do your goals and plans support the mission and vision of the unit? When will you begin? How will you know when you have succeeded? What will be happening that will be different? How will you hold yourself accountable? What do you need from me (unit leader) to support your success?"

According to Dr. Doss, "I always thought I had great relationships with my faculty and students because they smiled and were cordial. They just did whatever I asked. They respected me for my 40-plus years of experiences, and I used those experiences to tell them what I thought was the best solution, path, program, et cetera. After participating in Results

Coaching Global coaching seminars, I realized that the communication was primarily one way and only reflected my perceptions. In one of my favorite books, *Fierce Conversations*, Susan Scott states that the conversation is the relationship. As a coach leader, I must engage in conversations that are two-way interactions—not the old school 'my way or the highway.' I had to learn and hold a new expectation for myself and learn to allow myself to be vulnerable" (personal communication, December 8, 2015).

Leadership Coaching is emerging as a strong part of the culture of not only the unit headed by Dr. Doss but also the partner school districts with which the unit works. Seventy-five public school and UAM faculty have experienced Level I: Leadership Coaching for High Performance, or more advanced leadership training from RCG. The UAM School of Education Renewal Zone (ERZ) assumed the role of funding and coordinating Leadership Coaching seminars to create a larger culture that values, implements, and models effective coaching leadership mindsets as the "new essential for school leaders." Figure 6.4 charts the level of participation of ERZ partner school districts.

Figure 6.4 University of Arkansas, Monticello, Education Renewal Zone District Participation

Leadership Coaching Level I				
ERZ Partner District	**Cohort I**	**Cohort II**	**Cohort III**	**Total From District**	**Still in District or Moved Districts**
Cleveland County	0	0	0	0	0
Crossett	4	0	2	6	5
Dermott	4	1	3	8	7
DeWitt	0	1	1	2	2
Drew Central	0	6	1	7	7
Hamburg	2	1	0	3	2
Hampton	0	0	0	0	0
Hermitage	0	3	1	4	4
Lakeside	1	0	0	1	1
McGehee	0	3	2	5	5
Monticello	4	9	4	17	14
Star City	0	0	6	6	7
UAM	6	2	4	12	12
Warren	0	1	2	3	3

| Leadership Coaching Level I | | | | | |
ERZ Partner District	Cohort I	Cohort II	Cohort III	Total From District	Still in District or Moved Districts
Woodlawn	0	1	0	1	1
Did not complete	1	2	0	3	
ERZ Partner TOTAL COMPLETING	22	30	26	75	70

Used with permission. 2013–2016 Southeast/UAM Education Renewal Zone Leadership Coach Project Cohorts.

PATTERNS AND THEMES FOR TRANSFORMING CULTURE

As is clear from the variation of stories shared in this chapter, there are an abundance of possibilities for how to transform your culture to one that values coaching as the way to work. Each story is unique. Even with the diversity of approaches, some constants emerge. For those seeking guidance about starting this process, the following ideas are offered as possibilities:

- **Begin with self. The theme that individual transformation is the first step supports each of the stories of success shared here.** Leaders who fully embrace the mindset of a coach identity see its power potential and commit to integration of coaching attitudes and skills in all areas of their life. When others witness this change in their leader, they become believers, and they want it for themselves.
- **Presume positive intent**. We find over and over that this presumption alone changes cultures. When leaders presume the best in others, others give their best.
- **Commit to one conversation at a time!** As if it were action research for Susan Scott's work, story after story supports her assertion, "The conversation is the relationship." That's how it began in every story.
- **Grow others in the coaching mindset.** Count and capitalize on the phenomena of others wanting to be coach leaders. Coaching is experiential in nature. Once a person has experienced it for himself or herself, he or she will want more.
- **Move toward critical mass.** Working on the health of the subsets such as grade levels or departments will multiply one's efforts. Identifying and working with early adopters and allies who support coaching will positively influence the culture and advance the goal of creating a coaching culture. Dennis Sparks (2015) says it this way, "New cultures cannot be created by leaders acting alone. Indeed, a primary characteristic of high-performing cultures is that leadership is distributed throughout the school community. That

means that new, more effective cultures are co-created by leaders and community members, especially teachers."

- Gain support for the initiative. Implementing any new ideas or initiatives occurs more successfully when those impacted have clarity and certainty about how they will be personally affected. Leaders at any level may be the champion, and leadership definitely needs to be on board. Having a designated leader or leaders maintains focus and ensures consistency, continuity, and follow-up.

  Leaders must provide the necessary learning opportunities for leaders who will be coaching, be coached, or those who wish to pursue deeper understanding of the mindset and skills of coaching. There are numerous organizations that provide training. Onsite or virtual coaching is widely available. A plethora of books are available, written from various perspectives about coaching. Resources need to be screened to match the philosophy and mindset desired, so research is needed to select those appropriate to your specific setting.

> Keep coaching mindset and skills in the forefront as you build in ongoing conversations. These may take the form of book studies, scheduled practice of coaching skill development, intentional discussion and use in PLCs, faculty meeting focus, and the expectation that the essential skills of coaching are evident in everyday conversations.

- **Uphold standards and expectations.** Essential to the process of creating a coaching culture is the idea of commitment to identifying and articulating the standards and expectations that focus the heart of the work. Without clarity and certainty of focus, efforts can be disjointed and misaligned, and people are working really hard without getting the results they want, much like a hamster on a wheel.

  As you move from study to implementation, it is necessary to articulate clear expectations of how coaching will be provided and received. Definitions of what coaching is (partnering with another to increase self-reflection, self-efficacy, and self-direction) and is not (teaching or directing) need to be shared with all involved parties, including administration, coaches, teachers, and any other stakeholders involved.

- **Build trust and maintain confidentiality.** We strongly believe in the International Coach Federation definition of coaching, as stated in the ICF Code of Ethics. It states, "Coaching is partnering with clients in a thought-provoking and creative process that inspires them to maximize their personal and professional potential" (http://coachfederation.org/about/ethics.aspx?ItemNumber= 854). (Client is defined as the *coachee* or person being coached.)

In some instances, coaches are offered as a support and also expected to report back to the administration on what is happening or not happening in the classrooms they support. This undermines the critical component of trust and confidentiality that must be present in a true coaching relationship. The ICF Competencies found in the Resource section are our guideposts in developing the coach leader mindset, skills, and identity. Competency Number 5 is Establishing Trust and Intimacy. The ICF Code of Ethics also stresses the importance of confidentiality.

Clear guidelines are needed regarding what information will be shared with whom and under what conditions. For example, if an instructional coach visits a teacher's classroom and follows with a coaching conversation, the teacher needs to know with certainty whether or not any part of the observation or conversation will be shared with his or her evaluator to be used in an evaluation. The intent of coaching is for growth. As evaluation enters into the picture, the potential for lower trust and less transparency becomes part of the dynamic. If any information is to be shared outside the coaching conversation, all parties need to be clear and have an explicit agreement about the conditions for sharing.

Consider using external coaches if possible, because this enhances trust and transparency in many cases. Those being coached often have more certainty about the confidential nature of the coaching interactions when the coach is not an employee of the district. Another possibility is for leaders to coach across school sites rather than within the campus or site or to coach those they do not directly supervise.

- **Continuously establish working agreements that will guide how we will work together.** Working agreements are not only imperative for group work and development, they are necessary for each conversation, each meeting, each interaction we have with others. The most frequent discovery in our school improvement work is the absence of attention to how we will conduct our work, how we will treat one another when there is conflict, and what it is we will accomplish now and in the future.

Committed listening is the foundational skill for effective coaching. Establishing protocols that omit cross talk is one way of monitoring the expectation of full presence in meetings. It is also a way to practice the foundational skill of committed listening and paraphrasing. Meetings become more productive with use of the essential skills of coaching and contribute to the development of a coaching culture.

We have seen the importance of norms. Often, teams create norms together and then review or visit them infrequently. Norms are agreements of how people will work together that become expectations over time. Agreements and norms need to be revisited frequently once established and revised as necessary.

- **Assess the effectiveness or impact of coaching.** Check in frequently on the impact of coaching, using anecdotal methods as well as more formal interviews or evaluation studies. Data collection from the coach and those being coached provides a fuller picture of the impact, as the coach is as likely as the coachee to be transformed through the process.

SUMMARY

The above examples of schools, districts, and university units exhibiting strong coaching cultures are only a few of the many examples of individual and cultural transformation we personally experience. When one has experienced the joy of engagement within a coaching culture, that person takes the culture wherever he or she may find himself or herself. As individuals find new positions of influence, the vision and belief of the power of coach leadership is a seed that grows and flowers wherever it is planted. The larger message is that a seismic cultural shift can—and often does—begin with one person who captures the vision and transforms herself or himself first.

REFERENCES

Bambrick-Santoyo, P. (2012). *Leverage leadership: A practical guide to building exceptional schools*. San Francisco, CA: Jossey-Bass.

Block, P. (2009). *Community: The structure of belonging*. San Francisco, CA: Berrett-Koehler.

Brockman, B. (2015, December 17). Personal interview.

Bryk, A., & Schneider, B. (2002). *Trust in schools: A core resource for improvement*. New York, NY: Russell Sage Foundation.

Deal, T. E., & Peterson, K. D. (2002). Positive or negative. *Journal of Staff Development, 23*(3), 10–15.

Deal, T., & Peterson, K. (2009). *Shaping school culture: Pitfalls, paradoxes, and promises* (2nd ed.). San Francisco, CA: Jossey-Bass.

Filipkowski, J. (2014, October 1). *Building a coaching culture*. Cincinnati, OH: Human Capital Institute. Retrieved from http://www.hci.org/hr-research/building-coaching-culture

Filipkowski, J. (2015, October 8). *Building a coaching culture for increased employee engagement*. Cincinnati, OH: Human Capital Institute. Retrieved from http://www.hci.org/hr-research/building-coaching-culture-increased-employee-engagement

Kegan, R., & Lahey, L. (2002). *How the way we talk can change the way we work*. San Francisco, CA: Jossey-Bass.

Kegan, R., & Lahey, L. (2009). *Immunity to change*. Boston, MA: Harvard Business Review Press.

Markova, D., & McArthur, A. (2015). *Collaborative intelligence: Thinking with people who think differently*, New York, NY: Spiegel & Grau.

Peck, S. (2003). *The road less traveled, timeless edition: A new psychology of love, traditional values, and spiritual growth.* New York, NY: Touchstone Simon & Schuster.

Sparks, D. (2015). School culture matters. [Blog post]. Retrieved August 12, 2015. from http://wp.me/pDryL-zk

Resources

Coaching Mindset and Skills—Skill Self-Assessment

COACHING MINDSET AND SKILLS
Skill Self-Assessment   Date:_____

Scale 1-2-3-4-5   1: Not at all;   2: Occasionally
3: Frequently   4: Most of the time   5: All of the time

COACHING MINDSET

_____**Trustworthy:** I honor confidentiality; I do what I say I will do; I honor responsibilities and obligations; I can always be counted on.

_____**Nonjudgmental:** I offer reflective feedback that supports thinking and reflection and presumes positive intent; I consider multiple points of view; I seek opportunities to practice dialogue; I set aside and suspend judgment as I gather data and information.

_____**Results Focused:** I see people as whole and capable; I support others in taking action toward their goals; I partner with others to plan, reflect, seek solutions, and make decisions; my conversations with others mediate their resources and options for their self-direction and learning. I hold up the standards and expectations of the district and profession to guide and support high levels of learning and achievement for all. I set goals for my own learning and progress and reflect on my progress with a trusted colleague.

_____**Intentional:** I am intentional in how I "show up" for others. I use intentional language and continually reflect on my behavior and actions to ensure alignment with my goals to serve and support others to their most successful results. My listening reflects my intention and commitment to really hear and understand.

_____**Avoids Advice:** I am mindful of the temptation of advice giving. I monitor my thinking and words and offer options via reflective feedback, holding up standards, using the language of others, noticing their assumptions, perceptions, thinking, and decision-making processes.

_____**COACHING MINDSET: Coaching has become the core of my being. It has transformed from what I do to who I am (continuous and long-term goal).**

COMMITTED LISTENING

_____ I focus completely on what the speaker is saying and not saying, listening to both words and emotions to more fully understand meanings expressed by the speaker.

_____ I set aside unproductive patterns of listening that cause my mind to judge, provide solutions, become overly inquisitive, or focus on my personal experiences.

_____ I convey interest to the speaker both verbally and nonverbally (BMIRS).

_____ I genuinely honor the speaker's point of view even when it may be different from my own.

_____ I listen for patterns of language that connect to the speaker's values, beliefs, desires, goals, dilemmas, or obstacles.

_____I am comfortable with silence that allows others space to think and reflect.

Accredited Coach Training Program
International Coach Federation

PARAPHRASING

_____ I paraphrase the essence of what the speaker is saying and do so in an abbreviated way; *I LISTEN FOR* what the person wants.

_____ I paraphrase, and *I LISTEN FOR* both the content and emotions of the speaker. I recognize the importance of "witnessing the struggle."

_____ I paraphrase for clarity and understanding for the speaker; *I LISTEN FOR . . .* to summarize or organize the speaker's thoughts and ideas.

_____ I *LISTEN FOR* to REFRAME THINKING; from negative to positive; from problem to solution; from complaint to commitment.

_____ I intentionally paraphrase in my thoughtful conversations with others.

_____ I am comfortable and aware of my use of paraphrasing and witness the power of paraphrasing with others.

PRESUME POSITIVE INTENT

_____ I presume the speaker has positive intentions in all actions and behaviors.

_____ I presume the speaker has already thought, said, or done what I'm asking about and my language conveys this.

_____ I frequently use positive presuppositions in my own statements to demonstrate genuine belief in the positive thinking and actions of the speaker.

_____ I hold up the district standards and expectations in my language while presuming others are desiring to follow and adhere to them.

REFLECTIVE FEEDBACK

_____ I take time to reflect before offering feedback and choose my words with care to convey respect and sincerity of thought. I recognize the impact of SCARF on the brain and choose my words with care.

_____ I ask clarifying questions for mutual understanding.

_____ I am generous and specific with positive feedback. My feedback conveys the value or value potential that is crucial for repetition.

_____ I ask reflective questions that communicate concerns or suggestions as possibilities. My reflective questions for possibilities presume another person's knowledge, desire, and commitment. I use standards, research, common goals, core values, or data to frame my reflective questions rather than my opinion to provide nonjudgmental language and safety to another's thinking.

_____ I notice when I am about to use judgmental language such as great, wonderful, and so on; I modify my language to identify the specifics and value of what they have done.

_____ I am aware of the importance of feedback for growth, improvement, and motivation. I balance my reflective feedback with value and reflective questions.

Coaching
Standards

Core Competencies

A. SETTING THE FOUNDATION

1. Meeting Ethical Guidelines and Professional Standards—Understanding of coaching ethics and standards and ability to apply them appropriately in all coaching situations.

1. Understands and exhibits in own behaviors the ICF Code of Ethics (see Code, Part III of ICF Code of Ethics).

2. Understands and follows all ICF Ethical Guidelines (see list).

3. Clearly communicates the distinctions between coaching, consulting, psychotherapy and other support professions.

4. Refers client to another support professional as needed, knowing when this is needed and the available resources.

2. Establishing the Coaching Agreement—Ability to understand what is required in the specific coaching interaction and to come to agreement with the prospective and new client about the coaching process and relationship.

1. Understands and effectively discusses with the client the guidelines and specific parameters of the coaching relationship (e.g., logistics, fees, scheduling, inclusion of others if appropriate).

2. Reaches agreement about what is appropriate in the relationship and what is not, what is and is not being offered, and about the client's and coach's responsibilities.

3. Determines whether there is an effective match between his/her coaching method and the needs of the prospective client.

PCC MARKERS: Creating the Coaching Agreement

1. Coach helps the client identify, or reconfirm, what s/he wants to accomplish in the session.
2. Coach helps the client to define or reconfirm measures of success for what s/he wants to accomplish in the session.
3. Coach explores what is important or meaningful to the client about what s/he wants to accomplish in the session.
4. Coach helps the client define what the client believes he/she needs to address or resolve in order to achieve what s/he wants to accomplish in the session.
5. Coach continues conversation in direction of client's desired outcome unless client indicates otherwise.

B. COCREATING THE RELATIONSHIP

3. Establishing Trust and Intimacy With the Client—Ability to create a safe, supportive environment that produces ongoing mutual respect and trust.

1. Shows genuine concern for the client's welfare and future.
2. Continuously demonstrates personal integrity, honesty, and sincerity.
3. Establishes clear agreements and keeps promises.
4. Demonstrates respect for client's perceptions, learning style, and personal being.
5. Provides ongoing support for and champions new behaviors and actions, including those involving risk taking and fear of failure.
6. Asks permission to coach client in sensitive, new areas.

PCC MARKERS: Creating Trust and Intimacy

1. Coach acknowledges and respects the client's work in the coaching process.
2. Coach expresses support for the client.
3. Coach encourages and allows the client to fully express himself or herself.

4. Coaching Presence—Ability to be fully conscious and create a spontaneous relationship with the client, employing a style that is open, flexible, and confident.

1. Is present and flexible during the coaching process, dancing in the moment.

2. Accesses own intuition and trusts one's inner knowing—goes with the gut.

3. Is open to not knowing and takes risks.

4. Sees many ways to work with the client and chooses in the moment what is most effective.

5. Uses humor effectively to create lightness and energy.

6. Confidently shifts perspectives and experiments with new possibilities for own action.

7. Demonstrates confidence in working with strong emotions and can self-manage and not be overpowered or enmeshed by client's emotions.

PCC MARKERS: Coaching Presence

1. Coach acts in response to both the whole person of the client and what the client wants to accomplish in the session.

2. Coach is observant, empathetic, and responsive

3. Coach notices and explores energy shifts in the client.

4. Coach exhibits curiosity with the intent to learn more.

5. Coach partners with the client by supporting the client to choose what happens in the session.

6. Coach partners with the client by inviting the client to respond in any way to the coach's contributions and accepts the client's response.

C. COMMUNICATING EFFECTIVELY

5. Active Listening—Ability to focus completely on what the client is saying and is not saying, to understand the meaning of what is said in the context of the client's desires, and to support client self-expression.

1. Attends to the client and the client's agenda and not to the coach's agenda for the client.

2. Hears the client's concerns, goals, values, and beliefs about what is and is not possible.

3. Distinguishes between the words, the tone of voice, and the body language.

4. Summarizes, paraphrases, reiterates, and mirrors back what client has said to ensure clarity and understanding.

5. Encourages, accepts, explores, and reinforces the client's expression of feelings, perceptions, concerns, beliefs, suggestions, and so on.

6. Integrates and builds on client's ideas and suggestions.

7. "Bottom-lines" or understands the essence of the client's communication and helps the client get there rather than engaging in long, descriptive stories.

8. Allows the client to vent or "clear" the situation without judgment or attachment to move on to next steps.

PCC MARKERS: Active Listening

1. Coach's questions and observations are customized by using what the coach has learned about who the client is and the client's situation.

2. Coach inquires about or explores the client's use of language.

3. Coach inquires about or explores the client's emotions.

4. Coach inquires about or explores the client's tone of voice, pace of speech, or inflection as appropriate.

5. Coach inquires about or explores the client's behaviors.

6. Coach inquires about or explores how the client perceives his or her world.

7. Coach is quiet and gives client time to think.

6. Powerful Questioning—Ability to ask questions that reveal the information needed for maximum benefit to the coaching relationship and the client.

1. Asks questions that reflect active listening and an understanding of the client's perspective.

2. Asks questions that evoke discovery, insight, commitment, or action (e.g., those that challenge the client's assumptions).

3. Asks open-ended questions that create greater clarity, possibility, or new learning.

4. Asks questions that move the client toward what they desire, not questions that ask for the client to justify or look backward.

PCC MARKERS: Powerful Questioning

1. Coach asks questions about the client; his or her way of thinking, assumptions, beliefs, values, needs, wants, and so on.

2. Coach's questions help the client explore beyond his/her current thinking to new or expanded ways of thinking about himself or herself.

3. Coach's questions help the client explore beyond his or her current thinking to new or expanded ways of thinking about his or her situation.

4. Coach's questions help the client explore beyond current thinking toward the outcome he or she desires.

5. Coach asks clear, direct, primarily open-ended questions, one at a time, at a pace that allows for thinking and reflection by the client.

6. Coach's questions use the client's language and elements of the client's learning style and frame of reference.

7. Coach's questions are not leading, i.e., do not contain a conclusion or direction.

7. Direct Communication—Ability to communicate effectively during coaching sessions, and to use language that has the greatest positive impact on the client.

1. Is clear, articulate, and direct in sharing and providing feedback.

2. Reframes and articulates to help the client understand from another perspective what he or she wants or is uncertain about.

3. Clearly states coaching objectives, meeting agenda, and purpose of techniques or exercises.

4. Uses language appropriate and respectful to the client (e.g., non-sexist, nonracist, nontechnical, nonjargon).

5. Uses metaphor and analogy to help illustrate a point or paint a verbal picture.

PCC MARKERS: Direct Communication

1. Coach shares observations, intuitions, comments, thoughts, and feelings to serve the client's learning or forward movement.

2. Coach shares observations, intuitions, comments, thoughts, and feelings without any attachment to them being right.

3. Coach uses the client's language or language that reflects the client's way of speaking.

4. Coach's language is generally clear and concise.

5. The coach allows the client to do most of the talking.

6. Coach allows the client to complete speaking without interrupting unless there is a stated coaching purpose to do so.

D. FACILITATING LEARNING AND RESULTS

8. Creating Awareness—Ability to integrate and accurately evaluate multiple sources of information and to make interpretations that help the client gain awareness and thereby achieve agreed-upon results.

1. Goes beyond what is said in assessing client's concerns, not getting hooked by the client's description.

2. Invokes inquiry for greater understanding, awareness, and clarity.

3. Identifies for the client his or her underlying concerns; typical and fixed ways of perceiving himself or herself and the world; differences between the facts and the interpretation; and disparities between thoughts, feelings, and action.

4. Helps clients discover for themselves the new thoughts, beliefs, perceptions, emotions, moods, and so on that strengthen their ability to take action and achieve what is important to them.

5. Communicates broader perspectives to clients and inspires commitment to shift their viewpoints and find new possibilities for action.

6. Helps clients see the different, interrelated factors that affect them and their behaviors (e.g., thoughts, emotions, body, and background).

7. Expresses insights to clients in ways that are useful and meaningful for the client.

8. Identifies major strengths vs. major areas for learning and growth, and what is most important to address during coaching.

9. Asks the client to distinguish between trivial and significant issues, situational vs. recurring behaviors, when detecting a separation between what is being stated and what is being done.

PCC Markers: Creating Awareness

1. Coach invites client to state and/or explore his or her learning in the session about his or her situation (the what).

2. Coach invites client to state and/or explore his or her learning in the session about himself or herself (the who).

3. Coach shares what he or she is noticing about the client and/or the client's situation, and seeks the client's input or exploration.

4. Coach invites client to consider how he or she will use new learning from the coaching.

5. Coach's questions, intuitions, and observations have the potential to create new learning for the client.

9. Designing Actions—Ability to create with the client opportunities for ongoing learning, during coaching and in work/life situations, and for taking new actions that will most effectively lead to agreed-upon coaching results.

1. Brainstorms and assists the client to define actions that will enable the client to demonstrate, practice, and deepen new learning.

2. Helps the client focus on and systematically explore specific concerns and opportunities that are central to agreed-upon coaching goals.

3. Engages the client to explore alternative ideas and solutions, to evaluate options, and to make related decisions.

4. Promotes active experimentation and self-discovery, where the client applies what has been discussed and learned during sessions immediately afterward in his or her work or life setting.

5. Celebrates client successes and capabilities for future growth.

6. Challenges client's assumptions and perspectives to provoke new ideas and find new possibilities for action.

7. Advocates or brings forward points of view that are aligned with client goals and, without attachment, engages the client to consider them.

8. Helps the client "Do It Now" during the coaching session, providing immediate support.

9. Encourages stretches and challenges but also a comfortable pace of learning.

10. Planning and Goal Setting—Ability to develop and maintain an effective coaching plan with the client.

1. Consolidates collected information and establishes a coaching plan and development goals with the client that address concerns and major areas for learning and development.

2. Creates a plan with results that are attainable, measurable, specific, and have target dates.

3. Makes plan adjustments as warranted by the coaching process and by changes in the situation.

4. Helps the client identify and access different resources for learning (e.g., books, other professionals).

5. Identifies and targets early successes that are important to the client.

11. Managing Progress and Accountability—Ability to hold attention on what is important for the client and to leave responsibility with the client to take action.

1. Clearly requests of the client actions that will move the client toward his or her stated goals.

2. Demonstrates follow-through by asking the client about those actions that the client committed to during the previous session(s).

3. Acknowledges the client for what they have done, not done, learned, or become aware of since the previous coaching session(s).

4. Effectively prepares, organizes, and reviews with client information obtained during sessions.

5. Keeps the client on track between sessions by holding attention on the coaching plan and outcomes, agreed-upon courses of action, and topics for future session(s).

6. Focuses on the coaching plan but is also open to adjusting behaviors and actions based on the coaching process and shifts in direction during sessions.

7. Is able to move back and forth between the big picture of where the client is heading, setting a context for what is being discussed and where the client wishes to go.

8. Promotes client's self-discipline and holds clients accountable for what they say they are going to do, for the results of an intended action, or for a specific plan with related time frames.

9. Develops the client's ability to make decisions, address key concerns, and develop himself or herself (to get feedback, to determine priorities and set the pace of learning, to reflect on and learn from experiences).

10. Positively confronts the client with the fact that he or she did not take agreed-upon actions.

PCC MARKERS 9, 10, and 11: Designing Actions, Planning and Goal Setting, and Managing Progress and Accountability

1. Coach invites or allows client to explore progress toward what he or she want to accomplish in the session.

2. Coach assists the client to design what actions/thinking client will do after the session for the client to continue moving toward the client's desired outcomes.

3. Coach invites or allows client to consider her or his path forward, including, as appropriate, support mechanisms, resources, and potential barriers.

4. Coach assists the client to design the best methods of accountability for himself or herself.

5. Coach partners with the client to close the session.

6. Coach notices and reflects client's progress.

Supervision and Coaching

Glickman's Model of Developmental Supervision

Glickman's Developmental Model (1985, 1990) is direct assistance to teachers, which also includes staff development, group development, curriculum development, and action research. Supervisors must be knowledgeable in developmental supervision (supervision of pedagogy—science of teaching and learning), effective school characteristics, adult development, interpersonal skills, and technical skills. Developmental supervision requires the ongoing personal contact with individual teachers and groups of teachers. Glickman recommends five principles:

Principle 1—Supervision should encourage teachers to invest in a "cause beyond themselves."

Principle 2—Supervision should enhance teachers' feelings of efficacy in influencing student outcomes via classroom management and effective instruction.

Principle 3—Supervision should encourage teachers to share ideas and materials and support one another's efforts in improving common instructional goals.

Principle 4—Supervision should stimulate teacher involvement in staff development, curriculum, and instruction action research to strengthen collective action.

Principle 5—Supervision should challenge teachers to think more abstractly about their practice of teaching. This is accomplished by giving feedback, questioning, and confronting teachers to self-appraise, reflect, self-modify, and adapt their practices to the ever-changing needs of students.

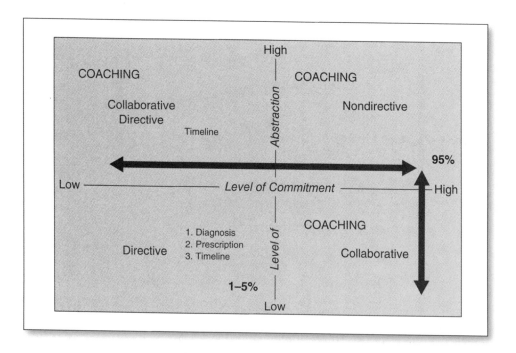

Glickman suggests that most teachers are unlikely to initiate or pursue change independently, due to the unchanging and controlling work environment of schools that constantly reinforce conformity and unimaginative thinking. Supervisors have an obligation to challenge the ineffectiveness of the traditional role of supervisor to a professional level that facilitates deep thinking and problem solving, reflection, and insights that will produce new ideas, solutions, actions, and continuously improved results.

SOURCE: Pajak, E. (1993). *Approaches to clinical supervision: Alternatives for improving instruction.* Norwood, MA: Christopher-Gordon; and Glickman, C. D. (1990). *Supervision of instruction: A developmental approach* (2nd edition). Newton, MA: Allyn and Bacon. Summary: Kathy Kee.

Supervision Practice Scenarios

SCENARIO 1: QUADRANT III

The teacher is in her 12th year of teaching Algebra I. She is completing a master's degree in education that includes hours of graduate-level mathematics classes. When you have asked her to participate in after-school math tutorials, she told you that she was too busy with her graduate classes and keeping up with her grading to commit the time. When you have questioned her about using more models and manipulatives in her classes, she told you: "I had a couple of education courses that talked about that, but that doesn't work with my students. They just play with them and it's a distraction to the good students. Some of that stuff is good theory, but it just doesn't work in a real classroom." At the end of the first semester, 20% of the 140 students had a failing grade and will need to repeat the first semester as a "trailer course" or in summer school. The average failure rate for other Algebra I teachers is 8%. On the ninth-grade spring state math test, this teacher's students had the highest failure rate in the school—more than 40%. When you have talked with her about her failure rates, she told you that her students' math skills were very weak and that the ones who failed were the ones who did not pay attention in class and would not do the homework. You have conducted three 15- to 20-minute observations during the past two weeks. One observation was at the beginning of the class period; the other two observations were at the end of the class period. Each of the three times you observed the following:

- There were 28 students in the class.
- The teacher was working algebra problems on a SmartBoard.
- All the problems were in an algorithmic (computational) format.
- As the teacher worked the problems:

- - Ten students were writing down the problems during the first observation.
  - Twelve students were writing down the problems during the second observation.
  - Eleven students were writing down the problems during the third observation.

- The teacher interacted (called on students with questions) with four students during the first observation, with seven students during the second observation, and with five students during the third observation.
- Of the 16 total students who were called on, six answered the teacher's question correctly.
- At the end of the third observation, the teacher assigned students to work the odd-numbered problems in a 30-problem set; there were 10 minutes remaining in the period.

  - The teacher began to walk around the room.
  - The first two students stopped her and asked her to help them, which she did.
  - As you walked around, you observed:

    - ❖ 8 students had their books closed and were doing nothing.
    - ❖ 2 students were working on class work for another class.
    - ❖ 18 students were working the problems;

      - ➢ Eight told you they did not understand how to do the assignment.
      - ➢ Ten told you that they did understand how to do the assignment.

- When the bell rang, the teacher was still working with the two original students.

SCENARIO 2: QUADRANT II

The teacher has been teaching for 2 years. The teacher willingly takes on extra-curricular activities and is always willing to participate in professional development training. The teacher arrives early and stays late, working on lesson plans and setting up activities for students. Last year, this teacher's students scored significantly below the campus, district, and state averages on the state reading test. You have just completed a 30-minute observation in the teacher's classroom. The data from your observation indicate that the teacher used a traditional, deductive lesson cycle to teach a Reading/ English Language Arts lesson. Your data indicate the following:

- The teacher was teaching a skill lesson on using commas in compound sentences;

- To check for student understanding, the teacher called on 7 of the 25 students; 5 of the 7 had difficulty answering the questions correctly;
- The teacher moved the students to guided practice;
- The practice contained sentences that were even more complex and difficult than the ones the teacher modeled during the explanation;
- When you left, the teacher was monitoring the guided practice and you counted 15 students who had stopped working and had their hands raised.

SCENARIO 3: QUADRANT IV

The teacher has been teaching high school English for 15 years. He has a master's degree in English and teaches one community college English class each semester. He has served in a variety of roles in the district including membership on both the campus and district improvement committees. He is the chairman of the high school English department and has been teaching only Advanced Placement and Pre-Advanced Placement English class for the past 5 years. Students generally make good grades in this teacher's class and all of his students have met expectations on the state achievement tests in the past 3 years. Almost all of his students take the AP English examination, and about 20% of his students score well enough to be awarded college credit for high school English. The teacher is popular with students and parents.

The teacher is an engaging performer in his classes and uses almost exclusively a lecture/discussion format. In your most recent visit to his classroom you saw what you typically see:

- Students had been assigned to read Shakespeare's *Othello*;
- Students were seated in a semicircle around the teacher;
- The teacher read (actually, performed) two of the soliloquies from the play;
- He then began asking individual students questions to interpret the meaning of various lines and the importance of some of the symbols that Shakespeare used;
- In the 30 minutes you observed, the teacher called on 9 of the 25 students, and all gave answers which the teacher acknowledged as being correct; the questions were all analysis and evaluation questions; and
- The other 14 students appeared to be listening to the teacher.

SCENARIO 4: QUADRANT?

This teacher is a veteran teacher from another district. In the previous district this teacher has served as a grade-level (departmental) team leader and as a member of the site-based decision-making committee. The teacher has a reputation as being a "tough teacher" and students love the class. You have just completed a 20-minute observation in this teacher's classroom. Your data from this 20-minute observation and an examination of the teacher's lesson plan indicate that the teacher used an inductive lesson cycle to teach a lesson on figurative language (similes, metaphors, personification, and onomatopoeia) and vivid descriptive language. During the observation, you observed:

- The teacher began the class period by saying, "Today, I want you to get into your triads and read the first three pages of Edgar Allan Poe's *The Cask of Amontillado* and tell me what you think about Poe's writing style."
- Students moved into their triads;
- After they organized their triads, the students began to ask questions: "What do you mean by his writing style?" "Why do we have to read Edgar Allan Poe again? We read some of his stuff last year."
- The teacher stopped the students and explained that they were to identify any words or phrases that the author used which painted a mental picture or evoked an emotional response;
- All of the students then engaged in the reading and in identifying descriptive words;
- The teacher walked around to monitor each group and asked questions such as "How did that word make you feel?" "What kind of mental picture did those words paint for you?" Have you ever used those kinds of words in your own writing?" "What other writers have you read who used these kinds of words and phrases?"
- When you left, each group was reporting the words they had identified and talking about how the words evoked an emotional reaction or painted a vivid mental picture.

1. What information tells you which quadrant the teacher is in?
2. What issues(s) do you want to have a conversation about?
3. How will you begin the conversation?
4. Assuming an "acceptable response," what will you do next?

SCENARIO 5: QUADRANT?

The teacher has been teaching for 10 years on your middle school campus. The teacher holds a master's degree in English and is taking doctoral courses at a nearby university. You hired this teacher 2 years ago. Parents have regularly complained that students are bored in this teacher's class. They have also complained that students frequently have long writing assignments to do at home and that students do not know what they are supposed to do. On the day of your observation in this teacher's classroom, you have looked at the curriculum document that the teacher printed out and turned in to you on Monday morning. The curriculum's essential knowledge and skills that the teacher turned in include:

7.12E—Compare communication in different forms such as comparing story variants, including:

- Connecting ideas
- Comparing and contrasting characters
- Comparing ideas
- Comparing themes

Your 25-minute classroom observation reveals the following data:

- Students were told to read the first chapter of a novel (everyone is reading the same novel); they are told that after they have finished reading, they are to go to a computer, pull up the questions on this chapter, answer the questions from the computer program, print out their score, and bring the score to the teacher for recording in the grade book (there are six computers in the classroom);
- You know that this novel is on the eighth-grade reading list;
- The teacher sits at the teacher desk while students are individually reading;
- As students finish reading the first chapter of the novel, they sit until the teacher reminds them to go to the computer to answer their questions;
- Some students wait several minutes until one of the six computers is free;
- You examine the eight questions on the computer program; all but one of the questions are knowledge/comprehension level, multiple choice questions.

1. What information tells you which quadrant the teacher is in?
2. What issues(s) do you want to have a conversation about?
3. How will you begin the conversation?
4. Assuming an "acceptable response," what will you do next?

RCG Coaching Conversation Frame

RCG COACHING CONVERSATION FRAME

ENTER THE CONVERSATION

- **Trust connections**
- **Agreements for**
  —time, topic, outcome, success measures, and why they are important for this conversation

THINKING
FEELINGS
INSIGHTS
CLARITY
NEW
PATHWAYS

EXIT THE CONVERSATION

- **Agreements met . . .**
  —topic, purpose, outcome
  ○ **Next steps**
  ○ **Benefits/value**
     of the conversation

Sample Language for
ENTERING THE CONVERSATION

- Given we have about 10 minutes, what would you like for us to focus on?
- At the end of our 15 minutes, what would you like to take away?
- What are you wanting to accomplish by the end of our 20-minute conversation?
- I'm here to be your thinking partner for the next 15 minutes. What would you like to focus on?
- What are you thinking would be the best use of our time?

Sample Language for
EXITING THE CONVERSATION

- What has been the most helpful in our conversation today?
- When we started our conversation you wanted_____; how did we do?
- Of all the things we have talked about, what has been of greatest value?
- What is clearer for you now that was not as clear when we began our conversation?

NEXT STEPS:

- When we began our conversation, your goal was to_____. How are you feeling about your great thinking? What will be your first steps?
- What actions are you ready to begin based on the plan you have designed?
- When we talk again where are you thinking you would like to begin?

Sample Language for the RCG – GPS

SOLUTION FOCUSED:

- If ideal, how would the situation be?
- When you have encountered this situation before, what did you do that resolved it successfully?
- What three things are you thinking would have the greatest impact on achieving your solution?
- Would it be helpful to generate numerous options to consider?
- How will you know (what data will you use) to evaluate your success with this situation?

GOAL FOCUSED:

- When this goal is achieved, what will the impact be?
- What people or resources are you thinking will be the greatest support in achieving your goal?
- What strategies [specific #] are you assessing will have the most influence on achieving this goal?
- What will be your first steps? What data will inform you of your achievement?

PLANNING FOCUSED:

- What do you want?
- What will it look like, sound like, be like when accomplished?
- What strategies are you thinking will get you there?
- How are you wanting to assess your success?
- As you consider your timeline, what are your first three steps?

REFLECTION FOCUSED:

- As you have reflected on this, what was the greatest insight (learning) for you?
- What did you do specifically that influenced the outcome?
- To what did you pay attention, to ensure your goals were accomplished?
- As you take this learning forward, what will you keep with you; what will you refine; what will you leave behind?

RCG Difficult Conversation Frame

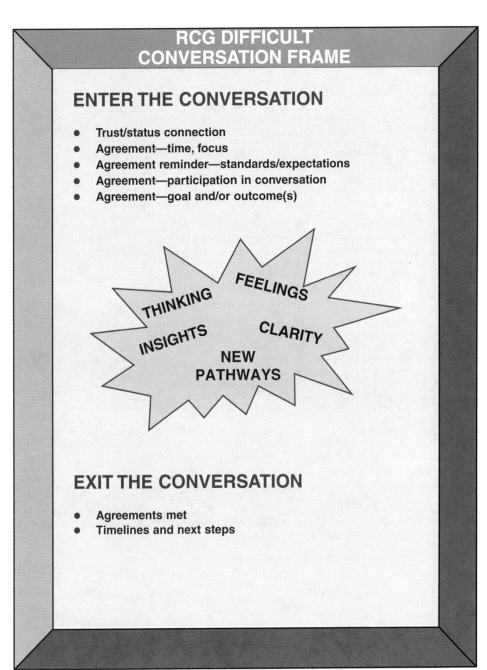

RCG DIFFICULT CONVERSATION FRAME

ENTER THE CONVERSATION

- Trust/status connection
- Agreement—time, focus
- Agreement reminder—standards/expectations
- Agreement—participation in conversation
- Agreement—goal and/or outcome(s)

FEELINGS

THINKING

INSIGHTS

CLARITY

NEW
PATHWAYS

EXIT THE CONVERSATION

- Agreements met
- Timelines and next steps

COACHING FRAME

SAMPLE LANGUAGE

QUADRANT I—DIRECTIVE

- You came into this profession to make a difference. You were hired because of your knowledge, skills, and/or tools—which are . . .
- The expectations of the position have been articulated to be . . .
- The urgency of your actions is . . .
- It is immediately critical to see the following . . .
- Some evidence of it would look like . . .
- Your timeline for it is . . .
- On a scale of 1–10, what is your commitment to this goal/action/timeline?
- I look forward to your success and reviewing your evidence on . . .

QUADRANT II—COLLABORATIVE/COACHING

- Your energy and commitment to your work are evident.
- This conversation is just to review and revisit the standards/expectations that will be so important to your success in the position.
- How are you assessing your success? What evidence are you noticing?
- What do you want to be celebrating about this in a couple of weeks?

QUADRANT III—COACHING w/specific follow-up timelines

- You came into this profession to make a difference and have been doing that for many years. Your years of service are . . . Your knowledge, skills, or gifts are . . .
- You are very aware of the huge accountability changes in our profession and the expectations that we face today; you are very aware of the standards we are held to; you have been at this long enough that you know . . .
- As you think about this requirement, what comes to mind as your best strategies or moves? How are you hoping to put this into action?
- With your knowledge and expertise, what will guide your self-assessment of your progress?
- Let's talk again in 10 days so you can share what you are seeing and how it has impacted your results.
- So your understanding of your focus and work is . . .?

QUADRANT IV—SELF-DIRECTED—COACHING

RCG Guided Pathways for Success—GPS

RCG Guided Pathways for Success GPS

Solution Focused

- "Witness the struggle"
- Listen for words, phrases, and metaphors that guide thinking
- Reframe from problem to solution focus
- Language of discovery and appreciation
- Ask questions to evoke talents, success discovery, dreams, and desires
- Ask powerful questions to make solutions possible

- Support thinking to create clear image of attributes of the solution

Goal Focused

- What do you want? Clarify and articulate goals—be explicit; what does it look like, feel like when achieved?
- Prioritize your goals
- Generate multiple pathways for achieving your goal; identify the top 10 strategies
- Create an action plan
- Identify resources (people and things) needed to facilitate your achievement
    - REFLECT AND CELEBRATE!

Planning Focused

- Clarify goals
- Determine success indicators
- Anticipate approaches, strategies, and decisions
- Identify the data for self-assessment
- Determine the plan for action
- Reflect on benefits of conversation

Reflection Focused

- Summarize impressions
- Recall supporting information
- Compare, analyze, infer cause and effect relationships
- Construct new learnings and applications
- Reflect on benefits of conversation and any refinements

207

Results Coaching Global ©2016

RCG Guided Pathways for Success GPS

Sample Language

Solution Focused

- You are really hurting from this.
- The broken trust has emptied your bank account.
- (Miracle ?) What would have happened to achieve the most positive outcome?
- You are seeking your most successful strategies to apply to this situation.
- What actions and strategies have given you success in the past that could be "regifted" in this situation?
- What compels you to ensure the solution you desire?

Goal Focused

- What do you want?
- What will it look like when you have achieved this goal?
- Of the four goals you want, rank them in priority and time commitment for yourself.
- What five strategies are you thinking you want to put in place to achieve your goals?
- What are three more ways you can do it? Two more?
- Of your 10 strategies, which 3 offer the most powerful steps to achieving your goal?
- What is your timeline for accomplishing your goal?
  - Who will you utilize to assist you in realizing your goal?
  - As you reflect on this conversation and your upcoming goal achievement, what will you be celebrating in 2 months?

N

W

- Your courage and commitment to your students have created a clear vision of your goal.

E

Planning Focused

- What are you wanting to achieve?
- How will you know when you have achieved it?
- What strategies have you determined will support your success?
- How will you know when you have achieved your mission? What data will affirm your accomplishment?
- What will be your first steps in your plan for action?
- How has this conversation been helpful?

S

Reflection Focused

- How do you feel about your performance?
- What data support your feelings?
- What did you do to get the results you achieved? What specifically impacted your results?
- If you were to do this again, what would you want to repeat? Refine? Eliminate?
- How has this conversation supported your reflective practice?

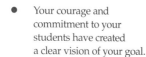

Index

A SAGE Publishing Company

CORWIN HAS ONE MISSION: to enhance education through intentional professional learning.

We build long-term relationships with our authors, educators, clients, and associations who partner with us to develop and continuously improve the best evidence-based practices that establish and support lifelong learning.

Solutions you want. Experts you trust. Results you need.